Courageous Visions:
How to Unleash Passionate Energy in Your Life and Your Organization

Martha Lasley

DISCOVER
PRESS

FIRST EDITION

Cover Designed by George Foster www.bookcovers.com

Publisher's Cataloging-in-Publication Data
(Provided by Quality Books, Inc.)

Lasley, Martha.
    Courageous visions : how to unleash passionate energy
in your life and your organization / Martha Lasley.--
1st ed.
    p. cm.
    Includes bibliographical references and index.
    LCCN 2004101625
    ISBN 0-9742000-1-8

    1. Leadership. 2. Creative ability in business.
3. Success in business. 4. Organizational change.
I. Title.

HD57.7.L37 2004   658.4'092
                             QBI04-200073

This book is dedicated to my extended family.
I love you all.

Contents

Acknowledgments

I have so much gratitude for all of you who contributed to my thinking and the writing of this book. I especially want to thank those who know this book wouldn't have been possible without you: my editor, Gene Kraybill; my writing coach, Steve Liebowitz; my business partner, Virginia Kellogg; and the woman who filled in all the blanks, Charlotte Morse.

I'm also deeply grateful to the people who reviewed parts of the book and acted as my sounding boards: Jane Moeller, Barbara Coyle, Sushma Sharma, Angelo John Lewis, Andrea Sigetich, Pierre Rochon, Elizabeth Crook, Phil Sandahl, Barbara Abrams, Richard Pope, Mary Mathias, Charles Jones, Katie Replogle, Neil Samuels, Barbara Carden, Alice Geiling, Peter Iglinski, Sarah Conlon, Richard Michaels, Roberta Dean, Kate Sholonski, Bobbie Camp, Martha Young, Ron Renaud, Louise Peabody, Maya Balle, Gail Taylor, Gregg Kendrick, Louise Aucott, Toni Risboskin, Sam House, Elizabeth Woodbridge, Angus McIntyre, Lucy Horton, Mary Kuentz, Carol Bruce, Jean Minielly, Usha Mathivanan, Carole Snyder, Leo Miller, Betsy Pickren, and Brian McDermott.

Part I Designing Your Future

It's never too late to be what you might have been.

— George Eliot

Chapter 1:
Envisioning a Better Future

Everyone has been made for some particular work and the desire for that work has been put in every heart.

— Rumi

Imagine leaping out of bed in the morning, full of passionate energy. You wholeheartedly know what you want, you focus on new possibilities, and you engage deeply in work and in life. As if that isn't enough, imagine that you inspire others, that you surround yourself with people who passionately work together to design a better future.

Envision working in an organization where everyone focuses more on what they want than on what they don't want. Picture all of you talking together spiritedly, sharing your ideas for a better future, and getting fired up about making it happen. Imagine your enthusiasm and creativity having a profound impact on the bottom line.

Sound ridiculous? Did you lose your idealism a long time ago, or do you still believe you *can* live the life of your dreams? Have you resigned yourself to living and working with people who grumble and groan, or do you know how to explore possibilities and shape the future you want? Are you half asleep yourself, or do you act as a catalyst for awakening heart and soul, both at home and at work?

Envisioning the future leads to a deep, courageous, rewarding journey. Whether you are crafting your personal vision, developing an organizational vision, or planning your next project, this book is your guide to creating the future *you* want. By sharing powerful tools that thousands of people have used to change their lives and their organizations, I invite you to unleash passionate energy in yourself and in others.

Courageous Visions serves as a springboard for awakening potential in individuals *and* in organizations. By connecting with what makes you feel most alive, you can discover new ways to manifest your vision while developing the courage to choose your destiny. This is not just a solo adventure, but a shared journey that releases the visionary powers of ordinary people who create extraordinary results.

Why think about something as intangible as your hopes for the future? In many organizations, gazing out the window is frowned upon. If you aren't busy putting out fires, your value to the organization is questionable. However, without a personal or organizational vision, direction is unclear, thinking is muddled, and people go through the motions uninspired. Instead of putting out fires, what if you *light* the fire, inspiring the passion people yearn for?

Your hope inspires others. Helen Keller once said, "No pessimist ever discovered the secrets of the stars, or sailed to an uncharted land, or opened a new heaven to the human spirit." When you imagine a better future and describe what you see, people feel drawn to the picture you paint. They inhale your passion. Your optimism is contagious.

Recognizing Visionaries

We recognize people with vision immediately. Fearlessly they share their hopes and dreams. They offer an irresistible image of the future. They know that the best way to predict the future is to create it, first in their minds, then in reality. Instead of following a prescribed path, they use their mind's eye to blaze a new trail.

Visionaries explore self-awareness unceasingly with curiosity and passion. By expanding the sense of what's possible, they communicate their desire to make life better for others. Because they embrace an optimistic outlook, they do far more than expected and inspire others to take bold action. Visionaries act as magnets for people who want to engage in something greater than themselves.

Leaders need competence, knowledge and experience to establish credibility, but communicating a compelling vision is the most important skill a leader can develop. While basic leadership skills win trust, a well-grounded achievable vision inspires the groundswell of support that changes people, organizations and the world.

The quest for a personal vision often begins with an internal struggle, or with a sense of dissatisfaction with the status quo. In Native American cultures, adolescents go on a vision quest as a rite of passage where they explore their hopes and fears. As young men, Mahatma Gandhi and Martin Luther King Jr. both went through long periods of reflection before they communicated their visions that changed the world.

Whether coming from a humanitarian, business, or political perspective, visionary leaders tell you where they are going and why you should come along. While powerful visions often evolve over time, occasionally sudden insights emerge. After visiting a trashy carnival with his daughter, Walt Disney wanted to create a magical place full of fun for the whole family. He expressed his dream of Disneyland in terms of discovery, nostalgia, joy, hope and beauty:

> It will be a place for people to find happiness and knowl-
> edge... for parents and children to spend pleasant times in one
> another's company... for teachers and pupils to discover greater
> ways of understanding and education. Here will be the won-
> ders of Nature and Man for all to see and understand.
>
> Disneyland will be something of a fair, an exhibition, a play-
> ground, a community center, a museum of living facts, and a
> showplace of beauty and magic. It will be filled with the ac-
> complishments, the joys and hopes of the world.... And it will
> remind us and show us how to make those wonders part of
> our own lives.
>
> —*Bob Thomas, Walt Disney: An American Tradition*

For Walt Disney, dissatisfaction with a local carnival sparked a fantasy that nourishes the souls of children of all ages. He became a worldwide success and a famous, wealthy man. But visions are *not* just for famous people or for the exceptionally bright and creative. Anyone disappointed with the status quo, or anyone brave or desperate enough to dream of a better future can recreate themselves and their organizations.

Visionaries come from every walk of life. Visions can be as common as world peace or as unique as the dream realized by David Whyte, author of *The Heart Aroused*, who brings poetry to corporations to help people find creativity and meaning.

Sometimes we make the mistake of thinking that only the leader of an organization should chart the future. In actuality, visionaries work everywhere from the boardroom to the boiler room. Some plans are small and some are huge. Maybe you envision all your files in perfect order. Perhaps you take part in Coca-Cola's vision to put their brand within arm's reach of every person on earth. Although I find the extent of their success inspiring, I fantasize about what would happen if we applied determination and talent of that scale to humanitarian causes. Imagine how the world would change if we applied the same resources toward ending violence against women, as envisioned by playwright and activist Eve Ensler. Picture street children in India with medical care, shelter, and a chance to go to school, which Jaimala Gupta envisions for the children of Jaipur.

Fueled by a sense of confidence, the realization of small dreams feeds the larger visions. Ultimately, the opportunities you pursue reflect the values and priorities you consider most important.

Whether you envision a better world, a better-run organization, or a better home life, you can expect people to do amazing things to turn a powerful idea into reality. Without foresight, managers wander around shaking their heads and wonder why their workers aren't motivated. Sadly, members of an organization without vision have no role in creating their own professional futures or in creating the organization's future. Building awareness of an individual's and an organization's sense of purpose helps people come alive in ways that revolutionize personal and corporate lives.

Creating an inspirational collective vision is one of the most dramatic ways to improve the health of your organization. Developing visionary leaders is a vital aspect of long-term growth. Peter Senge wrote *The Fifth Discipline* and was named a "Strategist of the Century" by the *Journal of Business Strategy*. He once said, "Every organization has a destiny: a deep purpose that expresses the organization's reason for existence. We may never fully know that purpose, just as an individual never fully discovers his or her individual purpose in life. But choosing to continually listen for that sense of emerging purpose is a critical choice that shifts an individual or a community from a reactive to a creative orientation."

Leaders who listen with deep curiosity have a strong sense of where the organization is headed. To get everyone headed in the same direction, leaders trust that each member's sense of purpose will further the organization's purpose. Collective planning helps create a culture of openness to new possibilities.

In most organizations we rely on the hero leader to determine the vision. We expect the words of an inspired leader to trickle down. We wait to be told what to do. I often hear, "We don't have strong leadership here." When I ask, "What are you doing about it?" I get a blank look. "What can I do? I'm just a..." In dynamic organizations everyone recognizes the leadership capacity in everyone else. Collectively they inspire each other, including the person at the top.

How does a sense of vision develop in an organization? Sometimes, the CEO creates the vision and communicates it enticingly. Other times the vision arises through a process involving every member of the organization. Usually the level of involvement lies between the two extremes. Involving *everyone* would prove challenging, but when you engage people at all levels to create a vision, you ensure a sense of joint ownership. Getting "buy-in" opens the door to wholehearted implementation. However, buy-in does not imply that the leader sells and everyone else buys.

Instead people explore their collective passion, and engage each other in designing their ideal future. Rather than accept the vision from above, they shape and guide the realization of the vision. Even when their ideas aren't used verbatim, people feel heard and understood because they contribute to the evolution of the organization.

Even people on welfare or in prison come alive using the power of their visions. Working in New York's Welfare to Work program, my business partner, Virginia Kellogg, found that many women feel deep hopelessness until they awaken to new possibilities. Invariably, what they want for their children excites and motivates them to make changes in their lives. Virginia also teaches coaching skills to prisoners who participate in a powerful program where they coach youth at risk, tapping their internal motivation to make their lives count.

Sometimes we conceive our visions with the help of dreams, meditation, or prayer. Rarely do visions blind us with sudden insight. Usually a vision develops over time, the elements emerging sometimes gently and sometimes urgently. The most compelling visions evolve slowly and require personal introspection and group exploration. Whatever we invest, the time spent crafting a vision offers multiple rewards.

Sharing My Vision

Before we go further, I'd like to share some of the details of my personal journey. I spent a large part of my life accepting what came my way without giving much thought to what I could create. Today, part of my vision is crystal clear:

I envision a world full of people who love their work, love the people in their lives, and passionately work to create a better future.

I haven't always had such clarity or been so centered. Some of my attempts to create a vision have been disappointing, even laughable. Still, I keep looking for opportunities to expand my sense of what's possible.

As co-founder of a firm that grows people, ideas, and businesses, I feel blessed to work with wonderful people who are so loving and nurturing that I want everyone else to experience a high-quality work environment where they let their light shine.

Our work together is filled with questioning, designing, and creating. I love the disappointment, the despair, the joy and the hope that surfaces in surprising ways as we wind our way through uncharted territory.

The people I work with call me forth and hold a vision of me that I find intoxicating, but grounded and supportive. I continue to feel amazed that our clients so deeply appreciate our work. Their bold dreaming touches me at the core, energizes me and inspires the daily actions that manifest my vision.

I have gone through a few "Let's kill the facilitator!" days that leave me wondering, "Why do I keep doing this work?" Pushed beyond my comfort zone, I become even clearer about my hopes and goals.

Working with individuals and groups to develop and live their ideal future—to become visionaries in the true sense of the word—is more rewarding than anything I can imagine. Progressive organizations hire us to coach their managers, encouraging them to use the time to discover their personal path as well as expand the organizational vision.

I have steadily gathered tools that help people awaken to their true potential. My quest has led me to a strong sense of my life purpose—to serve as a catalyst for transformation. I approach each day excitedly because I want everyone I know to find their right work—work they love with people they love.

One CEO told us that his managers worked 60-80 hours a week, and our job as coaches was to help them find a way to go home at night and get some balance in their lives. Another owner believed so strongly in the importance of self-awareness that he left it up to each employee to develop criteria to assess the value of coaching. A project manager at a university asked us to work with a new group, helping them design their dream team from day one. Few teams start with a powerful vision process, so working with a team from the start feels like a true gift, both for them and for us.

There's nothing like working with progressive clients, but we also get to work with groups and teams who struggle with issues of trust, inclusion, acceptance, and fear of failure. One woman described her team by saying, "We put the *fun* in dys*fun*ctional." Working with struggling teams feels exciting and fulfilling because we help people start imagining again, and they shift from despair toward creating the organization they've always wanted.

Creating visions becomes a way of life. It means daring to dream, to open to new spiritual understandings and directions. Years ago, I envisioned living simply, raising healthy kids, and growing fruit and vegetables. I still pursue that lifestyle, though my children are grown. At the same time, I'm constantly amazed by new opportunities to create a full, satisfying personal and professional life that take me far beyond my rural garden in the Endless Mountains of Pennsylvania. My favorite philosopher, Yogi Berra, once said, "The future ain't what it used to be." He reminds me of the unexpected humor around every corner. My view of the future keeps changing, and like the horizon, it continually moves. Since the journey toward the vision is far more inspirational than arrival, I focus on enjoying the ride.

Throughout this book, you will see many examples of inspirational visionaries, from the world-famous to people like Charlie, a teenager suffering from a severe eating disorder who used a simple vision process to break down his healing into small steps, starting with stirring his soup.

To protect the privacy of friends, colleagues and clients, in some cases, I have used first names only and changed some personal details, but the essence of each story is true.

Using this Book for Personal and Organizational Transformation

You can only create a compelling vision through serious exploration. To invest in yourself and in your future, use this book to open new vistas, new directions, and new wisdom.

After creating your vision in Part I, you'll use the tools and strategies in Part II to help you manifest your vision. This book offers a variety of activities to help you transform your work and your life. Although some organizations don't subscribe to the value of doing personal vision work, if you want committed, energized people, then invite them to share their personal visions!

Nothing will enliven an organization more than a collective sharing of hopes and dreams. It takes time to explore personal visions, but people engage at a deeper level and learn to bring out the best in each other.

In most organizations, if you ask individuals for their personal visions, you hear, "I've already done that," or you get a puzzled look. Organizations are full of people who have done extensive personal exploration, or they've done none at all. In many organizations, people can recite the company's vision, or they can "get it for you." Only outstanding organizations foster an environment where people talk with genuine excitement about their future.

Writer's block is a common barrier to vision work, but you can choose a remarkably simple antidote: If you can't write about what you want to see in the future, *talk about it or draw a picture of it.* Creating a vision is, after all, nothing more than seeing a picture of the future. Just like a blueprint provides a visual image of what a building will look like after construction, the pictures you draw or the stories you tell represent your ideal future.

In the computer world, the expression WYSIWYG means, "What you see is what you get." It refers to software with the capability of depicting on the screen what actually appears on paper when a document is printed. With WYSIWYG software, you can make changes to your screen image and know that your altered image will become reality when printed. The work of the visionary is the equivalent of using WYSIWYG software.

Once you can imagine a picture on your mental screen, you begin to develop the faith and confidence to translate your dreams into reality. What you *see* is, indeed, what you *get.* Where most of us fail is in the *seeing.* Using my internal WYSIWYG screen, I envision the simple but profound ideas in this book opening your mind's eye to a whole new way of living.

I wish I could take some credit for other's visions, but I actually contribute very little in the way of content. My gift is in creating safe space for emerging visions and stimulating dialogue for designing a better future. A book is not the best medium for dialogue, but my intention is to ask provocative questions to stimulate both your inner and outer dialogue.

One more note before we continue. I encourage you to write and draw in this book. Make it yours. No one becomes a visionary by simply reading a book; you must explore, excavate, sketch and scrawl to discover emerging visions.

Chapter 2:
Exploring Your Vision, in Seven Steps

...all change, even very large and powerful change, begins when a few people start talking with one another about something they care about.

— Margaret Wheatley

Most people understand the importance of being highly aware of their personal values, purpose, and vision. But get a group of people together, whether it's a family, a community, or an organization, and it's much more difficult to define a collective vision. The shared vision experience is more fun, more inspirational and more rewarding than doing the work alone.

How do you arrive at a vision for yourself or your organization? In this chapter, you'll tour the seven steps of the *Tell Your Vision* process. When you complete the journey, you'll hold a vivid image, deep within your mind's eye, which opens you to exciting new opportunities for yourself and your organization. In the following chapters, you'll see more details and suggestions about how to enhance each of the seven steps.

I encourage you to do the actual work for each step as you move through this chapter. Or, put your feet up and read the whole book for inspiration, and then come back to each chapter to do the work, alone or with your team. Whatever you decide, don't skip the work. Your reward is a much deeper understanding of yourself, your organization, what you value, and what you can achieve.

Instead of endorsing a static vision statement, engage in the *Tell Your Vision* process to get people excited about what's possible. The process awakens passionate energy and leads to a shared commitment to a bold new future. The first two steps of the process capture the best of what already exists and the next five steps help you paint a compelling picture of the future.

To get the most from this model, do the personal work as the foundation for the organizational work. The reason for doing both is simple: personal visions awaken passion that enlivens the organization. When ordinary people expand their aspirations to include family, company, and society, they broaden their sphere of influence and produce extraordinary results.

Sometimes people feel reluctant to start a shared vision process with a quest for personal vision. They value their privacy and fear exposure. These fears are real. However, once people get started, they enjoy the process because they want to contribute to each other's well-being. The beauty of a shared vision process is that people forge fulfilling bonds that connect them to a deeper personal purpose and a larger collective purpose.

The *Tell Your Vision* Process

Developing a powerful vision is easy if you take one step at a time. Start with history, a look at where you've been. End with the vision story, a strong sense of where you intend to go. In between, explore the values, environment, action, identity, and contribution that lie ahead.

Do you have to go through all seven steps exactly as prescribed? Of course not! No model, including this one, should be used as a cookbook. Instead, use the model as a navigation system, or a guide for expanding your thinking. In my experience, the most powerful results involve elements of the seven steps defined here. Still, I encourage you to customize the process and the language for your unique team or organization.

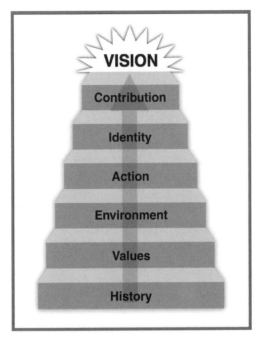

Tell Your Vision
The seven steps begin with a look at the past
and end with a story about the future

Step One: History — Sharing Milestones and Possibilities

Personal

Chart your history, by writing down important milestones in your life, or making simple sketches that illustrate your journey to date. Include high points, low points and milestones from the past. In small groups, tell your personal life story, sharing as much as you like. Ask the group to listen for themes in your life and reflect back what they hear. Then group members share three milestones they hope to reach in the future.

Organizational

Create a timeline from the organization's beginnings until the present, and divide the timeline into logical sections. Assign small groups to each era of the organization's history, and ask them to present the highlights and low points. Share your milestones, important events and "lessons learned" by telling stories, sharing drawings or acting out important events. Give people time to prepare their presentations, and then ask them to share stories in chronological order. Sharing milestones and acting out important events gives people a deep sense of how the organization evolved. This process lends itself to later identifying historic values and competencies.

In small groups, ask members to reflect on the following questions:

1. *What empowering traditions do you want to keep?*

2. *How does respecting the past help you embrace the future?*

Each group tells stories and acts out important milestones they'd like to achieve in the future, talking about them as though they've already occurred. For example: "In the year 2020, we opened offices in China and threw a big party with fireworks and gifts for new customers..."

In the large group, debrief by asking:

1. *What's attractive about the future?*

2. *What future milestones inspire you?*

Step Two: Values—Clarifying What Matters Most

Personal

Values are not wishes, morals, or "shoulds." Your values are your intrinsic beliefs about what is important in life. Make a list of values you currently live by. Determine what values you deem important, that you would like to honor more fully.

Organizational
Consider your present organizational environment and the values you collectively endorse. Envision the most desirable future imaginable. Observe how people publicly declare the values of the organization, and hone in on which values guide the actions of the organization. There isn't one single "right" set of values for individuals or for organizations. Visionary companies do not identify values they "ought" to subscribe to. They identify the values that already give heart and soul to the organization, and their members commit to living those values more fully.

In small groups:

1. *Share a peak experience and ask others in the group to listen for your values.*

2. *What personal values do you hold dear that people in the organization also value?*

In the large group, debrief by asking:

1. *Share the stories that you tell repeatedly about your organization. What organizational values do these stories highlight that you would like to perpetuate?*

2. *How do you ensure that both personal and organizational values are honored?*

After the group has brainstormed a list of values, use "dot voting" to determine and prioritize the five core values that matter most. The way it works is this: Write all the values on a large sheet of flip chart paper. Then each person gets five dots to place on the values they think are most important. Each person has the option of using all their dots on a particular value or spreading them out among several values.

Separately chart the top five values based on the most votes. On a scale of 1-10, where 1 is low and 10 is high, each individual scores the values in terms of how strongly the organization honors or embraces each of the values right now. Ask yourself what behaviors have to change so that desired values become honored more fully. Instead of asking how others need to change, ask yourself, "What can *I* do to honor my values and the organization's values more fully?"

Step Three: Environment—Choosing What You Want

Personal

Picture your ideal future environment and every aspect of your surroundings. Picture your home, your community, and the place where you work. Don't limit yourself to what's practical. Get a feel for your ideal environment and notice what it looks like. Consider your ideal possessions, climate, living space, artwork, people, music, scents, and ambience.

Organizational

Imagine that you visit your ideal workplace ten years from now. Picture a place where you and everyone else choose to come each day, passionate about what awaits you. Allow your imagination to run wild. Don't limit yourself to what you deem realistic or within your budget. Notice what's different about your desired future and what stands out. Look for evidence that your workplace is a great place to work.

In small groups:

1. *Describe your environment in the perfect future. What surrounds you that is important to you?*

2. *Visualize the ambience you want to create.*

In the large group, debrief by asking:

1. *What do you see in your current environment that you want to maintain in the future?*

2. *If you had a magic wand, how would you change the physical and emotional environment of your workplace?*

Step Four: Action—Shaping Behaviors and Capabilities

Personal
Think about your ideal future and your behavior. Notice what you *do* in the ideal world. In your ideal future, determine what capabilities you have mastered. Build your awareness about what you especially enjoy *doing*.

Organizational
Thinking again of your ideal picture of the future, notice the actions that you and others take in the future. Compare your ideal future with the actions and behaviors in the present. Look for behavioral changes that contribute to your ideal future. Notice how you handle the good times and how you handle stress. In the ideal workplace, imagine an environment where everyone in your organization has mastered new competencies. Surely, you all have a new set of technical skills, but think about what other skills you will need in your preferred future.

In small groups discuss:

1. *What personal capabilities do you already have that you will use even more in the future?*

2. *What competencies do you hope to master within the next five years?*

In the large group, debrief by asking:

1. *What behaviors and capabilities do people already demonstrate that you want to see even more of?*

2. *What new competencies do people need to master to meet future challenges?*

Step Five: Identity—Honing Your Image

Personal

Hone in on what's special about you. In an ideal world, imagine the short phrases people use to describe you. Determine the unique strengths and talents you offer that others find particularly valuable.

Organizational

Consider what makes your organization unique and how you provide value. Create a metaphor or visual image that describes your organizational identity. Instead of a dry mission statement, create an identity that resonates with people on an emotional level.

In small groups:

1. *What is your organization's competitive advantage?*

2. *While thinking about your ideal future, brainstorm the identity or nicknames you would like to earn. Imagine that you overhear people talking about your organization. What do you want them to say?*

In the large group, debrief by asking:

1. *Ten years from now, what does your organization do better than anyone else in the world?*

2. *Create an agreed-upon metaphor that captures the organization's future identity.*

Step Six: Contribution—Serving Your Purpose

Personal

Think about how you wish to serve. Imagine your ideal contribution. Picture yourself in balance with giving and receiving. Envision that you take care of yourself so that you can contribute fully.

Organizational

Imagine how your organization could impact the greater community. Envision your organization's contribution and how it serves the highest good. Picture your ideal image in your own backyard. Notice how your future products, services and ideas impact clients, your family, your community, your city, your country, and your world. Build on your metaphor from Step Five and describe how the imagery contributes to the betterment of humanity.

In small groups:

1. *Identify all the potential ways that you would like to make a contribution. What do you contribute in the short term? In the long term?*

2. *What do you consider the most important contribution that you could make in your life time?*

In the large group, debrief by asking:

1. *Who cares about your organization's future and what's in it for them?*

2. *How can your organization ensure a better future for your children and grandchildren? What will you do that will impact seven generations into the future?*

What impact do we want to have?

Step Seven: Vision—Picturing Your Future

Personal

Describe your ideal future, choosing words or phrases that energize you. Notice what's exciting or compelling about your future. Write your personal vision story in a way that is clear, brief, and comes from the heart.

Organizational

At the capstone stage of the process, open your collective hearts to intuition and feelings, and get in touch with your deepest aspirations. Imagine a cover story written about your organization. Regardless of your role now, picture yourself as one of the key players interviewed for the article. Talking about the future as though it has already happened makes it more tangible. Dialogue or write about the future in the past tense to unleash passionate energy and inspire confidence.

In small groups discuss:

1. *What headline introduces the cover story?*

2. *You are quoted in the article. What do you have to say about the success of your organization?*

In the large group:

1. *Share the highlights from your cover stories.*

2. *Building on your personal wishes, create an organizational vision, a story that captures the energizing elements of your shared future.*

Notice the ways that personal and organizational visions support each other. The most creative vision work generally happens in a group, with the help of a facilitator, but you can do it on your own. As simple as the *Tell Your Vision* process sounds, a facilitator ensures that group members feel understood and own the results. An external facilitator is especially useful when the group doesn't have a history of openness, or when group members have a strong personal stake in the outcome.

As you conclude this chapter, do you hold a new outlook of yourself and your organization? Acknowledge your success, and open the door for deeper work. In the next several chapters, you'll get more guidance and some exciting tools in your quest for a better future.

Chapter 3:
Setting the Tone for Your Work and Your Life

If I were to wish for anything, I should not wish for wealth and power, but for the passionate sense of the potential, for the eye which, ever young and ardent, sees the possible. Pleasure disappoints, possibility never. And what wine is so foaming, what so fragrant, what so intoxicating, as possibility!

— Soren Kierkegaard

Applying Appreciative Inquiry to Vision

Weaving vision into the fabric of our lives leads to hope and confidence that permeates the core of our interactions. An exciting way to tap personal and organizational potential is Appreciative Inquiry. This approach helps us explore the past and present so that we can design a better future. In this chapter we look at the four phases of Appreciative Inquiry: discovery, dream, design, and delivery. We'll explore how to use this technique as a means of focusing on possibilities, learning from past mistakes, and engaging the heart.

What exactly is Appreciative Inquiry? Appreciative Inquiry is a provocative approach to organizational learning and change developed by David Cooperrider and Suresh Srivastva from Case Western University. Inquiry into the "art of what's possible" begins with appreciation of the past and present, leads to a positive image of the future and inspires collective action. Appreciative Inquiry uses storytelling to affirm people, identify the life-giving forces, and accelerate learning at all levels of the organization. Appreciative Inquiry produces new perspectives and unleashes a powerful energy that increases the value of the organization. The process serves as an uplifting power tool for organizational growth.

Appreciative Inquiry emphasizes the positive, engages people's hearts, transforms inner and outer dialogue, and stimulates creativity. It differs from other approaches to organization development which focus more on the negative or deficits in the organization: i.e. what's wrong and how can we fix it.

Traditional vocabulary related to organizational deficits includes:

- Bureaucratic red tape
- Downsizing
- Missed commitment
- Sexual harassment
- Churn
- We/them mentality
- Debug
- Performance evaluation
- Distrust
- Gap analysis
- Inter-group conflict
- Trouble report
- Job dissatisfaction
- Labor management
- Employee turnover
- Low morale
- Customer complaints
- Organizational stress
- Group think
- Reorganization
- Down time
- Silos
- Delayed orders
- Turf battles
- Burnout
- Negativity and distrust

In contrast, Appreciative Inquiry focuses on dialogue about:

- Benchmarks
- Innovations
- Shared values
- Peak experiences
- Turning points
- Proud achievements
- Best practices
- Leveraging strengths
- Empowering traditions
- Inter-generational wisdom
- Moments of courage
- Learning from difficult times
- Organizational capacity
- Hopes for the future
- Organization's founding story
- Wishes and dreams
- Leadership at all levels
- Organizational legacy
- Tests of integrity

Wait a minute. Surely we need to resolve our problems and fix what is not working. If we focus on problems, we tend to give birth to even bigger problems. When we identify and fix a problem, it feels great which leads to short-term euphoria and we may become addicted to the high. The danger then becomes that we need to find new and more difficult problems to solve. For the same reason that pyromaniacs join the fire department, your best problem solvers become your worst nightmares, as they continue a crusade to uncover ever bigger problems.

At any moment, we can choose to focus on what's going "wrong," or we can turn our attention to what's going well. When we look for instances of people doing good work, we find many people actually doing good work, and we begin to see trends moving in the right direction instead of in the wrong direction. The direction we look in leads us to where we most often end up.

You do not have to remain a victim of problems, or spend your time focusing on potential problems. You do not need to keep your perspective rooted in the problems of the past. Appreciative Inquiry gives you the tools to move into an inquiry about your future. You have the power to break the ancient habit of letting your past eat up your present and future, by asking new questions and changing your focus.

When you look for life giving forces, you bring out the best in people. Instead of using traditional problem solving processes that separate, dissect and pull apart, look for forces that integrate and pull people together. By focusing on vitality, aspirations and ideas, the proverbial glass won't be half empty. It won't even be half full. It will be overflowing.

To get a feel for this technique, start by noticing where you habitually focus your attention. Do you focus on your good fortune and blessings, or do you pay attention to the clutter, busyness, disappointments, lack, worry, or fear? Consciously choosing where you put your attention requires self-awareness, decision-making and perseverance until you change the habit. Expect to learn a lot about yourself by simply noticing where your attention goes.

Build your awareness of where you focus by setting an alarm to ring every half hour during the day. Keep a log of your current thoughts each time the alarm goes off. Try it—you might surprise yourself with your findings.

- *Do you focus on the past, present or the future? Do you focus on possibilities or limitations?*

- *Ask yourself: How could my current situation change if I focused on possibilities instead of paying attention to perceived limitations, problems and barriers?*

You can't just give up paying attention to limitations without thinking carefully about how you will replace old ways of thinking. Where would you rather focus?

A problem-solving approach works well in the short run, but if you are looking for profound cultural change, Appreciative Inquiry creates an environment that fosters personal and organizational transformation with long lasting effects. Appreciative Inquiry gives you the opportunity to replace distrust, frustration and blame with mutual respect, cooperation and the desire to create. This affirmative process plants the seeds of the future and generates sustainable, systemic change.

Now let's look more closely at the four phases of Appreciative Inquiry. This approach serves as the philosophical foundation of *Courageous Visions*.

Exploring the Four Phases of Appreciative Inquiry

1. Discovery—Appreciating

In the discovery phase, we clarify values and use storytelling to capture the best of what is. We discover what gives life and energy to the organization. Start by asking people to interview each other in pairs to gather stories that capture memorable experiences, and discover organizational strengths and assets. Sharing and collecting these stories helps build organizational capacity by valuing and expanding on the best of what already exists.

As you collect these stories, ask yourself the following questions:

- *When it comes to your organization, what do you take pride in?*

- *What energizes people?*

- *What are the best stories about the organization?*

2. Dream — Envisioning
In the dream phase, we get out our magic wands and imagine what might be. Together we think big and share our hopes for our work and our relationships. We look at individual and organizational calling to explore our greater purpose and deepest wishes. In this phase, we act out our dreams to dramatize the possibilities and stretch the imagination.

Questions for this phase:

- *What is the world calling your organization to do?*

- *If you had no constraints, what new possibilities would you explore?*

- *If you surrounded yourselves with life-giving forces, what would that look like?*

3. Design — Co-constructing
In the design phase large numbers of people come together to co-create the organization. In small groups we explore the lofty images of the dream stage and determine what's possible. We align values, structures, systems and mission with the ideal by talking about what should be. In this phase, the team crafts provocative propositions which stretch the organization. We design by

exploring possible actions and making choices that will create a more desirable future.

Questions for this phase:

- *How does each piece look in an optimal system?*

- *To create a more desirable future, what actions do you choose?*

4. Delivery—Sustaining

In the delivery phase we develop action plans to realize the provocative propositions. In an open forum, ask people to determine their contribution and how they wish to serve. Establish personal and organizational commitments to fulfill these contributions. Create small groups to collaborate on the new initiatives that grow out of this process.

Because people are deeply involved in the first three phases, commitment and alignment come easily in the fourth phase.

Questions for this phase:

- *What action plan do you need to put into place to create a wonderful future?*

- *How can you bring about lasting cultural change?*

- *What do you need to do to sustain your preferred future?*

Focusing on Possibilities

Few organizations know how to change well. Using the traditional approach, they focus on the failures, define the problems and fix what's broken. Looking at "History," Step One of the *Tell Your Vision* process, does not mean focusing on what went wrong in the past. The problem with focusing on mistakes or failures is that whatever we put our attention on grows. When we focus on problems, mistakes and limitations, our limitations grow. When we focus on new possibilities, the possibilities grow. The latter is far more productive and exciting.

Most people recognize that when we continuously criticize children, they develop an inferiority complex. Many people don't know that the same happens to organizations. When people continuously critique the organization, structure, work processes, leadership, systems and each other, an inferiority complex develops and low energy predominates. An unconscious air of disempowerment seeps into the bones of the organization, stifling risk taking and shutting down options.

Learning from Mistakes

Many leaders tout the value of learning from their mistakes, but all we learn from our mistakes is what we *shouldn't* do again. Our mistakes don't tell us what we *should* do. Organizations move in the direction of what they study. But don't get the impression that Appreciative Inquiry means dancing around the issues in rose-colored glasses. Instead of glossing over problems, or avoiding unpleasant facts, we use them as powerful learning opportunities. Rather than wallowing in the past, we look at the positive aspects of our problems. What did we learn? How did we overcome adversity? We seek out the vital learning and build on existing strengths to create a bold desirable future. When we fail individually or as an organization, instead of casting blame or doubt, Appreciative Inquiry helps us transfer the learning to present practices.

Most consultants wouldn't dream of working with an organization without a thorough analysis of the problems. They argue that a pie-in-the-sky approach ignores the crumbling foundation, and no amount of designing the future will resolve the issues without looking at the causes of a distressed organization. In contrast, Appreciative Inquiry recognizes the crumbling foundation, but puts even more emphasis on exploring the resources available for rebuilding.

Appreciation means to express thankfulness, gratitude, or admiration. When we frame our questions positively, the inquiry results in "organizational appreciation," which means to grow or appreciate in value. The same way that the assets of the organization appreciate, people can appreciate.

Applying Appreciative Inquiry at Home and at Work

Many people I've met in the Appreciative Inquiry field exude hummingbird qualities, living on sweet nectar and appreciating beauty. Jamie Sams, a Native American spiritual writer, says that people with hummingbird "medicine" dart from one flower to another, tasting the essences and radiating the colors. They love life and its joys. They bring out the best in people and help them taste the succulent nectar of life.

To live an appreciative lifestyle is to pay attention to sources of energy. At my house, the best parties always end up in the kitchen. Even when we've all had plenty to eat, and we could choose more comfortable seats, we seek out life-giving forces. Sometimes a group ends up in my husband Dave's shop amidst the sawdust, tools and half-finished projects. With all the comfort of leaning against a table saw, people gravitate toward the creative energy of Dave's work. We are drawn toward what nurtures us.

Jane Magruder Watkins, who co-authored *Appreciative Inquiry: Change at the Speed of Imagination* with Bernard Mohr, gave me my first taste of using the methodology not just at work, but at home. Dave and I went to an Appreciative Inquiry couples retreat and learned how to celebrate and recreate our relationship.

She isn't the only practitioner who uses Appreciative Inquiry both at home and at work. Pierre Rochon from Ottawa says that his children warn their friends about the dinner ritual ahead of time, and tell them to just play along. Instead of asking, "How was your day," Pierre asks, "What was the best part of your day?" At first, the guests feel "weird," but it doesn't take long for them to jump into the conversation wholeheartedly.

When Pierre Rochon led an Appreciative Inquiry process for the Human Resources department of the Canadian National Defense, his boss held a 3-hour meeting to brief the executives on the process. His enthusiasm was boundless, and by the end of the meeting, he committed to gathering 300 people together for three days to get them excited about a shared vision. Surprised that his boss would leap in with both feet, Pierre feared that such a bold commitment might be a dangerous move. As enthusiastic as Pierre was about the process, he thought it somewhat suicidal to attempt to get 300 people energized using an approach that they had only recently heard about and of which they knew little.

That didn't stop him from proceeding. He recorded the process, and the first time I watched the video, I couldn't get the sound on my VCR to work, but the facial expressions said it all. The excitement of the participants ran deep, and they experienced a new energy. Collaboratively they designed initiatives that changed the way they communicate, how they work together and how they provide services. A year after the summit, they came back together to celebrate and filled a wall with one-page success stories.

Pierre Rochon and his wife also do volunteer work with couples engaged to marry, supporting them in designing and creating their ideal life. Later the couples come back to share the best stories of their first few years together. Pierre says, "I like using Appreciative Inquiry because it matches my outlook on life."

Bernard Mohr calls Pierre Rochon and Ginette Danis, "two of Canada's finest Appreciative Inquiry practitioners." In part, Pierre earned his reputation because he doesn't shrink from the naysayers, and particularly enjoys leading the turnaround with people who say, "Look, we know all about Appreciative Inquiry, and we think it's useless. It's just a silly feel-good approach and we need something more serious!" After they've been with Pierre for a half hour, they experience the rigor of the approach and the power of using Appreciative Inquiry for sustainable organizational change.

Engaging the Heart

> *Love in organizations, then, is the most potent source of power we have available.*
>
> — *Margaret Wheatley*

The quest for vision is not a problem to solve, but a mystical journey. The wisdom of the heart is crucial to the work because our hearts open the gateway to our deepest values, passions, and connection to others. Our hearts provide a source of clarity, humility and compassion, and become a vital resource for engaging in a more fulfilling future.

When James Kouzes, who co-authored *The Leadership Challenge* with Barry Posner, researched excellence in organizations, he met with outstanding leaders who often spoke about loving their work and loving their people. At first, he thought they spoke euphemistically, and that they *really* loved their families and their weekends. After hearing the word "love" mentioned so many times, he became convinced that the best leaders passionately love their work and their people. Kouzes and Posner also wrote *Encouraging the Heart,* an inspirational book about heart connection in the workplace.

In most corporate cultures, the "L" word is taboo even though people inherently recognize the value of love in any setting. Even people in the most macho work cultures know about the importance of love. Tim Gallwey, who wrote *The Inner Game of Tennis*, tells the story of sitting on a panel with three of the greatest coaching legends of all time, George Allen of the Washington Redskins, John Wooden of UCLA, and Red Auerbach of the Boston Celtics. The panel discussion focused on what great athletic coaches could teach business leaders about motivating people.

Gallwey noticed that the three coaches struggled to articulate how they successfully coached people to the top of their game. The interviewer pressed them for advice, but they only came up with a few anecdotes and no real principles.

After half an hour of banter, Red Auerbach grew increasingly frustrated and said, "How do I do it? Goddamn it, I'll tell you how I do it. I love the bastards."

That's when George Allen blinked in surprise and said, "Nothing we've said so far is important... until now." Auerbach thought for a second and continued, "And I'll tell you how I know that's how I do it. Because five years later, after these guys are no longer on the team, they're calling me up to tell me how things are going."

Red's language reminds me of Tim Sanders' book, "Love is the Killer App." How ironic and amusing that both Auerbach and Sanders talk about love in conjunction with words like "killer" and "bastards." When people in the workplace mimic the Budweiser commercials and say, "I love you, man," I hear their sarcasm, but I also recognize the value of this big four-letter word.

In the workplace and in life, many people fear intimacy, especially self-intimacy. Reluctance to love runs rampant. Fear of disappointment or loss might explain the reluctance to love others, but it doesn't explain the aversion to self-love. Jack Canfield, author of the *Chicken Soup for the Soul*, says the majority of executives have great difficulty looking in the mirror and saying, "I love you." Unconditional love of self and others awakens a great source of vitality that helps people collectively realize their potential.

Our deepest fear is not that we are inadequate. Our deepest fear is that we are powerful beyond measure. It is our light, not our darkness, that most frightens us. We ask ourselves, "Who am I to be brilliant, gorgeous, talented, fabulous?" Actually, who are you not to be? You are a child of God. Your playing small does not serve the world. There's nothing enlightened about shrinking so that other people won't feel insecure around you. We are all meant to shine as children do. We were born to make manifest the glory of God that is within us. It's not just in some of us; it's in everyone. And as we let our own light shine, we unconsciously give other people permission to do the same. As we're liberated from our own fear, our presence automatically liberates others.

— Marianne Williamson

Listen to the heartbeat of love by recognizing the inherent worthiness of others, but also explore the value of self-love, an essential ingredient that opens us to the love of others. Focusing on what you love about yourself and what you love about your organization fuels the fire.

- *List 50 things you love about yourself, including your gifts, talents, and uniqueness. Keep going until you get to 50! If you need help, ask people you know for ideas.*

- *Now list 50 things you love about your organization.*

Looking Within for What's Possible

Your vision will become clear only when you can look into your own heart.... Who looks outside, dreams; who looks inside, awakes.
— *Carl Jung*

It takes more than luck to find a profession that draws on your core aliveness and the rapture within. To explore your inner landscape is to ask the questions, "What purpose do I serve?" and "How can I impact the future?" The answer to so many questions comes from a gentle probing of self. Like bears, we enter the cave to hibernate and digest our experience. By entering silence, we discover our capacity to envision alternatives and know which path will lead us to our goals. Unique gifts and values cannot be borrowed, absorbed, or copied. Offering one of life's keys, John Miller says, "People who take time to be alone usually have depth, originality and quiet reserve." Introspection uncovers the surest route to a centered life.

Recovering from a few broken bones after an auto accident, I wistfully looked out the window at the best snow I'd seen in years and longed to go skiing. I asked, "Why me?" Instead of stopping there, I used Appreciative Inquiry to look for the learning in the experience, the value of the accident, the opportunity for a breakthrough.

Inaction has never come easily for me. On crutches, I couldn't do much. Without my roles in the world, without a full schedule, I thought I'd feel miserable. Instead, I kept concentrating on all that I felt grateful for, each breath filling me with peace. I learned how deeply I care about everything I *do* — working with clients, cooking great food, and helping others. I also became more aware of my hunger for learning, my love for family and friends, and my desire for personal growth and inner calm.

By sharing the Appreciative Inquiry process, I'm hoping you have a sense of the foundational philosophy of *Courageous Visions*. Attuned to continually opening to a fuller experience of what's possible, let's turn our attention now to the details of each of the seven steps of the *Tell Your Vision* process.

Chapter 4:
Attuning to the Heart

Storytelling has the capacity to directly engage the heart and imagination in such a way that a deeper level of listening is activated, which opens the eyes of perception.

— Laura Simms

Our stories provide us with a sense of appreciation and connectivity. When we explore our history, we bring collective memories to life and catalyze new ways of thinking about the future. Stories awaken our imagination and our courage. People see their history as a resource for possibilities, not a problematic series of events.

When we tell our stories, we convey our values and share the lessons we've learned, which builds community. In this chapter we capture the values from stories, define benchmarks, identify barriers to values, and differentiate between espoused values and lived values. We explore organizational values and seek alignment between personal and organizational values.

Sharing History

The best stories move us deeply because they touch us emotionally, teach us, and help us create shared meaning. Think of the stories you tell again and again, and discover what

> **Step 1:**
>
> History —
> Sharing
> Milestones and
> Possibilities

makes them your favorites. Your stories say a lot about who you are and what you care about.

One of my favorite life experiences happened in an unlikely place, the Jersey shore. At dawn before it fills up with umbrellas, babes, and people who have answered the call of the ice cream hawkers a few too many times, the beach feels tranquil and inviting. My mother and I walked from the dunes toward the water, which looked glassy, stiller than I'd ever seen it. We saw a huge school of dolphins about a half mile off shore, traveling north. If we acted quickly, we might reach them.

Dropping my book and towel, I said, "Let's go! We have just enough time to get out there." My mother had just turned 70, but she swims a mile a day, so it surprised me that she said, "I'll just slow you down—you won't get there in time if I go."

"There's no time to argue—come!" I said running backwards. I dove through the surf, and one more time looked back at her and shouted, "Now!" But she paid as much attention to my orders as usual.

Putting my head down, I swam hard for about 15 minutes. Figuring I had almost arrived, I looked up to find that I had only swum about half way. I had underestimated the distance; the dolphins now seemed about a mile from shore. Looking back, my mother looked the size of a dot, which startled me. I knew I had to keep up my pace if I hoped to reach the dolphins.

Exhausted, I reached the area where they were swimming— hugely disappointed that I had just missed them. Watching the dolphins leaping 50 yards north of me, I thought, "How wonderful it would have felt to swim with them!" I floated, caught my breath, and watched the school disappear.

As I thought about heading back, a dolphin suddenly leapt out of the water right in front of my face. Eyeball to eyeball, I felt a surge of fear—fear so intense that I could hardly breathe. I felt foolish to have ventured out so far all alone. I could drown. Boats could run over me. Most of all, I felt frightened by the dolphins. I could hear them talking. They sounded friendly, but the dolphins did not seem a bit like Flipper, the television show I'd watched years ago. Undoubtedly, the lifeguards still lay in their beds. The huge massive wild animals that ruled the ocean made it clear I didn't belong.

Before long, the dolphins circled around and came back to check me out. That's when I realized the size of the school—hundreds of them leapt all around me. My mother, who has swum with manta rays and humpback whales, and is sometimes called "the shark lady," would not have felt any fear in this situation. But I felt terrified! I had always thought of myself as the great daredevil, so my fear startled me. At the same time, I felt blessed, loved, and lucky to belong. For twenty minutes I swam with them, both mesmerized by their beauty and semi-paralyzed by my fear. As I calmed down, they swam away.

At my core, I believe that we only have two choices, two places to come from—fear or love. I always considered doubt and wonder opposites, but when I swam with the dolphins they showed me how to embrace both.

What values do you hear in my story? If you guess that I value adventure, spirituality, and connection, we're on the same wavelength.

Why bother exploring values? In the *Tell Your Vision* process outlined in Chapter 2, we saw how a clear understanding of history (Step 1) and values (Step 2) set the stage for development of a vision (Steps 3-7). When we share our personal values, we throw a pebble into the pool of awareness, which has a ripple effect on discovering organizational values.

Discovering Values in Peak Experiences

To deepen your sense of what matters most, and to set the stage for the future, share a few of your peak experiences with others. You don't have to limit yourself to the big turning

Step 2:

Values—
Clarifying What
Matters Most

points in your life; peak experiences range from noticing a flower to giving birth to a child. Look for times when life seemed sweet, when you danced on top of the world, when you felt totally "on" or inspired.

Your peak experiences and favorite stories say a lot about your values. What themes or common threads do you notice? What insights do your stories offer about what's most important to you? What do these stories say about your values?

Powerful work in the discovery and affirmation of values often happens in small groups because people see and understand each other more intimately through stories. As people tell their stories to friends or colleagues they trust, they experience the power of deep listening. The author Mary Rose O'Reilley talks about how listening like a cow helps people establish radical presence. She says, "Cows cock their big brown eyes at you and twitch their ears when you talk. This is a great antidote to the critical listening that goes on in academia, where we listen for the mistake, the flaw in the argument."

Critical listening crushes the spirit. Empathic listening builds awareness and encourages the talents of others. Empathic connections help us attune to our values and needs, which becomes a powerful tool for implementing change. When people see and hear us at a deep level, they create marvelous opportunities for personal transformation. Deep listening at a personal level becomes the precursor to personal and organizational change.

Leaders find the common thread that weaves together the fabric of human needs into a colorful tapestry. They seek out the brewing consensus among those they would lead. In order to do this, they develop a deep understanding of the collective yearnings. They listen carefully for quiet whisperings in dark corners. They attend to the subtle cues. They sniff the air to get the scent. They watch the faces. They get a sense of what people want, what they value, what they dream about.

— James Kouzes and Barry Posner

To listen the way Kouzes and Posner suggest is to listen for the scattered bits of courage—courage that fuels inspiration.

Exploring Valleys

Another approach to deepening awareness of values involves looking for the opposite of the peak experiences, by exploring the valley experiences. Think of times when you felt sad or disappointed or downright angry. List the times that stand out in your memory when you seemed most down and out.

Earlier I said that what you focus on grows. So why would I ask you to look at times of failure or sadness? Getting out the flashlight and looking in the darkness tells you even more about your values, because when you explore feelings of anger, fear, or despair, you usually find a value just under the surface. When others seem to squash your values, you might feel disturbed, but when you squash your own values, you feel miserable. Looking at what's missing helps you flesh out what's possible. What do your valley experiences say about your values?

When people in your life want to focus on the negative, the worst of what exists, you can use the valley experiences to point them toward what's possible. If they complain about problems without offering solutions, instead of feeling discouraged, say, "When you say that the teamwork around here is terrible, you must have an idea what good teamwork would look like. Will you tell me about that?" That way you get in touch with their pain, their needs, *and* their hopes.

Clarifying Values

Often people attempt to live their lives backwards: they try to have more things, or more money, in order to do more of what they want so that they will be happier. The way it actually works is the reverse. You must first be who you really are, then, do what you need to do, in order to have what you want.

—Margaret Young

When my colleague, Jackie, first started coaching Clint, she thought he was the most arrogant person she'd ever met, but kept coaching him anyway because she felt moved by the power of his vision. As a corporate turn-around artist, he lived out of a suitcase, worked until 1:00 a.m. seven days a week and rarely flew home on weekends. A true cowboy and a bit of a lone ranger, Clint spent his vacations herding cattle.

He saw the future clearly and intensely, but he couldn't communicate it well. Lots of visionaries underplay their passion because they're afraid that they will intimidate people. Clint didn't have that problem. Fired up about almost everything he did, he couldn't reach people because they spent all their time avoiding his heat and steering clear of the flames.

His executive team struggled and rarely spoke to him because they couldn't quite figure out what the boss wanted. Instead of risking doing something wrong, they played it safe and avoided Clint.

Jackie helped him work on his communication skills and tried to get him to tone down the arrogance. With practice, Clint began to translate what he thought and felt into terms that others understood. He also developed a deeper awareness of how others responded to his words. Without his arrogance, he seemed like a person with something missing—an amputee who could no longer kick, but could still feel all the sensations in his missing leg.

Like all turn-around practitioners, Clint's massive and swift restructuring strategies sometimes saved companies and sometimes decimated them. Smarting from a recent failure, he drove himself hard to achieve success and gain financially. For months, Jackie hoped to see a glimmer of altruism, that he cared about saving the company and saving people's jobs, but not once did any evidence emerge.

When the company started to turn around anyway, Jackie got a glimpse of the positive side of arrogance, not just the isolating side. For the first time, she realized the value of his strengths, how his palpable self-confidence and intense energy got results. Fully conscious of his arrogance, not once did he apologize for the fear he stimulated. His bravado was integrally woven into his plan to save the company.

Appreciating the power of his boldness, Jackie started working with him to develop his strengths, instead of focusing on turning weaknesses around. She told me that his pride helped her become more open, and that she now tries to look beyond her initial judgment when someone seems obnoxious, rude, or crazy. By exploring their inner world, she helps people identify their gifts so that they make a more powerful contribution and fulfill their purpose.

Jackie helped Clint identify the ways his confidence served him, which helped him clarify his strengths and hopes. Once he felt seen in all his glory, he shifted his perspective and made important changes in his life. He re-established a spiritual practice with a group of men in his hometown, which grounded him in a positive way. Clint became much clearer about both his business and his personal vision, and learned to articulate it in a way that others found attractive. He expanded his pursuits to make a significant contribution in the lives of young people, and he began teaching business skills to high school kids on the side.

Today Jackie holds deep respect for his ability to bring about radical change. Enthused about his personal values, Clint completed the turnaround and took a year off to run a Senate campaign for a woman he really believed in. He hadn't lived at home in years, nor had he lived without a regular paycheck, but he began to do both. His spiritual life came alive and he found new meaning in his work.

Clarifying personal values deepens self-awareness and adds richness and stability to your life. In a world of continuous change, your core values remain relatively constant. Often you'll find a big difference between what you think you "should" value and what you actually value. While family, culture, and tradition influence your values, every individual has a unique set of values. Clear, prioritized values help you remain true to yourself. When you continuously clarify what is most important to you, you practice the discipline of personal mastery.

If you have built castles in the air, your work need not be lost; that is where they should be. Now put the foundations under them.
> — *Henry David Thoreau*

Values hold the essence of your experience. They form the building blocks of your personal foundation. Values answer the question, "What do you stand for?" When you look at what you *must* have in life, beyond your basic needs, you usually find a value. When you align with your values, your mission and vision become clearer and easier to define.

Values List

Values are often summed up in a word. The list that follows includes some of the most frequently held values, but don't limit yourself to this list!

Accomplishment — productivity, advancement, triumph, acquire, predominate, attain, quality, recognition, mastery, expertise, dominant, superiority, greatest, set standards, excellence

Adventure — risk, danger, gamble, experiment, unknown thrill, speculation, endeavor, exhilaration, daring, quest, venture, courage

Catalyst — influence, impact, spark, stimulate, move forward, encourage, energize, touch, coach, alter, uplift, arouse, enlighten

Challenge — problem solving, competitive, fast pace, variety, growth opportunities, frequent changes, resilience, success, discovery, learn, uncover, high expectations

Contribution — serve, assist, facilitate, provide, improve, endow, minister to, foster, augment, strengthen, grant, assist, improve society, benefit others

Environment — aesthetics, ambience, beauty, grace, attractiveness, comfort, cleanliness, neatness, artwork, pleasant working conditions, well-designed workspace, opportunity for expression, orderliness

Independence — individualistic, self-directed, self-reliant, maverick, entrepreneurial, ownership, developer, authentic, empowered, free-spirit, freedom to choose, full self-expression

Innovation — creative, progressive, design, imaginative, conceptual, perfection, inventive, ingenuity, assemble, synthesize, originality, build, inspiration, artistic, vitality, idea generation

Leadership — take charge, direct, delegate, teach, educate, inform, prime, instruct, prepare, guide, cause, reign, persuade, govern, encourage, rule, model, power

Pleasure — fun, entertainment, bliss, play games, amusement, recreation, sports, relaxation, joy, time for family, friends, community, health, sensuality, well-being, tranquility, zest

Relationships — responsive, teamwork, harmony, connection, unity, bonding, part of family or community, nurture, integrated, intimacy, empathize, support, collaboration, comradeship

Security — commitment, high earnings, careful, planning, comfortable, low pressure, few constraints, predictability, leisure, assurance, prosperity, certainty, loyalty, tradition, trust

Spirituality—aware, relate with God, honor, accepting, devoted, passionate, awake, holy, religious, attuned to energy, ethics, integrity, honesty, compassionate

Prioritizing Your Values

The following technique can help you identify and prioritize the values that mean the most to you:

- *Begin by listing your most important values. You can choose from the preceding list, but search within to identify the values that you uniquely own. Write your 10 most important values, using clarifying words to flesh out the description of each value.*

- *Once you list your values, prioritize your top five values by crossing off the values that matter least, until only five remain. Your degree of discomfort in doing this will reveal the importance of the value. To test the ultimate importance of a value, envision a situation where you cannot honor the value.*

- *Imagine that you carry your five most important values in your boat as you travel down the river of life. The type of boat you envision tells you a lot about your values, too! As people join you on your journey, imagine that you need to lighten your load, and each of you gives up one value. Which value do you abandon first? Second? Keep throwing your values overboard until you only have one left. What one value can't you live without? Pay particular attention to how you feel when you are asked to abandon one of your top values.*

- *What single value would you like to pass on to your children (or other people's children) as the most important foundation for a wonderful life?*

Defining Benchmarks and Choosing Metaphors

Athletes keep track of their "personal best." True athletes don't always depend on the competition to bring out their excellence. That's why a personal record feels more rewarding than winning. When I coached competitive swimming, I marveled at the swimmers who nearly always swam a "personal best." Serious swimmers had a strong sense of time, and could guess their time within a few tenths. The inconsistent swimmers always baffled me. They didn't have a clue how fast they swam, wouldn't dare to guess their times, and had huge variances from one meet to the next.

After each race, I asked the swimmers for their official time, mostly to make sure they kept track. Until they turned 10 or 11 years old, they usually cared only about what place they came in and quite often answered, "I forgot to get my time."

"The race isn't over until you've gotten your time," I'd remind them, encouraging them to notice and track their improvement. As they got older, I'd ask them to predict their time before the race. At the end of the race, mature swimmers showed an intense look of apprehension until they got their actual time. Once in a great while, when a swimmer made a significant breakthrough, when the person felt "on" in every sense, the fist would go up or a full smile would break out across the swimmer's face even before they saw their time.

A "personal best" experience defines your own record-setting performance that embodies your individual standard of excellence.

- *What is the benchmark of your personal best experience? If you have more than one, write about the one that you smile about most.*

To honor your values fully means that nothing stands in the way of living a rich, fulfilling life. Even when you know what you believe, it isn't always easy to direct your thoughts and actions toward the realization of your convictions. To take values out of the nebulous realm of philosophy, try using benchmarks and metaphors as powerful tools for getting in touch with the energetic qualities of your values. A benchmark indicates a high point, a pivotal experience. To determine the benchmark of a value, think of a time when you honored the value fully. Name the event and use a word picture—a metaphor to describe the importance of the value.

Example of benchmarks and metaphors that capture personal values:

- Benchmark: A project manager for a software conversion fought for and won bonuses for every team member for bringing the project in on time and under budget.

  Metaphor: *Solidarity pays dividends*

- Benchmark: An AIDS prevention activist who values connection above all else, remembers bringing the AIDS quilt to her community as her touchstone.

  Metaphor: *Fragments joined by compassion*

- Benchmark: A marathon runner who values spirituality as his top priority, remembers a race in the pouring rain where every runner ended up covered with mud, but that only invigorated the runners and the crowd.

  Metaphor: *Earth, air and water encourage fire*

- Benchmark: A minister who values compassion, when robbed at gunpoint, radiates love and concern for his attacker.

  Metaphor: *Rainbow prism reflects love and light*

- Benchmark: A mentor learns much from the troubled teens he guides, and envisions himself as a rudder attuned to the changing river.

  Metaphor: *Listen to the river*

- Benchmark: An operations manager holds accomplishment as her dearest value and remembers the party-like atmosphere when her team went to a customer site to clean up the damage from a flood and helped them get back on line in 24 hours.

  Metaphor: *Gratitude fills the well of our souls*

For each of your values, remember a time when you fully honored your top value. A perfect ten.

- *What benchmark epitomizes each of our top values?*

- *What metaphor helps you visualize the value?*

Identifying Barriers to Values

Often people tell me they don't have enough time to honor their values. Nonsense. They have 24 hours a day, just like everybody else. What *real* barriers keep you from honoring your values? Sometimes "shoulds" or other people's values stop you cold, but most barriers come from within. Make the distinction between what you value and what others tell you to value.

Now that you've identified your values, the next step is to identify the internal or external barriers that prevent you from living fully in your vision. The following chart helps you identify and overcome barriers to your values:

1. *List your top values using a metaphor or phrase*

2. *Rate yourself on a scale of 1–10 as to how well you honor each of your top ten values right now.*

3. *What gets in the way of honoring your values fully? What barriers or obstacles keep you from honoring each value fully?*

4. *On a scale of 1–10, how strongly do you experience the barrier? What action can you take to honor the value fully?*

5. *What actions can you take so that each of your values becomes a "10"?*

1. Value	2. Score	3. Barrier	4. Strength of Barrier	5. Action to Honor Value

Identifying Barriers to Values

Differentiating Between Espoused Values and Lived Values

Consider the difference between espoused values and lived values. What we *say* is important is often different from how we *live. Lived* values tell us more about what we stand for right *now*, while *espoused* values tell us more about who we hope to *become*.

From a family with nine children, my husband Dave grew up with the value of serving others. Selfishness wasn't tolerated and everyone in their family put their personal needs last. I get to receive the benefits of his generosity, and occasionally I forget that he has another purpose besides serving me. Ouch.

Dave's work involves buying properties, fixing them up and renting them out. Sometimes I get involved with the decision-making when it means borrowing money. Stunned by his eagerness to spend lots of time and money for little or no return, the words out of my mouth aren't so encouraging. "You want to spend *how much money* on a new kitchen without raising the rent?" Occasionally he reminds me that he doesn't ask about my return on investment when I go to a conference, but I continue to ask him questions about his business that sound like the equivalent of, "Are you crazy?"

Once I said, "You'll never get your money out of those replacement windows," and his impassioned response stuck with me. He said, "Would you want to live in a place where the windows rattle every time the wind blows? Some guys spend their extra money on boats or cars; some spend their money on a girlfriend and some buy drinks for everyone at the bar. I buy houses and fix them up. That's my calling... to create great spaces for people to live. I don't care if I don't get rich doing this. I love turning a dump into a highly functional space where people *want* to live."

Oh. Now I understood. I'm skilled at hearing other's values and encouraging them to honor their values fully. So it surprises me when I don't do this with my own family. As much as I encourage a values-driven lifestyle in the workplace, I wasn't walking my talk at home. I envisioned all of our savings going into other peoples' homes, but that's no excuse.

Clearly I value security and stability. The values I espouse but *don't* honor are respect for Dave's calling and acceptance of his choices. I *say* that I value the vitality of every person's calling, so

I'm grateful that my family helps me bridge the gap between what I *say* I value and how I *live* my values.

- *What differences do you notice between your espoused values and your lived values?*

- *How can you start living your espoused values now?*

Becoming grounded in your core values enhances your authenticity. Last spring I realized that I didn't have much adventure in my life, and since I strongly value adventure, I decided to do something about it. I scheduled three white water trips, which looked exceptionally challenging. Dangerous would be more accurate.

During a trip down the la Poudre, I caught a glimpse of my oldest son's terror when he got dumped in the river. He looked terrified as I pulled him back into the raft, and I felt surprised because I'd always considered the water a friend.

A few minutes later, when the river pulled me into the froth, I understood his fear. The water moved much faster than I'd imagined, slamming me into rocks, and shaking my confidence. Later that night, he told his friends that I'd saved his life, and I laughed along with his joke. The next morning when we read in the paper that an experienced kayaker had drowned on the same river, he expressed a lot of emotion and made it clear that he believed he would have been seriously hurt if I hadn't grabbed him when I did.

This came on the heels of a canoe trip where a friend got caught in a helicopter eddy. I sent the throw rope sailing way beyond her reach and allowed the other end to slip out of my hand. The look on her face horrified me, reminding me of her reluctance to take me because of my inexperience. The third trip I went canoeing with my daughter after a heavy rain, and although we didn't swim or experience any close calls, our silent fear stayed with us the entire trip.

That's when I sat down and redefined my values. Yes, I want a lot of adventure and fun in my life, but I'll pass on the life-threatening kind. I re-visit my values often and hone them a couple of times a year, recreating metaphors that speak to me because they help me explore my core.

A finely-tuned understanding of my values simplifies my decision making. When asked to join a board of directors, I made the decision easily, referring to my list of core values that hangs by my computer. After a rigorous two-way interview with the nominating committee, I joined the board because I foresaw an opportunity to honor my value to contribute. I make the best decisions when I tune into my values.

- *Think of a decision you have avoided. Your decision could honor one value, but squash another. How will the decision honor or dishonor your values?*

Mining Organizational Values

A strong commitment to personal values leads to a strong commitment to organizational values. If we lead our lives based on other people's expectations, we don't approach our work or our life with the same spirit as when we're solidly connected to our own unique values. High awareness of our values helps us approach our work with full vitality.

Organizations can't establish a unified set of values without discovery and dialogue. Turning over the organization's historical soil allows new insights to emerge. Storytelling offers one of the best ways to discover both personal and organizational values.

- *Think about the stories you tell about an organization where you've belonged. What do the stories say about the organization's values?*

I will always remember the day I started a training program for a small manufacturing company. I asked Dominick Maria, the plant manager, to kick things off by saying a few words about the value of training. He looked at me like he didn't have a clue what I meant. So I suggested a few lines he might use. When we got into the training room, he didn't use any of them.

Instead, he looked at the floor, shuffled his feet and mumbled a few words. Shop talk. I felt clueless, out of the loop. I kept watching him because his language and style sounded far from dynamic, but I noticed every eye in the room riveted on him, hungry for connection with Dominick. I got the sense that the group would do anything for him. It felt like an honor to share the room with him, but I couldn't figure out what they saw.

I thought his words would lull them to sleep, but the group showed wide-eyed admiration. Dominick put his hands on the shoulders of one manager and began giving him a backrub as he spoke, which seemed out of step with his Jersey gangster accent and macho image. He had them in the palm of his hand, and I felt awe because I knew he hadn't done it with words, but with something much more elusive.

I felt the power of his presence, but he seemed unlike any influential leader I'd ever met. Later that afternoon, I asked him his secret, and he said, "My secret? I love people." Everyone in the room seemed visibly moved by his words, but no one displayed more emotion than Dominick himself. He seemed overpowered by the depth of his love.

A few weeks later when Dominick went out for dinner for his birthday, he walked into a restaurant to a surprise party thrown by his entire management team. The team showered him with gag gifts, but he had another surprise when he came into work the next morning and found his office painted pink. Bright pink. Not to be outdone, Dominick looked around the room slowly and said, "I like pink," and went to work.

One story about Dominick and his organization tells us more about their values than a list of words ever could. If I told you that they valued relationships, fun and hard work, you might believe me, but the story provides solid evidence of their values.

In my twenties, I worked for a utility company, and my co-workers fondly told stories that gave me insight about the culture and its norms. One story goes that they wanted to hire a new lineman, and the clerk setting up the interviews asked one prospect, "Can you come in Thursday for an interview?" He responded, "Sure. I'll just take a sick day." The clerk responded, "Don't bother. We don't hire people who take sick days when they aren't sick." It didn't matter that other organizations have different norms about how employees use their sick days; the applicant was rejected because he'd violated the organization's value of integrity.

One day I took one of my children to the hospital unexpectedly, and called in to say I could not come to work that day. My boss's secretary shared with me, "I think it would be better if you told him that *you* were sick, not your *child*." She had worked there 20 years, so I didn't doubt the validity of her advice, but I felt confused.

From everything I'd heard, I believed that telling the truth was one of their most important values. I learned that this male-dominated company had an even more important value than honesty — that employee loyalty to the company comes before loyalty to family. Ultimately, I left the company because I had no desire to align my values with the company's values. I felt like a fish out of water in an environment where people expected me to come to work when my children needed me most.

Many organizations have an unwritten rule that they only share favorable organizational stories during recruiting. If the company starts orphanages in the Ukraine, gives needy children jackets and toys during the holidays, or sends an employee's child to college, don't expect to hear much about it after your first week on the job. Once you join the ranks, only disparaging stories get told. That's the culture. It takes a lot of courage to change the culture, and only rarely do organizations change their values.

An engineer who works for a progressive firm that's number one in its industry, surprises me because he loves to share stories about how poorly the company is run. "We've changed our e-mail addresses three times in the last two years, and each time we do it, everyone in the company has to print new business cards. Now we're changing it a fourth time, back to our original e-mail addresses, but of course, not one of us kept our old business cards." He never had a good thing to say about this company, until I said, "But you work for this company. What does that say about you?"

Listening to the stories people tell reveals both their personal and organizational values. How the organization rewards and punishes tells you a lot about their underlying values. Pay particular attention to what happens during stormy times, because that's when the true values emerge as the compass.

- *The stories we tell about our organizations reveal a lot about ourselves, and a lot about the organization. List a few stories that you've told about your organization. What underlying organizational values do you hear imbedded in the stories? What themes do you notice?*

- *After sharing organizational values in small groups, list the organization's values on a flip chart and then come together as a single group and prioritize the values using a dot vote.*

One organization called my partner and me in to help team leaders develop coaching skills. On the first day of training, every team leader walked in wearing a hardhat. The underlying message was, "We're different from you." When we started organizational values work with them, I wasn't surprised that they mentioned hard work in many different ways. Jack timidly said, "I think we also value family," but he didn't think anyone else would agree with him. He told a story about how people in the plant helped raise money for a co-worker's legal battle. Apparently the co-worker shot a bear 50 feet from his house, out of season, because it came close to his young children as they played on a swing set. The gun was unlicensed, so the legal authorities treated him like a dangerous criminal. Still wearing his hard hat, Jack told the story with deep-felt emotion, and when it came time for the vote, everyone in the room chose family as the organization's most important value.

Aligning Personal Values with Organizational Values

Choosing the organization you work for can seem like a hit-or-miss affair. A few people know their destiny at an early age, get the education they need and excel in the profession of their choice. More often, a friend of a friend tells you about a job, or you keep accepting the raise until you end up in a job that has no meaning for you. Imagine that instead of waiting for a position amongst a field of contenders, you turn the tables, *you* make the choice and *you* make the offer. You interview a series of ideal organizations and choose which one gets to have you based on how their values align with yours.

- *What criteria do you use to choose your ideal job? Surely the organization has to value their employees and pay them well, but what else matters to you?*

- *Does the organization show signs of innovation or are they steeped in rich tradition? Do they take risk or plan cautiously? Do they care more about people, profits, or a cause?*

A human resources director decided to leave her job in manufacturing and go into education. She wanted to honor what she valued most: exploring new ideas with brilliant colleagues, making a difference through mentoring, spiritual growth, and curiosity. She felt surprised when the new job offer included a raise, and had no doubt that her improved physical health was a direct result of joining an organization where she could honor all of her values.

You don't have to honor every one of your values at work, but the closer your values align with the organization's values the more fulfilling your career. A psychologist who values adventure doesn't get much opportunity to honor that value at work, but she fills her weekends with rock climbing and kayaking. She fulfills her other values of serving, uplifting and connection when she meets with clients during the work week.

- *Which of your values align with the values of your organization?*

- *Which values do you find it difficult to honor in your line of work?*

- *What do you need to do to honor all of your values?*

Compelling personal visions become the building blocks for a strong organizational vision. Depending on one charismatic person at the top to create a vision that inspires loyal followers suggests a short-lived approach. In dynamic organizations, everyone takes the role of the visionary. The collective outlook mobilizes the life forces of the organization.

When you and your organization identify your most important values, you've successfully completed Step Two of the *Tell Your Vision* process. From here, go on to Step Three: looking at your environment to formulate a sense of what you want to create in your personal life and in your organizational life.

Chapter 5:
Shaping Your Environment

Our comprehensive personal visions encompass our whole life. Ideally we can integrate our work life with our home life, relationships with accomplishments, and personal development with service. We enjoy life when we feel balanced, fulfilled and purposeful. Even when we get out of balance occasionally, awareness comes easily and we consciously seek greater balance.

Instead of taking what comes our way, we can choose what we want to have in our personal life and our work life. Then we go after what we want. In this chapter we envision our whole life, look for what we want, affirm our intentions, immerse ourselves in gratitude, and design our ideal life.

> Step 3:
>
> Environment —
> Choosing What
> You Want

Envisioning Your Life as a Whole

May you live all the days of your life.

— *Jonathan Swift*

When we explore *all* our options, we envision a better future for all aspects of our life. The following are some components of personal visions from people who dare to dream:

Relationships
- "I live in a community with close friends where we listen to the Grateful Dead and care for each other into old age."
- "My work team cultivates boisterous relationships in a frat house environment."
- "I live a healthy life without financial concerns. Friends accept me for who I am and not for what I do for them."
- "As a first generation immigrant, my family is fully melted into the new society while celebrating our Japanese heritage."

Career
- "In ten years I have completed my Masters, and ventured out to work in the creative department, specializing in graphics and design."
- "I love my job in electronics. I interact with a wide range of people and we have a lot of fun!"
- "I make a positive and lasting contribution by providing organizations with innovative, valuable advice to industry-leading clients. My firm is recognized internationally as the highest quality professional services firm."
- "My inventions give people more free time to enjoy their families."

Contribution
- "I envision a world free of AIDS and I serve as a volunteer in the hospice program."
- "Every girl in our community will have the opportunity to participate in Girl Scouts."
- "I volunteer and give money to organizations that make a difference, such as Big Brothers Big Sisters and the Cancer Society."
- "My business creates jobs all over the world, allowing individuals and communities to prosper and enjoy a higher quality of life."

Environment
- "My office looks out over the lake. I have fresh cut flowers every day, and the eclectic artwork on the walls gets my creative juices flowing."
- "My business products and services help me protect the planet and the people on it."
- "My husband and I have our dream house in Vermont. We retire and raise dogs on a small farm where we have many other animals."
- "I have a big responsibility toward the natural environment. I work to make this world a better place to live—not only for me, but also for my children and great-grandchildren— through solid ecological education. "

Development
- "In seven years I have my PhD and I start writing my first book on the economics of war and peace."
- "To develop myself, I mentor kids on the robotics team and I really enjoy seeing their awkwardness turn into self-confidence. "
- "I can afford to take all the voice lessons I want and people from all over the world enjoy my music."
- "I serve on the board of directors of progressive nonprofits where I learn best practices that I apply in my job."

Recreation
- "My partner and I enjoy teaching seminars across the United States and we camp along the way, enjoying nature's beauty state by state."
- "In the next 10 years, I see the revival of the original feelings I had for music. I see myself sitting at a piano playing, not because I have to, but for the pure joy of it."
- "I will visit most of the countries in the world so that I experience other cultures."

- "I will upgrade my boat engine and get a ski mobile, and all the kids in the neighborhood play in our yard because it's a fun place to hang out."

Lifestyle
- "I have total control of my mind, body, and spirit so that I am at peace with my surroundings and myself."
- "My priority is to take care of the needs of my brothers and sisters back home in Peru."
- "I have no debts, have built financial security and have the freedom to travel to visit family."
- "I do my work from my deck, looking toward the mountains, and each evening I share a cigar and a cognac with the sunset."

Spirituality
- "Through faith and spiritual growth, I maintain good health, have an exceptional quality of living and the freedom to spend the utmost quality time with my family."
- "My activities in the church help people honor the divinity in every soul, and priests are no longer necessary."
- "I open myself to spirituality and sexuality and breathe life into the hearts of others."
- "I am a talented songwriter who inspires spiritual growth."

All these people chose to envision a life that they wanted. Living consciously means choosing consciously. The desire for work and life balance can be one of the toughest challenges we face, or it can be as easy as making the choice to follow our hearts. When people recreate their lives, they often start out wanting to change one aspect, but end up focusing on another. A few examples:

- A CEO in Kenya needed help with strategic planning. Just before the planning summit, she found out that her husband had another wife, which he'd hidden from her for many years.

- A boisterous marketing executive worked on building his sales team. He called full of fear because his son had trouble breathing, on life support after a car accident.
- A woman struggling to pay her debts received an unexpectedly large inheritance from an aunt who lived in a converted chicken coop.
- A plant manager wanted a more cohesive team. After taking his father to a nursing home, he got a call that his father had committed suicide.

Even though each of these people got professional help elsewhere (family support network, medical team, financial planner, and therapist) they still wanted to talk about what's most important during their coaching sessions. They explored how they feel, what they need and what they want to change. Everyone faces tough issues at one time or another, which impacts their ability to function both on and off the job. People who take the time to look at the big picture appreciate the opportunity to envision all aspects of their life. Often what's happening at work impacts what happens at home and vice versa.

Look at your whole life, and in a phrase or a sentence, describe your ideal for each area.

- *Relationships: What kinds of relationships do you want with family, friends, and colleagues?*

- *Career: What is your ideal career?*

- *Contribution: How do you want to serve?*

- *Environment: What do you want your surroundings to look like?*

- *Development: What skills and capabilities do you want to master?*

- *Recreation: How do you want to spend your leisure time?*

- *Lifestyle: What are your fundamental priorities?*

- *Spirituality: What do you want in your spiritual life?*

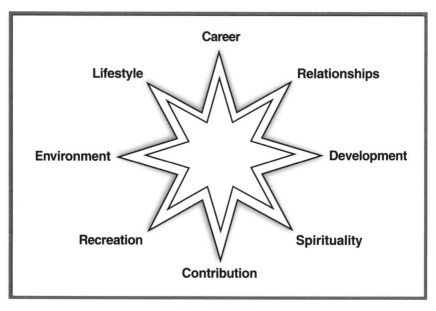

Your Ideal Life
What do you need in your life so that you shine?

Make your choices based on the inner experience you desire. Imagine living your ideal life, and explore what inner feelings you'd like to experience. You can choose to have that inner experience right now, even before you've achieved your vision.

Reawakening What Might Have Been

Perhaps the most distressing words of all are, "I wish I had..." Instead of regretting the past, harvest it for insights. Mine the past by asking, "What might I have done? What is still possible? What am I still willing to work for?" What we want remains elusive if we tell ourselves:

- I don't deserve it.
- I can't have what I really want.
- I don't know what I want.
- What I want isn't all that important.
- People won't like me if I achieve my goals.
- It won't be fair unless everybody else also gets what they want.

If any of these lines sound familiar, rewrite them! For instance, when you hear yourself saying, "I don't deserve it," what could you say instead? Perhaps: "I deserve happiness," or "I choose to live a fulfilling life." Getting grounded in your desires helps you tap your passion.

- *Make a big bold wish list of what you want and hang it on the wall. Think big! Keep your wish list visible to remind you of the infinite possibilities.*

Going After What You Want

The word "want" sounds crass. The word "need" feels desperate and the word "desire" implies out of reach. To avoid appearing selfish, lots of people stop expressing their desires and quietly suffer. Soon they don't even know what they want or know why they do what they do. Every action we take is an attempt to fill a personal need. If that sounds selfish, take comfort in knowing that the need to contribute to others' well-being is one of the most dominant universal needs.

Reawakening to what you want changes your life. Focusing on what you desire actually attracts what you want. Instead of silently hoping that others will guess what you want, and blaming them for lack of fulfillment, find out what happens when you start asking for what you want. Instead of ignoring your desires, become deeply aware of the changes you want.

A pharmacist gave me permission to tell her story and suggested I use the pseudonym "Stands with Fist." She had a long, dazzling relationship with a mentor that ended miserably because she couldn't get what she needed most—respect. A year later her old mentor asked her to sign off on the rights to a patent they jointly held. Although willing to turn over her rights, she wanted to stand up to her old mentor and keep her name on the patent. I sent her a quick note saying, "Is that all you want?" After a lot of churning and dancing around her wants, Stands with Fist decided to ask for *everything* she wanted. Her mentor sat in stunned silence as she painted the best-case scenario. Although she admits she didn't get *everything*, she kept her rights to the patent and created a new joint venture with her old mentor to make their product more available. They both walked away from the negotiations deeply satisfied, in awe of each other.

Invigorated by her success with the patent, Stands with Fist started looking deeper at what else she wanted in her life. She looked at her relationships, her work, and her dreams of radically improving health care. At first, she vacillated between wanting to create the perfect career and wanting to stay in the city she loved. It didn't surprise me a few months later when she created a new position for herself. "Where am I moving?" she laughed, "No where!" Her fist symbolizes the fierce determination to get what she needs, but she's just as tenacious about addressing others' needs. From unabashed passion to infectious humor, her wide range of emotions invites full expression from others.

Consider your own passion and your deepest wants. What do you want that clenches your fist? What do you want that releases your fist?

Answer the following questions spontaneously. Don't ponder the question, but instead trust your intuition to identify the kernel of truth. Look at your whole life for your answers.

- *What do you want?*

- *When you have that, what do you want that you consider even more important?*

- *When you have that, what do you want that you consider even more important?*

- *When you have that, what do you want that you consider even more important?*

Connirae Andreas and Tamara Andreas in their book *Core Transformation* say that when they repeatedly ask a similar question, "What do you want through having that?" people shift from wanting things on the outside to wanting things on the inside. They start out wanting a car or security or protection, but they shift to wanting a deep, inner, core-feeling state. "What will that get you?" is another question that takes us to the core.

The words people use to describe their deepest desires vary, but they tend to center on grace, awareness, inner peace, fulfillment, oneness, and love.

If you keep asking "What do I want?" you'll notice that you keep building your awareness. With a partner, dig deeper and clarify what you really want. Ask each other, "If you could have it now, would you take it?" This question helps you eliminate things you don't truly value. Now ask each other, "Imagine you have it now. What's different?" This question helps you reflect on and confirm your underlying values.

Making Affirmations Happen

Your crown has been bought and paid for. All you must do is put it on.

— James Baldwin

One way to get what you want is to practice using affirmations. Simply repeating a positive phrase whether journaling, speaking in front of the mirror, or listening to a tape, can enhance both your personal and work life. A common affirmation is, "Every day in every way I'm getting better and better." A few more include:

- I am filled with energy and vitality.
- I can achieve whatever I want.
- My vision attracts people who want to contribute.
- Meeting my goals is fun and easy.
- I am passionate about contributing to the world.

Sounds easy, doesn't it? Some people teach that you need only have the goal in mind and affirm it often enough and it will magically happen. But first ask yourself, do you actually believe in the possibility of reaching the goal?

Suppose you affirm every day that you will become a motivational speaker who earns $20,000 per engagement. You would love to have that happen, but not one cell in your body believes in the possibility. Every time you say your affirmation, the words come out, "I am a highly paid motivational speaker," while your mind affirms a different message, "That's impossible!" Because you brace against the possibility, you create a tension in your body. When tension exists between what you want and what you believe is possible, you shrink from the goal, because what you want seems too far away. No one becomes inspired by unreachable goals, so make sure you choose stretch goals that you believe you can attain.

One way to stretch yourself is to build your affirmations incrementally. Instead of starting with "I am wealthy," start with "I am becoming wealthier each day," or "My wealth is growing."

You can create a healthy state of mind by writing your affirmations in the here and now, in the first person. Make sure your affirmations state what you do want, not what you don't want. Instead of saying "I will quit smoking," say, "I breathe fresh air with every breath." Or find your own words that appeal to you. Repeat your affirmations first thing in the morning and last thing in the evening so that you start and end your day well.

- *Look at the world around you and notice what's available. Make a wish list of all that you want.*

- *Write your affirmations in the positive, present tense, describing everything you want in your ideal future.*

- *Use music or movement to get yourself in a positive frame of mind when you say your affirmations.*

- *Write your affirmations on cards and either put them on the wall, record them and play the tape daily, or say them in front of the mirror each morning and evening.*

- *Write shared affirmations with your team. What do you collectively want?*

Becoming Immersed in Gratitude

There are only two ways to live your life. One is as though nothing is a miracle. The other is as though everything is a miracle.
— Albert Einstein

Choosing to live in a state of wonder, awe, and gratitude brings magic into the world. Writing about life's daily miracles forms a wonderful practice that brings even more miracles to life. Keeping a gratitude journal, describing everything you feel thankful for, helps you attract the things you desire. So consider taking an inventory of your life's assets. When you start noticing all that you appreciate, life's bounty multiplies.

- *What do you feel grateful for?*

Designing Your Ideal Life

In his late thirties, Joe loved his job in operations, enjoyed the respect of his peers, made great money, and lived a good life. Asked to join a band, he decided to start living his life-long fantasy of writing and playing music. Reluctant to give up all that he'd worked for, he coasted uneasily through the highs and lows of a transition period. He started spending long weekends in Nashville where he lived on Doritos and good vibrations. Increasingly full of energy, he practiced and recorded with the band, living on three or four hours of sleep each night.

When he showed up at work on Monday tattooed, and driving a Harley, his co-workers chalked it up to a mid-life crisis. Joe knew better. His new lifestyle epitomized the opposite of crisis. He was living passionately, fully attuned to his heart's desire. He gave notice, but the CEO begged him to stay another year to execute the strategic plan and train his replacement. Joe said he'd give them three months, but jazzed by another weekend of upbeat music, he came back the following week and gave a firm two weeks notice.

He hated the thought of staying caged up in an office when he could be playing music. After more arm-twisting, Joe agreed to help with the transition, but on his own terms and his own schedule. He wanted to spend five days in Nashville and two days a week in the office, and much to his surprise the company agreed to all of his requests. A month later he came back to work singing a different tune. The musician's life offered an addictive high, but sleep deprivation and lack of nourishment took its toll. He remembered what he loved about his job, and took great comfort in the familiar. Re-examining his passion he realized he wanted it all... the cut and thrust of running operations and the full tilt of the music that made his heart soar. He crafted a new life for himself that included the best of both worlds. More importantly, he slowed down, consciously eliminating sources of potential burnout.

- *What do you need to have in your ideal life? Specifically include who and what surrounds you — important people in your life, your possessions, and your ideal environment.*

- *Now imagine a future where you experience life fully, you do what you want to do, and you have what you truly want. Find the core place inside where your energy comes fully alive and vibrant. Notice where desire lives in your body. The heart of developing your vision means finding that spark inside and discovering what you need to change for that spark to burst into flame. Find the place within where your passion runs deep, but also find the quiet and calm that helps you relax and fill the well of your soul.*

When you answer the big questions, you'll have a wonderful view of your ideal environment—and will be well on your way toward forming a plan worthy of your life. Now that you've looked at your ideal environment, let's explore Step Four: looking at actions and capabilities as part of formulating a vision for both your personal life and your work life.

Chapter 6:
Choosing Developmental Opportunities

To do is to be. *– Nietzsche*
To be is to do. *– Sartre*
Do be do be do. *– Frank Sinatra*

What you do defines your experience. Your actions provide evidence of your values and help you get what you want.

You'll remember that Step 4 in the *Tell Your Vision* process is "Action – Shaping Behaviors and Capabilities." In this chapter, you'll explore the behaviors and capabilities you want to master in your ideal future. Some of the ways we'll look at shaping future actions include assessment tools, SWOT analysis, 360° Feedback, leadership development plans, and coaching.

> ## Step 4:
> ## Action – Shaping Behaviors and Capabilities

By changing your behaviors and developing new skills, you can travel to new heights. To start, examine what you are already doing. Notice which actions have heart and meaning. When you ask Don Juan's question, "Does this path have a heart?" you take a step towards determining right livelihood and right action. Hone in on what you do that energizes you. What would you like to keep doing, stop doing, and start doing?

What could be more important than filling your days with actions that honor your values and contribute to your and other's well-being? Imagining what you will do in the future helps you create that future. Some people easily change their behaviors but many more love their habitual ways of doing things, whether those behaviors are working for them or not. Ridding yourself of old behaviors is much easier when you replace them with new behaviors.

I once worked with Jen, an executive known for high competency. She always got the work done efficiently, but nobody wanted to put up with her harsh criticism. The people who reported to her kept leaving her department, and when one of them told her, "Nobody wants to work for you," she decided to change. She wanted to become more compassionate, warm and connected, but struggled with changing her ways. Taking the time to build relationships conflicted with her drive to produce results. Yet she knew that stronger people skills would make her a better leader and ultimately she would accomplish even more.

Intellectually, Jen easily made the shift from her head to her heart, and she became very creative about brainstorming new ways to become a better leader. She decided to ask for input instead of barking out orders, and when things went wrong, she sought understanding instead of finding who was to blame. It all sounded so easy. The trouble was that she never took action. She continued to take over when someone didn't do it her way, and people walked on eggshells in her presence.

Stuck in the comfort zone of doing things the way she had always done them, she only fantasized about better relationships. Her breakthrough came when she started applying her task-oriented skills to the people side of her life. She put people on her calendar and turned relationship building into a project with checklists and deadlines. Eventually relationship building came naturally, and Jen said, "People don't avoid me now. I used to like it that they avoided me because I thought I got more work done. Now we're getting more done in less time, and people like coming into my office!"

Some of the tools that Jen and other leaders use to help them change their behaviors are developing organizational

competencies, leadership skills assessment, SWOT analysis, 360°
feedback, DISC profile, leadership development plan, and building
a coaching culture. To help you prepare for a better future, I'll
share details about each of these tools.

Developing Organizational Competencies

The buzzword "competency" is widely used to mean
knowledge, skills and abilities, but the term encompasses all the
characteristics that contribute to successful performance and
results. Our values, motivation and initiative influence our ability
to master a competency.

An organization needs people to develop hundreds of
competencies, but they also need to focus on the most important
competencies that will propel them into an ideal future. To focus
on too many at once feels overwhelming. A cross-functional team
can collaboratively choose 8 to 12 competencies that they'll need
in the future based on trends, opportunities, and projections. Don't
limit yourself to the list that follows, but choose the competencies
of highest importance to your future organization:

- Accountability
- Change Management
- Coaching and Mentoring
- Communications
- Conflict Management
- Critical Analysis
- Customer Orientation
- Decision Making
- Delegating
- Developing People
- Emotional Intelligence
- Entrepreneurial Orientation
- Financial Analysis
- Future Trends Analysis
- Global Thinking
- Goal Setting
- Interpersonal Relationships
- Leadership
- Negotiation Techniques
- Networking
- Organizing
- Planning
- Presentations
- Problem Solving
- Strategic Focus
- Team Building
- Technology
- Time Management
- Training
- Vision

Assessing Leadership Skills

After analyzing future needs, one organization chose eight core competencies that they wanted their leadership team to master, and then developed a self-assessment tool to give leaders a visual picture of their personal level of satisfaction with each competency. The following example shows the eight core competencies and lists a description of each area.

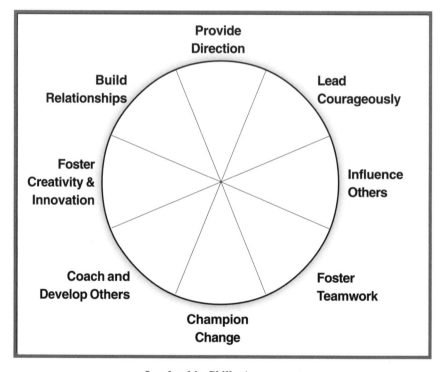

Leadership Skills Assessment

With the center of the wheel as 0 and the outer edge as 10, rank your level of satisfaction with each leadership skill area by drawing a curved line to create a new outer edge. Identify your strengths. Determine what actions you will take to improve your scores.

- Provide Direction
  Foster development of shared vision
  Define priorities and plan strategically
  Promote systems thinking

- Lead Courageously
  Take a stand for your values
  Confront issues and concerns promptly
  Challenge others to make tough choices

- Influence Others
  Win support to broaden your impact
  Provide feedback that inspires action
  Negotiate and get others to act

- Foster Teamwork
  Build team spirit and get results
  Encourage interaction among members
  Celebrate team accomplishments

- Champion Change
  Enlist change agents
  Manage resistance to change
  Sustain a culture of continuous change

- Coach and Develop Others
  Identify and groom talent
  Offer developmental challenges
  Develop leaders at all levels

- Foster Creativity and Innovation
  Stay ahead of industry trends
  Use technology innovatively
  Explore new options creatively

- Build Relationships
  Build networks
  Leverage diversity
  Manage conflict

This self-assessment tool gave their leaders a sense of their developmental needs with each competency. Although a self-assessment provides a limited perspective, the competencies that each leader wanted to develop were intrinsically motivating, and the driving force behind organizational change.

- *What are the core competencies that your organization will need to create your desired future?*

Analyzing Personal and Organizational SWOT

Both individuals and organizations can find a SWOT analysis useful. In my approach, SWOT stands for:

- Strengths
- Wishes
- Opportunities
- Threats

The traditional SWOT analysis looks at strengths, weaknesses, opportunities, and threats. Instead of looking at *weaknesses*, we can focus on *wishes*. From an appreciative perspective, looking at wishes inspires us far more than looking at what we don't want. Instead of saying "My weakness is poor time management," it can be more inspiring to say, "I wish for excellent time management skills." When people express a wish, listen carefully to their words, because wishes already imply movement. Strengths and wishes point to the internal landscape, the things we have control over. Opportunities and threats focus on the outer landscape, the things we do not control.

	Strengths	Wishes
Inner Landscape		
Outer Landscape	Opportunities	Threats

Appreciative SWOT Analysis

Traditionally the left side of the SWOT analysis lists the positive and the right side lists the negative. Instead, withhold evaluation and state your observations in each quadrant. Each quadrant holds valuable useful observations. As ominous as the word "threat" sounds, awareness of threats reveals positive options. For instance, you probably consider competitors threatening, but without strong competitors, organizations become complacent and wither away to nothing. Likewise, an overused strength can cost you dearly. If your presentation skills are outstanding, you may neglect to develop that skill in others. People and businesses that want continuous growth need balance in each quadrant. Threats often become opportunities, and wishes often become strengths.

Exploring the Inner Landscape

Reflecting on the inner landscape deepens your awareness of all that you value about yourself and your organization. For your personal strengths, include the skills you've mastered, your internal characteristics, talents, and experience. Your personal wishes include the skills you want to master, the knowledge or experience you wish to gain, and any areas you wish to improve. When you examine the internal landscape of the organization, you look at the collective strengths and wishes.

Exploring the Outer Landscape

Exploring personal opportunities can be exciting and stimulating. By looking at where you can stretch and how you can have greater influence, you can prioritize your opportunities. Then anticipate the threats or obstacles that might keep you from reaching the peak. From there, take a look at the opportunities that your organization can take advantage of and determine how you can use threats as a source of inspiration.

A scan of your situation and surroundings reveals what's new and unexpected in your environment, giving you a feel for the larger context. Opportunities and threats that warrant attention, especially at the organizational level, include these wide-ranging areas:

Capital Availability
Competitors
Demographics
Diversity
Economics
Education
Energy Availability
Environmental Conditions
Food
Global Influences
Governments
Health and Human Services
Housing
Information Access
International Relations
Labor Force and Employment
Life-style
Management Philosophy
Multiple Cultures
Natural Resources
Politics
Religion and Spirituality
Security
Strategic Partners
Technology
Transportation

- *After you've identified your strengths, wishes, opportunities, and threats, analyze and prioritize the lists in each quadrant.*

- *What themes and trends from your SWOT analysis deserve your attention?*

- *Identify personal opportunities to stretch yourself, broaden your impact, and position yourself, all for the sake of realizing a better future.*

- *Conduct a team or an organizational SWOT analysis by taking a look at the wider landscape and notice what themes and landmarks stand out. Looking through an appreciative lens, notice what's possible.*

- *How can you use individual SWOT analyses to contribute to the team or organizational SWOT analysis?*

Using 360° Feedback for Professional Growth

Consider that providing meaningful feedback is a life skill and receiving feedback is the highest honour. It means that person is invested in your growth and development.
— Ron Wiens, Consultant

Feedback used to travel a one-way street, from boss to employee. Performance reviews caused more anxiety than skydiving. Today, more and more organizations use a 360° feedback survey as a tool to help managers become more aware of their talents and developmental opportunities. We call it "360° feedback" because you ask for and receive feedback from people all around you. When you get feedback from your manager, peers and direct reports, you gain a more rounded view of your performance and impact. Some companies include feedback from customers, board members, suppliers, and even family members.

Feedback provides information for evaluating your actions and developing competencies. You can choose from hundreds of 360° feedback surveys on the market, some rigorously tested, and others tailored to the specific needs of your organization. Many people value rigorous testing because recipients get to compare their scores to averages. However, a customized approach to 360° feedback provides the most useful information and lets people know which competencies are most important to the organization.

Choosing which competencies to focus on shapes the future of the organization, whereas generic language produces leaders with generic skills. Since most leadership skills transfer easily to any workplace environment, feedback on generic leadership skills will offer plenty of insight. Some organizations identify future competencies important to their unique organization and wisely include them in their survey. Most 360° surveys ask respondents to score performance on a 1–7 scale on a multitude of skills, with a few open-ended questions. The numeric scores give people a sense of the value of their contribution, but the open-ended questions provide the most useful, substantive information.

When Gary, an executive in a manufacturing firm, received his generic 360° report, he turned pale. His peers and boss gave him high scores, but the two people who reported directly to him rated him an average of 3.5 on a scale of 1–7 on all 64 questions. Even though his employees went through training on how to give useful feedback, their open-ended answers ranged from "He's the best manager I've ever had," to "Absolutely no personality." Looking deeper, he noticed that the rating ranged from 1–7, which meant that one person rated him a "1" and one person rated him "7" on every single competency. Although his raters were anonymous, he had no doubt about who said what. Instead of seeking clarification, he struggled with the implications of the feedback. He wasn't the only one on the team stumped by the 360° feedback. What does it all mean? What do we do with the information?

Typically, people give more honest feedback when they give it anonymously, but with no name attached to the comments, getting clarification becomes difficult, and trust within the organization often deteriorates. I've heard managers complain that it can take months to deal with the wake of the 360° feedback process. Even with mature leaders, anonymous feedback can be vindictive. Participants get discouraged unless they have opportunities to get more information about their performance.

That's why my colleagues and I developed a 360° feedback survey that incorporates the Appreciative Inquiry philosophy. The feedback inspires people to act on the information they receive. Instead of a numbered rating system, people get real observable feedback including the wishes that others have for them. When participants choose contributors (traditionally known as raters) to give them input, we encourage them to select people whose opinions they value. The result is that people get feedback they willingly act on, and they experience far less anxiety and rivalry. Instead, they establish camaraderie and develop alliances as they invest in each other's development. The survey is just the beginning; after identifying developmental opportunities, peers coach each other to realize their goals.

The *360° Feedback Survey Using Appreciative Inquiry* that follows is an Internet-based survey that you can easily customize based on the competencies that your unique organization wishes to develop.

Leadership that Works
360° Feedback Survey Using Appreciative Inquiry

Over time, people have recognized two methods for change: focus on what you do wrong and do less of it, or focus on what you do right, and do more of it. The latter usually yields far greater results.

In one fascinating experiment, a bowling match was videotaped. One team viewed an edited video of everything they'd done well, and the other team viewed a video of everything they'd done wrong. The second team used the traditional training method of analyzing all its mistakes and strategizing how to correct them. While both teams improved, the team seeing what they did right demonstrated more than 100 percent greater improvement than the team that examined its mistakes. (Cooperrider 1990)

This 360° Feedback Survey is an Appreciative Inquiry tool designed to help team members learn about the value of their performance and heighten awareness of their potential. Appreciative Inquiry does not assume the glass is full, but looks at how it became half full (root cause of success) vs. half empty (root cause of failure). Instead of putting on rose-colored glasses, imagine a person's full potential to benefit the organization.

Your answers help participants become more aware of their assets and how they can develop their full potential. You may find it difficult to answer some questions, or find that some don't apply, so please answer only the questions that you expect the recipient will find useful.

Most people give 360° feedback anonymously, but we believe that open, honest communication fosters trust and inspires growth. The people to whom you give feedback deserve to know that you have invested in their future! We encourage you to put your initials after each of your responses, and that way the recipient can get additional clarification. This survey was adapted from *A Guide to Appreciative Upward/360° Feedback Conversations* by Neil Samuels and is influenced by the work of many Appreciative Inquiry practitioners.

Name the person for whom you are providing feedback:

1. Give examples of times when you've found it especially enjoyable or exciting to work with this person.

2. How has this person contributed to your success? In what ways has this person enabled you to do your best work?

3. Think about times this person has impacted performance within your organization or within client organizations. What significant things did this person do as a catalyst for success?

4. Can you describe something progressive or innovative that this person did this year? What key challenges did this person face? What impact did this person have?

To heighten awareness of this person's full potential, describe a time when this person demonstrated strengths in each of the competency areas for lines 5-12. Then offer this person one wish for developing this competency even further.

5. Making Decisions: Identifies important issues, helps the team analyze complex situations, and makes wise choices.

6. Creating a Vision: Inspires a desirable future and helps to weave a collaborative vision.

7. Fostering Creativity and Innovation: Creates a culture where innovation flourishes, and finds better ways of getting things done.

8. Developing Teamwork: Leverages talents within the team and with other internal or external groups.

9. Building Relationships: Encourages and supports diversity, recognizes peoples' contributions.

10. Communicating Powerfully: Listens to ensure understanding, connects authentically and fosters effective communication throughout the team.

11. Developing Self and Others: Gives and receives feedback as a gift, and effectively develops self and others.

12. Integrity and Honesty: Demonstrates trustworthiness and follows through on commitments.
13. When you think of this person overall, what strengths stand out? How could this person better utilize those strengths to benefit the team or the organization?
14. What's the biggest positive change you've seen in this person this past year?
15. What three wishes do you have that would make this person even more effective?
16. What requests would you like to make of this person?

Appreciating Diverse Work Styles

Nothing is so powerful as an insight into human nature... what compulsions drive a man, what instincts dominate his action... if you know these things about a man you can touch him at the core of his being.

— *William Bernbach*

Learning to appreciate different behavioral styles is one of the most powerful ways to build team spirit in the workplace. High performing teams consist of people with radically different styles, and when they learn to value different styles, team spirit soars.

The DISC profile offers a simple approach to helping people understand different behaviors and preferences. The DISC does not measure intelligence, values, or personality, but instead looks at behavioral style preferences. The tool is based on the work of Jung and William Marston, and many others have contributed to the field. Hippocrates, known for observing people, noticed four basic types of people. Today, the four behavioral types are known as Dominance, Influence, Steadiness, and Conscientiousness.

The DISC helps individuals and teams deepen self-awareness and understand each other's behavior. Learning about the DISC helps people acknowledge diversity (in behavior, opinions, ideas) and deepen their appreciation for other styles. Instead of ignoring, changing, or shutting down others, the DISC helps people celebrate human differences.

I had a real aversion to the DISC when I first saw it. I didn't believe that there were only four types of people, and I certainly didn't want to stereotype people or have them put *me* in a box. I've always seen people as unique individuals, but the DISC helps me understand a variety of behavioral preferences.

One dominant team leader found the DISC profile especially useful because she'd always worked hard, and "didn't respect people who engaged in chit chat when there was so much work to be done." After learning about the behavioral preferences of her team members, she discovered new ways to value both people-oriented and task-oriented members on the team. She built mutual respect that impacted the quality of relationships both inside and outside the organization.

Interestingly, the DISC's four behavioral types have strong correlations with archetypes and animal totems of Native American and indigenous cultures. According to Native American tradition, when you need support, you can call on animals for guidance, similar to the way people call on angels for protection or to explore life's lessons. In Jungian psychology, archetypes serve as symbols to help people understand the collective unconscious. Animal totems have the same significance, but animals mean different things to different tribes. Traditionally, animal spirits help us face the Jungian shadow and integrate the things we cannot accept about ourselves. Among Native Americans and other tribal peoples, animal totems are the enduring animal symbols that help spiritual seekers embrace the path of self-exploration.

The Warrior archetype represents the *Dominance* style because they act ambitiously, forcefully, and decisively. They communicate directly, cherish their independence, and challenge the status quo. In the U.S., where independence is considered a virtue, the dominance type represents 18 percent of the population. The animal totems are the decisive antelope, the active beaver, and the aggressive badger. Every team needs Dominance types to make decisions and get results quickly.

The Visionary archetype represents the *Influence* style because they express themselves easily, exude enthusiasm, and demonstrate friendliness and openness. Natural storytellers, they represent 28 percent of the U.S. population, and their animal totems are the visionary eagle and the joyous hummingbird. Influencers bring a lot of creative, fun-loving energy to the team and they enjoy sharing their vision of the big picture.

The *Steadiness* type connects with the Healer archetype because they nurture others, act reliably, and hold deep loyalties. They bring calm energy to the team and take pride in finishing what others start. Highly modest, these methodical people get the job done using a systematic approach. There are more Steadiness types than any other, with 40 percent in the U.S., and even higher in eastern cultures where values of family and teamwork come first. Their animal totems are the elk for its steadiness and the dog for its loyalty. Because the bear "dies" and is reborn each spring after hibernation, it's known as a powerful source of transformation and healing. Without Steadiness people on the team, the work doesn't get done. We need their quiet, stable energy to realize the vision.

Conscientious types serve as the Teachers of the tribe because they enjoy analysis and contemplation. Others see them as compliant, conservative, exacting, deliberate and highly ethical. Their animal totems are the mouse that pays attention to detail, and the owl that has uncanny ability to ferret out deception. They represent only 14 percent of the U.S. population. They're not always the most popular of the four styles because they insist on ethical behavior and tend to analyze issues to death, but they think and care deeply.

Effective teams enjoy a balance, appreciating the advantages that all four types bring to the mix. One production manager told me, "Before I understood the value of each style, I was spinning my wheels, trying to get others to work at my fast and furious pace. The DISC helped me appreciate people who take their time to analyze our decisions, and the people who build team spirit. They're the glue that holds us all together."

After people steep themselves in appreciation for the four different styles, they learn to value every member of the team as a unique individual, which opens people to expanding their contribution.

- *After delving into your 360° feedback and the DISC profile, you may see dozens of competencies you'd like to develop, but which competencies do you deem most important to creating your ideal future?*

- *After choosing 8 to 12 competencies for your organization to develop, choose 3 to 5 competencies that you personally would like to develop.*

Creating Your Leadership Development Plan

Your 360° feedback helps you get grounded in your strengths and points you toward new possibilities and developmental opportunities. You can also use your SWOT analysis, DISC profile, and other feedback as the foundation for building your leadership development plan. Listen to others' desires, but make sure you reflect your own needs and desires when you write your Leadership Development Plan. External motivation pales in comparison to internal motivation, so explore the options and choose a development plan that makes your heart sing.

An example of a personal leadership development plan follows. It is based on two components: leveraging your strengths and developmental opportunities. The two-fold plan starts with developing your strengths, so that you can accentuate and build on your unique talents. The second phase helps you explore developmental opportunities based on what you need or wish to improve.

Leadership Development Plan Part I Using Strengths as the Foundation for Development			
Step 1: **Leveraging Strengths**	Step 2: **Action Plan**	Step 3: **People who can help**	Step 4: **Target Dates**
Strength: Empower Others Objectives: -Give others more authority -Communicate high expectations -Challenge direct reports to resolve problems they identify	1. Shadow managers who empower others. 2. Ask for additional feedback from direct reports. 3. Listen to tape on empowerment. 4. Identify three projects to delegate.	Visit Shaun at another plant Alicia, Gary, Melissa Ask HR for advice My boss	Next quarter 5/25 Today 3/14
Strength: Communications Objectives: -Write reports that are easier to read -Improve presentation skills -Run more effective meetings	1. Read book on effective business writing. 2. Join Toastmasters to give presentations. 3. Attend meetings run by people known for efficient meetings. 4. Serve on the Boy Scouts Board of Directors.	Librarian Ask Sara to search Internet Zack or Barb Ask bowling buddy	This week Friday Next month By end of year
Strength: Conflict Resolution Objectives: -Become a better mediator of disputes across departments -Use conflict as a source of opportunity and growth	1. Volunteer to train as a mediator. 2. Address conflict in a timely manner. 3. Join a listserv on conflict resolution. 4. Identify conflict resolution strategies.	My boss Spencer and Jean Mentor Cory	Next year Today 7/14 Tuesday night

Sample

Leadership Development Plan Part II Targeting Needs as Development Opportunities			
Step 1: **Developmental Opportunity**	Step 2: **Action Plan**	Step 3: **People who can help**	Step 4: **Target Dates**
Need or Wish: Establish Trust and Integrity Objectives: -Treat people fairly and reduce perceptions of favoritism -Communicate honestly and realistically	1. Take a class on authentic leadership. 2. Share ethical dilemmas and ask for input. 3. Admit mistakes, make realistic promises and keep them. 4. Volunteer for service organization.	Mentor Spiritual advisor Spouse Rotary	5/24 7/4 Tonight Next meeting
Need or Wish: Influence Others Objectives: -Become more assertive -Give compelling reasons for ideas -Win support from others	1. Practice assertive messages before delivering them to others. 2. Pay attention to reactions when delivering message. 3. Get continuing feedback on persuasiveness. 4. Take a class to improve negotiation skills.	Dane Peter and my children Tests and Mary Local college continuing ed dept	Before Monday meeting Monday Ongoing Next semester
Need or Wish: Provide Direction Objectives: -Develop a clear vision for the department -Define priorities -Clarify roles and responsibilities	1. Solicit input from employees on departmental objectives. 2. Ask team members to share expectations of each other. 3. Discuss priorities during goal-setting sessions. 4. Review and update job descriptions.	Whole department Team members Get advice from Ethan Human Resources	3/15 5/16 7/12 1/31

Sample

Leadership Development Plan Part I Using Strengths as the Foundation for Development			
Step 1:	Step 2:	Step 3:	Step 4:
Leveraging Strengths	**Action Plan**	**People who can help**	**Target Dates**
Strength: Objectives:	1. 2. 3. 4. 5.		
Strength: Objectives:	1. 2. 3. 4. 5.		
Strength: Objectives:	1. 2. 3. 4. 5.		

Leadership Development Plan II Targeting Needs as Development Opportunities			
Step 1: **Developmental Opportunities**	Step 2: **Action Plan**	Step 3: **People who can help**	Step 4: **Target Dates**
Need or Wish: Objectives:	1. 2. 3. 4. 5.		
Need or Wish: Objectives:	1. 2. 3. 4. 5.		
Need or Wish: Objectives:	1. 2. 3. 4. 5.		

Developing a Coaching Culture

Although a few people have the initiative and support they need to take themselves to the top of their game, most people need a lot of help. A coaching culture empowers authentic strong leadership at all levels of the organization. Whether you choose professional coaches or develop peer coaching relationships, a coaching culture helps people bring their heart and soul to work. Coaches hold people accountable for the actions that they say are important to them. Organizations that establish coaching cultures encourage 360° connections where people seek out coaching relationships in all directions. They proactively coach their peers, direct reports, bosses, customers, and family members.

The GROW model developed by John Whitmore, author of *Coaching for Performance*, provides a simple process for encouraging action, learning, and growth.

GOAL setting for the session as well as short and long term.

REALITY checking to explore the current situation.

OPTIONS and alternative strategies or courses of action.

WHAT is to be done, WHEN, by WHOM and the WILL to do it.

Different from mentors or consultants, skillful coaches rarely provide solutions or advice. Instead, a coach facilitates what's most important to the person being coached by asking rigorous questions. The coaching relationship helps people focus, analyze the present situation, explore new possibilities, and choose an action plan. Attuned to values and vision, a coach helps people realize their full potential.

When Boyd became plant manager in a progressive manufacturing firm, the CEO asked me to coach him because, in the CEO's words, "He's incredibly talented, but he has no people skills." When clients get "sent" to a coach, they often feel awkward. Some perceive coaching as remedial. Some call it going to charm school. They regard coaching as punishment for poor performance or suspect that it's the first step out the door. Boyd thought of coaching as a minor annoyance and claimed, "I get great results, but the CEO doesn't understand me."

He reeked of cockiness, and described himself easily. "I trust my own judgment. I don't have a high need for approval. I implement new projects quickly and some people get left behind." He even said with pride, "Part of going full tilt ahead means leaving dead bodies in your wake, and that's the price you pay."

Even though his boss made it clear that Boyd needed help with his people skills, Boyd told me bluntly, "I don't need coaching. People take way too much of my time. They're a real nuisance and they slow me down." Giving him a taste of his own medicine, I left saying, "I value my time. So I only work with people who want to make changes. Call me when you're ready. "

Invaluable to the organization, he considered himself personally responsible for growing the business by 22 percent the previous year. A week after our meeting, a union member filed a grievance against him for unfair treatment, and his CEO told him, "As much as I value your contribution around here, this is the last mess of yours that I'm going to clean up for you. Ever. If anything like this happens again, you're done." Still in shock, Boyd called me to relay the message from the CEO, but he couldn't quite spit out the words that he needed help.

Despite the CEO's ultimatum, it took a while to get Boyd to look at anything other than what mattered most to him—cooking up new ideas, jumping into projects, and getting immediate results. He had a vague sense that he needed better listening skills, that he needed to gain support before plowing ahead, but he still believed that changing his ways would only cramp his style.

When he explored his values, vision and purpose, he said it helped him to "stop and smell the roses, and look at where I've been and where I'm going." His wrinkled nose told me the scent wasn't all that pleasant, and I guessed that he'd rather smell smoke while battling a forest fire. He loved the heat of the action and prided himself on results.

He kept his antenna up some of the time, but my feedback had little impact and he did little to change his behavior. At one meeting, he interrupted a peer three times and seemed oblivious to the effect he had on others. I intervened. "Boyd, I've got some feedback for you about your impact. Would you like to hear it now, or later in private?"

Immediately he said, "Now."

"I've noticed that you interrupt people repeatedly and that no one here looks at you when you talk. I'm wondering if that happens because you don't acknowledge their contributions to the discussions." He opened his mouth to refute this, choked back his words and looked around the room, taking them in slowly.

Although reluctant to pour salt into his wounds, I added one more piece of feedback. "When you take your intensity for getting the work done, and start applying that same passion to understanding people... you will be unstoppable."

The compassionate looks from the group melted his stiffness. Finally he said, "I'm ready to listen now." For the rest of the meeting he didn't say a word, but his body language communicated openness and encouragement.

Not every intervention works like this one, but in Boyd's case, he went on to work with his team, coaching them individually and as a group. Out of anger and frustration, members of the team had always expressed themselves passionately, but what a difference it made when they actually heard each other! Occasionally they still remind Boyd to slow down, but each year they get requests from people in other departments who want to join their team.

Sometimes people ask, "Why would a company pay for personal coaching? Doesn't that just encourage employees to leave?" Well sometimes they do leave. They leave for a better job, or they start a new venture, but most people stay with visionary companies. Even people who do not intend to leave their position find it worthwhile to explore their ideal job. What if you could do whatever you wanted *and* get paid well for it?

Joe, a salesman in his late 40s, came alive when he described his ideal career of playing professional basketball. His voice took on a deeper, resonant tone as he talked about his passion for the game and the joy of playing with a great team. He played in a league twice a week, and vividly described how it would feel to play for the Knicks, hitting every 3-pointer, getting the team in the zone, hearing the roar of the crowd.

On a good day, he stood 5'11" so he didn't suffer from the illusion that he would ever play with the NBA. Exploring his fantasy career led to a breakthrough at work. Instead of competing against the rest of the sales force, he began to develop them as a team. By tuning into the energy of his team on the court and in the office, he fostered an environment where he could bask in his stardom *and* in the accomplishments of others. Sales picked up along with his renewed enthusiasm.

When he did some vision work, he discovered his real gift— fostering team spirit and holding the energy. He explored the possibilities of transferring the game energy to the workplace. He learned how to uplift his work team the same way he inspired his basketball team. Playing in the zone became more and more frequent at work. He also switched from the over-40 league to a more competitive league. What a thrill for him when a former Knicks player joined his team, a little taste of the dream come true.

- *What's your dream job? How can you revise your current job to include aspects of your dream job?*

Now that we've looked at competencies, the leadership assessment tool, the 360° feedback survey, DISC, the SWOT analysis, the leadership development plan, and the power of coaching, we've explored Actions and Capabilities—Step Four of the *Tell Your Vision* process. Next is Step Five—Defining Your Identity.

Chapter 7:
Defining Your Identity and Contribution

Shaping Personal Identity

There is a vitality, a life force, a quickening that is translated through you into action, and because there is only one you in all time, this expression is unique. And if you block it, it will never exist through any other medium and will be lost.

— Martha Graham

To explore your unique expression, imagine yourself alone on an island, where you have no possessions, no responsibilities and no relationships. Strip yourself of your roles, gender, age, life style, ethnic group and profession. What's left? What truths do you know about yourself?

Each of us has a unique identity and our own strategies for contributing. In this chapter, we shape personal and organizational identity, explore our purpose, define the legacy we'd like to leave and choose how we wish to serve.

Step 5:

Identity —
Honing Your
Image

Your identity is who you are at the core, without all the trappings. That's why identity — personal and organizational — occupies Step Five in the *Tell Your Vision* process. Identity encompasses values, purpose, self-image, and reputation. The feedback you receive from others often affects how you feel about yourself, but ultimately, whether you are having a good day or a bad day, your identity remains the same. How you perceive your identity depends on how you see yourself and how you process your experience. Consider how an employee saw herself and responded to the world around her in the following story.

Although Pat was on a steady upward path before she became a VP, she believed she had little control over her destiny. She thought of herself as a victim of organizational circumstances, someone whose next move up the career ladder depended on a promotion by her superiors. She saw herself as self-aware, politically astute, passionate, and willing to change. Now, looking back, she says she had no vision and was "lazy about designing the future."

Pat's transformation began when she was given a senior role in a pharmaceutical research lab. She wanted to ask, "What am I supposed to do?" She knew that would be like Thomas Edison asking, "How do I make a light bulb?" Nobody had an answer.

After promoting her to a new position, the president expected her to build without a blueprint. Disturbed about a lack of quality in the lab's processes, Pat knew she wanted to serve as a catalyst for change. She became a spark plug in the organization, enlisting people in a change initiative, getting funding, earning ISO 9000 certification, and generating significant contracts with new customers.

As Pat pursued her vision of what the organization *could* become, she felt tempted to become a workaholic. Instead, she stayed attuned to what was most important in her life, performed at energized effectiveness during reasonable hours, and enjoyed leisurely vacations with her family, without her cell phone.

Pursuing her own potential and passions at work unleashed her creativity in all areas of her life. She became aware of her priorities in a new way. Her teenagers noticed that she more readily accepted their choices. Having identified and pursued her passion, she wanted her children to do the same. Her son wanted to be a football official. Her daughter wanted to cook. Pat never would have chosen these roles for them, but she determinedly supported their ambitions, their friends, and their hobbies. In supporting their visions, her relationship with her children flourished, and they all experienced family in a new way.

In her job today at the pharmaceutical lab, Pat enjoys more opportunities than ever. Her influence continues to grow. Headhunters call her routinely. With her newfound confidence, she stops them cold with a simple question, "Is your organization ready to completely change its identity and culture?" She's happy to stay where she is, in a culture where people understand the value of remaking themselves, both personally and organizationally. Pat's official title is Senior Vice President, but her internal title — her motivating self-identity — is, "Change Catalyst." And it all started when, troubled by the chaos and confusion of her new position, Pat gave herself permission to envision the future she desired. She changed her personal identity and went on to change the identity of the organization.

To change your own personal identity, you need to be acutely aware of your greatest strengths and unique talents, but you also need to focus on how you add value. Cultivating a personal image does not mean applying a veneer. A strong identity has depth, based on values, purpose, and meaning. The key to establishing a strong personal identity is to define yourself instead of letting others define you. If you don't like your image, you change it.

If you find incongruence between how you envision yourself, and how others see you, re-position yourself in the minds of colleagues and clients by choosing how you wish to contribute to their well-being. What offer do you envision making? Unless your goal is to blend in, you need lots of visibility to establish your identity. Visibility gives people the perception of quality.

- *How do you differentiate yourself from the pack?*

- *How do you want others to think of you? Fill in the blank: I am the one who:*

- *What do you want to be better at than anyone else in the world?*

- *What is memorable about you?*

- *What core strength or talent would you like to specialize in?*

- *How does your identity leverage your true personality?*

- *How can you express your identity distinctively?*

Crafting Organizational Identity

Organizational identity goes way beyond graphics, colors, logos, and slogans. Although buildings and ambience help shape an organization's identity, reputation and image represent the major components.

What you stand for, what's unique and distinctive about you personally, helps shape your self-concept and impacts the organizational identity as well. The people in an organization convey the identity, which affects the customer's concept of your organization. Individual reputations contribute to the organization's track record. Reputation creates value because it attracts like-minded people and the resources you need to establish the identity you want.

Strong leaders create strong identities, which results in unified action. Clear direction, a single culture, aligned teams—all these merge to create a strong identity. But identities often change, and both people and organizations struggle at times with identity crises.

Once-successful companies like Kmart, Lucent, Howard Johnson's, Nortel, and Polaroid have struggled to reinvent themselves. In the whirlwind of changing environments, they seem unable to create a new identity. When people are too busy running the company to discover *why* they're running the company, that's the first indication that the organization suffers from an identity crisis. People fill their days with activities, but few people seem to connect action and purpose. In times of rapid change, people who take time to reassess their personal and organizational identity become revitalized and focused.

Organizations with longevity embrace a deep sense of purpose. Increasing shareholder wealth doesn't inspire commitment the way that a genuine purpose or cause does. A few organizations that easily communicate their purpose are:

- 3M: To solve unsolved problems innovatively.
- U.S. Geological Survey: Minimize loss of life and property from natural disasters.
- Disney: Create happiness.
- Mary Kay Cosmetics: To give unlimited opportunity to women.
- Wal-Mart: To give ordinary folk the chance to buy the same things as rich people.
- Wakefield Library: Open the door to knowledge and imagination.

Most people want to contribute to the betterment of humanity. It feels good. What if your company collects bills or manufactures rat poison? One way to deepen your sense of personal or organizational purpose is to ask, "Why is that important?" Keep asking the question until you carve out an identity that fires the imagination, excites spirit, and evokes commitment.

Authors of *Awakening Corporate Soul*, Eric Klein and John Izzo say, "The soul does not require a chance to save the world to find purpose and fulfillment. Rather the soul awakens in response to serving, no matter how 'small' the effort."

Whether your organization builds houses or evaluates the stock market, a fulfilling purpose includes a human element, such as making life easier for people or making it possible for people to live better lives. Unless they own part of the company, not many people get excited about increasing shareholder value, but they do get fired up about working together to make their customers' lives better.

According to Hamid Bouchikhi, of France's ESSEC Business School and John R. Kimberly of the University of Pennsylvania's Wharton School, some companies never adapt to shifts in the competitive environment, because the required change is inconsistent with the company's core identity. Their research also indicates that poor decision-making is often rooted in deeply-held beliefs about the company's identity that emerged early in its history.

The same way an individual's identity often links to gender, religious beliefs, generation, life style, ethnic group or profession, a company's identity can be strongly rooted in a product, an area of expertise, a founding leader, a customer base, a community or a core philosophy. Changing a company's identity can be especially difficult when the change shifts the power base.

Few companies successfully change their identity, but Corning, Inc. did an astonishing job. They sold their plodding house-wares division and shifted focus to glass technologies. At one time, the Corning name conjured images of cookware, but today, Corning is a leader in optical fiber, cable systems, flat glass, and photonic technology for the telecommunications industry. Though their stock plummeted in 2001 as did all the stock in their industry, they've launched a successful comeback.

General Electric was once known for their remarkable strategic planning, but the company that once thrived on detailed plans has developed a new culture where receptivity to change is the essence of their identity.

Johnson & Johnson has had a strong reputation for decades, but years ago when I joined the board of directors of our local abuse and rape crisis center, my first meeting focused on a debate about J&J's presence in apartheid South Africa. The company had advertised that they would donate funding to abuse and rape crisis centers like ours.

Our board members argued about whether to accept the $500 donation; some believed the money was tainted, while others focused on the good J&J could do by contributing to crisis centers. The board tabled the decision, but when word of the controversy got back to the survivors of abuse staying in the shelter, they expressed their outrage at apartheid by removing every J&J product from the building.

The board voted 6-4 to refuse the grant money as did several other crisis centers in Pennsylvania. An authority on business ethics, Oliver Williams, wrote *The Apartheid Crisis*. He singled out Johnson & Johnson as one of the most responsible American companies for dealing creatively to change apartheid.

With their identity at stake, J&J was under tremendous pressure to leave South Africa, and CEO Jim Burke asked his people to examine whether they should leave. Although J&J paid taxes to a racist government, they repeatedly broke the law when they promoted black managers, put black members on the board and assisted blacks in buying homes in white neighborhoods. J&J donated money for education, medical care, and hospital equipment in black communities.

A few years later in 1982, their fast, compassionate handling of the Tylenol poisonings helped Johnson & Johnson solidify a powerful identity as a company that does the right thing. They briefly lost market share and then recovered from the tragedy. They still take in 1.3 billion in annual revenue from Tylenol alone.

Identities don't change easily. Denny's Restaurant was once synonymous with racial discrimination, but today their image has changed. More than half their employees are minorities, and their parent company, Advantica, tops Fortune magazine's "50 Best Companies for Minorities."

Instead of relying on tragedy or bad press to awaken your desire to change your identity, consider your ideal identity now.

- *What do you want customers to think when they hear the name of your organization?*

- *What does your organization make possible for people?*

- *What makes your organization appealing compared to your competitors?*

Serving Your Purpose

Some of us wish to wait until our gift is potent and comprehensive enough to solve all the world's problems. Seeing that our gift does not stop all the suffering, we decide it is inadequate. But every gift is a drop of water on a stone; every kindness, every flash of color or melody helps us remain hopeful and in balance. Each of us knows some part of the secret, and each of us holds our small portion of the light. We can thrive on the earth only if we each bring what we have and offer it at the family table.

—Wayne Muller

Although many people choose their life work strictly to meet their financial needs, others connect deeply with their purpose and find their work intrinsically rewarding. When people work energetically, enthusiastically and creatively, it's often because they contribute to a larger purpose.

> **Step 6:**
>
> **Contribution — Serving Your Purpose**

Few people know their life work at an early age. Discovering your calling usually requires a long period of incubation. What could be more important than tuning in to how you wish to serve? That's why gaining a sense of your purpose and contribution occupies Step 6 in the *Tell Your Vision* process.

I've noticed that the most successful business people lead with a servant's heart. One of the best ways to step into leadership is to discover new ways to put your heart and soul into your work through service. To create an environment where everyone embraces work wholeheartedly, you can set the tone by serving others.

Author of *Fire in the Soul*, Joan Borysenko, says, "We don't know yet where we are called to go. We leave anyway because some inner voice tells us that if we do not, there will be hell to pay.

Then we wander for a while in the strange place called 'don't know.' Don't know where I am going. Don't know what is coming next. Don't know who I am anymore. This is courage, not confusion; it is wisdom, not folly. It creates the space for something new to be born."

Many of us are called; perhaps we each get a call at one time or another, but how often do we listen to the call? We push the snooze button, or sleep through numerous opportunities to follow our bliss. We want undeniable proof of what will bring meaning to our lives, and lacking that, we lead unfulfilling lives.

How do you cut through the confusion and answer the wisdom of the call? Do you hear a call toward a new beginning? Starting a business? Furthering a cause? Beginning a family? Changing your career? Going back to school? Or are you called away from something old? Ending a destructive relationship? Leaving a failing business? Changing your place of worship? Moving away from the city?

Following the call means listening to your intuition and heeding guidance from multiple sources. Turning the call into action involves tuning in to your inner voice and stepping out with courage. You already have many clues about your calling. Which clues have you ignored and which have you responded to?

• *What is your purpose or calling?*

Becoming More Aware of Impermanence

It's only when we truly know and understand that we have a limited time on earth — and that we have no way of knowing when our time is up — that we will begin to live each day to the fullest, as if it was the only one we had.

– Elisabeth Kubler-Ross

Great teachings come from those whose lives are suddenly shortened. How we change when we live each day as though it could be the last! The Buddhist practice of marasnasati, or "death awareness," encourages us to become conscious of our eventual death, and use this awareness to enrich our life. Knowing we will die, how do we live life to the fullest? Awareness of our impermanence helps us determine which parts of our life are worth living, and which are worth letting go.

The Buddha told this parable:

A man traveling across a field encountered a tiger. He fled, the tiger after him. Coming to a precipice, he caught hold of a root of a wild vine and swung himself down over the edge. The tiger sniffed at him from above. Trembling, the man looked down to where, far below, another tiger was waiting to eat him. Only the vine sustained him.

Two mice, one white and one black, little by little started to gnaw away at the vine. The man saw a luscious strawberry near him. Grasping the vine with one hand, he plucked the strawberry with the other. How sweet it tasted!

- *Imagine yourself on a vine hanging over a cliff. Perhaps there is a strawberry within your reach. If you could taste one sweet thing, right now, what would you reach for?*

Leaving a Legacy

When Alfred Nobel's brother died, a newspaper accidentally printed Alfred's obituary instead. It explained that he'd invented dynamite and explosives and become rich by enabling people to kill each other in unprecedented numbers. This assessment led Nobel to change his life and use his fortune to benefit humanity. Today he's best known for the Nobel Peace Prize.

- *After you are gone, what would you like people to say about you? Imagine that you are at the end of your life, and you have the opportunity to write your own eulogy. Take the time to let the world know about all your gifts. Include your accomplishments and whatever ways you have impacted the lives of others.*

- *What did your life stand for?*

- *What legacy did you leave behind?*

Describing Your Ideal Life

Imagine a life where all your dreams come true. When you dream, you wake up your desires in a way that brings them closer to reality. Consider designing several lives for yourself, each one more wonderful than the last. Why not create several scenarios before choosing? You don't have to limit yourself to one ideal life! By seeing the variety of what is possible, you more fully own the choices you make.

- *If you had only one year to live, how would you live it? Describe your surroundings, your actions, and your companions. Capture the sights, sounds, smells, colors, and the mood of this ideal time. Write a detailed journal of your one-year ideal life scenario.*

- *What themes do you notice about your dream life?*

- *What keeps you from making your fantasy a reality?*

- *After you've described your ultimate fantasy, divide everything into three lists:*

  1. *Can't live without it.*
  2. *Optional, nice to have, willing to work for.*
  3. *Frills I can live without.*

Choosing How to Serve

The great and glorious masterpiece of man is how to live with purpose.

— *Michel de Montaigne*

When Nicolae Ceausescu, the leader of Romania during the 1980s, banned contraception, social workers and HIV screening, AIDS ravaged the country. Thousands of children were inoculated with the same needle. When they contracted the AIDS virus, authorities took them from their homes to live in cages, warehoused in institutions.

When Susan saw the children on *Prime Time*, she turned to her husband Bill, and said, "Do you think I should go?" Without hesitating, he said, "Yes."

Walking into the orphanage, she found the silence chilling. The babies were quiet because no one had responded to their cries in the past. Tiny Loredana, two years old and only 8½ pounds, gave a little laugh, the only sign of hope. Susan converted a corner of the orphanage into a home for Loredana and four other children, all of them about two years old.

When Bill came to visit, he fell in love with the children. Starting small, Susan suggested adopting one child, but Bill wanted them all. That's exactly what Susan hoped he would say, so she stayed in Romania, working to secure adoption, battling hepatitis and severe weight loss. Bill visited her every couple of months and called his legislators, fighting for the right to bring his HIV positive children home.

Eighteen months later the Belfiores brought four children home. The fifth child was able to go back to his family because he tested HIV negative. Over the next couple of years, Loredana prayed for a baby. Gently, Susan explained, "Mommy can't have children." Sweethearts since age eleven, she and Bill had tried to have children and had given up. Loredana insisted that she would have a baby brother. So when Susan went to the clinic to discuss menopause, she felt shocked when the doctor confirmed her pregnancy.

Inspired by the work of International AIDS Activist, Brother Toby McCarroll, Susan believes, "There are only a few times in our lives that we are called. Hopefully we are able to hear the call." Over a thousand people volunteered for Brother Toby's project but only five were chosen to go. Susan said, "I'm sure my letter was very similar to all the others, but I never had any doubt that I would be chosen to go." She says, "A feeling came over me, and I just knew I would go."

She had a similar feeling about going to Africa to address the AIDS epidemic there. Well-meaning friends and family suggested that she stay home. They said the numbers were too overwhelming. It's too far away. The culture is so different. But none of these comments deterred Susan from her purpose. She took pictures of her healthy HIV positive teenagers to give people hope. Currently Susan is raising funds for the Elizabeth Glaser Pediatrics AIDS Foundation, to reduce the mother-to-child transmission of HIV.

The phrase to "make a difference" sounds like a platitude, but almost everyone wants to contribute. Stating specifically what difference you wish to make can inspire people to take action. With so many great causes that need people to serve, choosing where to serve can feel overwhelming. So many options! To get past bewilderment, consult with your heart, which has even more insight to offer than your brain.

- *Tapping the wisdom of your heart, how does your heart want you to serve?*

- *What shakes your heart?*

- *What breaks your heart?*

- *What awakens your heart?*

Chapter 8:
Painting Your Vision

Many executives thrash about with mission statements and vision statements. Unfortunately, most of those statements turn out to be a muddled stew of values, goals, purposes, philosophies, beliefs, aspirations, norms, strategies, practices, and descriptions. They are usually a boring, confusing, structurally unsound stream of words that evoke the response "True, but who cares?"
— *James Collins and Jerry Porras*

Living in a fast-paced environment leaves little time for vision, even though we recognize it as a leader's most important task. Without time devoted to planning an ideal future, busy people get stuck in the reactionary roles of problem solvers rather than becoming inspirational leaders. Most organizations have plenty of people highly skilled at finding and solving problems, but only a few know how to translate problems into a compelling vision.

To develop organizational capabilities, we start by inviting individuals to define and savor their own personal vision. Personal vision work stretches the canvas. Individuals add color and life to an organizational vision. As artists, we paint our visions for everyone to appreciate, offering a sense of hope and beauty. In this chapter we start by looking at other's visions, then visualize our future, stimulate our right brains, and paint the picture using visual imagery to tell our vision story.

Sharing My Journey

At age 16, I went on a vision quest in the Rocky Mountains of Colorado as part of a month-long Outward Bound trip. I brought only my clothes and a match. For three days I sat by a little pond. The time alone was meant to be a rite of passage, but nothing spectacular happened. Not one part of me could bear to sit still. I sadly waited for the three days to pass, and could not get the ache out of my body. Every bone, every muscle longed for action.

Back in the group, I learned of others' personal transformations and sensed that I had missed out on something rich and wonderful. I had not been afraid, excited, or awakened by spirit of any kind. Instead, I felt profoundly bored. To make matters worse, words my mother used to say, "Only boring people get bored," echoed in my mind and cast a lingering sadness on my quest. Others uncovered their courage. I uncovered my emptiness.

Many years later, I went on another quest, this time in the Endless Mountains of northern Pennsylvania. Inspired by the Native American writers Jamie Sams, Brooke Medicine Eagle, and Denise Linn, I felt determined to discover a personal vision. I spent a month in preparation, cleansing my mind, my emotions, my spirit, and my body. I even cleaned my house and my office thoroughly — a rarity.

By the time I got to the mountains, I felt ready and open. Wanting to feel comfortable in mid-October, I brought a sleeping bag, a poncho, and a jug of water. I climbed high into the mountains, marked my circle with stones, and sat expectantly. In the darkness, I slid into my down bag and waited. Falling asleep, I was startled by a bright light shining through the trees from the top of the hill. I thought to myself, "You idiot! You walked miles in the wilderness and you ended up choosing a spot under a yard light, smack in the middle of someone's backyard!"

Before long I realized it was the moon casting its light over my private spot. Watching the "yard light" soar into the night sky, I laughed at myself over and over. My spirit began to lift. The moon reminded me that my quest for significance often blinds me to simple truths, and that laughter is indeed my true friend.

The next night, as I lay in my sleeping bag, an owl swooped down 50 feet away, and swallowed the squeal of a mouse. This happened repeatedly all night long. Sometimes the owl landed only a few feet from my head. Many Native Americans and like-minded souls believe that when animals visit someone on a vision quest, each animal embodies special meaning. An animal spirit represents an invitation to recognize the animal medicine or power from within. A brush with an owl, for instance, suggests that you harbor special insights, the ability to comprehend the inner life of others. Repeated contact with a mouse suggests that you examine the small details of your life.

Lying there in the woods, I reminded myself that owl medicine helps me see right through deception and ulterior motives. I wondered whether this brush with an owl held an important message, or whether it represented nothing more than a nightly search for food by one hungry bird. Then my mind turned to the mice. Always a big-picture person, I have never paid much attention to detail, which often gets me into trouble. The mice swallowed by the all-knowing owl suggested that attention to detail in my life would nourish me, give me strength and lead to wisdom.

The following day a bald eagle flew overhead. I napped and had a wonderful dream of an eagle showing me that I would work in the rain forest of South America. Was this vivid dream the vision I was questing for? Uncertain, I stayed on the mountain, wanting to complete my three days in the wild.

It rained so hard the last day that my poncho didn't keep the rain out. I was soaked to the bone. Determined to stay my last night, I hunkered down and suffered. At dusk, a deer brought unexpected clarity to my quest. She ran up to me, looked me right in the eye, and gave me a startled look that said, "What are you doing here?" She snorted loudly, ran around in a circle, came back to the same spot, and repeated the question.

That's when I got my vision—I saw myself at home in a dry bed, sleeping peacefully with my loving husband. That glimpse of comfort gave me all the urging I needed. I gathered my things, ran down the mountain, rushed home, fixed a sandwich I'd been craving, and crawled into bed.

At the time, I considered my second vision quest almost as disappointing as the first. Although I had come away with a vague feeling of well-being, I emerged with no clear sense of where to point my toes. I still haven't gone to the South American rain forest, but I remain open to that possibility and many others.

In the end, the vision process is not about the destination. It's about the journey. I trust that my travels down the river of life lead me to tributaries filled with intrigue, mystery, adventure, opportunity, and peace. The destination keeps changing, but my trust and faith in my path keep me grounded, centered, and in a state of wonder.

Using Vision Examples for Inspiration

The same way that artists learn to paint by imitating the masters, we can learn to envision an inspirational future by studying visionaries. When we study other's visions, we can also learn what we *don't* want.

When an organization puts together a vision statement, too often the result looks like something spit out of the mission statement generator on Dilbert's web page: "It is our mission to conveniently enhance ethical catalysts for change as well as to dramatically create competitive deliverables to stay competitive in tomorrow's world."

The U.S. Poultry & Egg Association's vision sounds less generic, but no more inspiring, "A national organization which represents its members in all aspects of poultry and eggs on both a national and international level." Not only small organizations suffer from uninspiring visions, but large companies suffer from the "Who cares?" response. Target could easily exchange their generic vision statement with almost any other company, a sure sign that it lacks inspiration, "We are in business to please our customers and to provide a greater value than our competitors."

It's not all that different from Nordstroms' vision, although the two companies cultivate very different images. Despite their success, Nordstroms' outlook seems pretty lackluster, "To become the quality, service and leadership department store of the future." To their credit, Nordstroms has a unique list of rules for employees: Rule # 1: Use your good judgment in all situations.

Some organizations leave no doubt that they have a strong vision of where they're headed:

> We believe that Images and Voices of Hope is first and foremost a web of relationships, a network of conversations. As we engage in these appreciative conversations, we seed a shift in awareness. With this new awareness we see the world with new eyes. Our new vision of the world causes us to tell different stories and to produce different images. Out of these new stories of the world, we will produce a different world. This, we believe, is the power of a living dialogue to ignite social change.
>
> *— Images and Voices of Hope*

> We pledge to provide the finest personal service and facilities for our guests who will always enjoy a warm, relaxed yet refined ambience. The Ritz-Carlton experience enlivens the senses, instills well-being, and fulfills even the unexpressed wishes and needs of our guests.
>
> *— Ritz-Carlton*

> The Sacred Space Institute is a group of intimate peers with the common commitment of supporting each other's spiritual evolution as well as planetary transformation. Toward this end, we freely share resources, including information, technical skills and equipment, love, wisdom, nurturing, erotic energy, and financial opportunities.
>
> *— The Sacred Space Institute*

> Georgia Tech will be a leader among those few technological universities whose alumni, faculty, students, and staff define, expand, and communicate the frontiers of knowledge and innovation. Georgia Tech seeks to create an enriched, more pros-

perous, and sustainable society for the citizens of Georgia, the nation, and the world.

— Georgia Institute of Technology

Free the Children is dedicated to eliminating the exploitation of children around the world, by encouraging youth to volunteer in, as well as to create programs and activities that relieve the plight of underprivileged children.

— Free the Children
founded by Craig Kielburger at age 12

Although John F. Kennedy could have capitalized on getting to the moon before the Russians, his vision focused on exploring a new frontier. He said, "I believe that this nation should commit itself to achieving the goal, before this decade is out, of landing a man on the moon and returning him safely to Earth."

Powerful visions send an uplifting, positive message, but several companies successfully run negative campaigns. Focusing on the competition can inspire the troops, such as Pepsi's aspiration, "Beat Coke," and Nike's, "Crush Reebok" and Honda's, "We will crush, squash, and slaughter Yamaha."

Beating the competition unleashes passion, but despite some notable exceptions, negative campaigns rarely produce long-lasting positive results. After all, they're in the same business. If you really believe that your organization's contribution has value, and your competitors contribute something similar, do you really want to destroy the competition? Most politicians have an innate desire to serve, but mudslinging rivalry makes it harder and harder for quality candidates to give up their peace of mind to enter the ring.

If I wrote a negative vision statement for our company, instead of squashing the competition, I'd choose "Hurt Prozac and Maalox." Prozac and Maalox aren't direct competitors of course, but I believe the transformative nature of our work reduces the need for medication, so part of my vision includes putting a dent in the escalating usage of drugs. With the use of anti-depressants skyrocketing, I'm concerned that we're turning into a world of

Stepford robots with frozen smiles, taking Aldous Huxley's soma pills.

I envision a world where sadness and other shadow emotions aren't off-limits, and instead we explore the emotions that nudge us to change our behavior. But "Hurt Prozac" is not my vision, because I'm far more focused on what we can create, not on what we can destroy or dominate.

The vision of our company used to read, "We are the catalyst for personal and organizational transformation." All those long words felt a little daunting, so we changed it to, "We awaken the passion that grows people, ideas, and organizations." Our vision is always evolving and every time we tell the story of our future, it changes:

> *Awakening potential is at the heart of our work. Our passion comes from the stand we take for learning and growth. We engage deeply and act as midwives to the change process. Our work helps leaders set intentions, enlist support and get astounding results.*
>
> *Fun, creativity, and laughter jump out at us. We create safe space for doing the daring personal work of change. We harvest the learning that comes from failure and celebrate new ways of working together. Practicing radical authenticity, we make it easy for leaders to be vulnerable and get what they want. Listening for potential transformation, we build the bridge between actual impact and desired impact. Wherever we go, money flows freely. We aren't in business just to make money and neither are our clients. Every day we explore how we can serve and inspire other leaders to ask, "What do I have to give today?"*

Making Your Vision Simple, Powerful and Compelling

Many people subscribe to the concept that an inspiring vision has to be short and memorable. A vision statement can be as short as "To put Coke within arm's reach" or "The World's Favourite Airline" from British Airways, but vision *stories* generate a greater sense of inspiration and hope.

Few people create visions as grand as Henry Ford's, "I will build a motor car for the great multitude. It will be so low in price that no man making a good salary will be unable to own one. The horse will disappear from the highways; the automobile will be taken for granted...[and we will] give a large number of men employment at good wages. "

A powerful, shared vision touches us at the core and expands our imagination. When we share our vision as a story, we help people carry a vivid picture of the future in their heads and hearts. George Merck thought about his vision during the difficult years of the Depression, but he still carved out time for thinking about the big picture.

Merck's old vision stated, "Merck will be number one in its core businesses through innovations created by talented, entrepreneurial employees," and goes on to use inspirational language that sparks hope, "We will be the first drug maker with advanced research in every disease category. Our research will be as good as the science being done anywhere in the world. Our drugs won't be used by a single person who doesn't need them. Merck will continue to grow on a steady basis, bringing forth worthwhile products..."

Merck's old vision strikes a chord because of the explicit reference to what they won't do, "Our drugs won't be used by a single person who doesn't need them." Contrast that with the vision on their website in 2003:

> *We focus our activities on business segments in which we achieve competitive advantages through excellent quality of our products, services and systems. We want to achieve this through concentrating our activities on innovations and research in the pharmaceuticals business and on higher grade products in the chemicals business. In the future Merck will be positioned as a pharmaceutical company with an attractive chemicals business.*

What happened to the passion and energy of Merck's original vision?

Sony created one of the most compelling visions of all time in 1950, to "Become the company most known for changing the worldwide poor-quality image of Japanese products." They describe the future using vivid imagery:

We will create products that become pervasive around the world ...We will be the first Japanese company to go into the U.S. market and distribute directly.... We will succeed with innovations that U.S. companies have failed at — such as the transistor radio.... Fifty years from now, our brand name will be as well known as any in the world... and will signify innovation and quality that rival the most innovative companies anywhere... "Made in Japan" will mean something fine, not something shoddy.

Sony established this vision more than 50 years ago which guided and energized the organization toward worthwhile pursuits. Continuing the tradition by talking not so much about their image, but about what they will do, Sony's recent vision carries the torch. Instead of labeling themselves with adjectives, they fill their vision with action verbs that inject a sense of movement. Their story of their future:

Sony is a company dedicated to the celebration of life. We create things for every kind of imagination.
Products that stimulate the senses and refresh the spirit.
Ideas that always surprise, and never disappoint.
Innovations that are easy to love, and effortless to use.
Things that are not essential, but hard to live without.
We're not here to be logical.
Or predictable.
We're here to pursue infinite possibilities.
We allow the brightest minds to interact freely, so the unexpected can emerge.
We invite new thinking, so that even more fantastic ideas can evolve.
Creativity is our essence.
We take chances.

We exceed expectations.
We help dreamers dream.

Sony's chairman, Akio Morita, envisioned the Walkman as a way to listen to his beloved classical music without imposing on other commuters. The Walkman became Sony's signature product because it reinforced Japanese cultural values by encouraging harmony and respect for others. Another reason the product became so successful is that Westerners could listen to music without being bothered by others, reinforcing their values of autonomy, choice, and individuality.

Microsoft's website sets a distinctively visionary tone:

At Microsoft, we see no limits to the potential we all might reach because we see no limits to human imagination. That is what inspires us. And that is why we create software that helps people and businesses reach their potential. It's not just our purpose. It's our passion.

Examining both weak and strong visions inside and outside your industry can give you a sense of what you don't want your vision to look like, but others' visions can also inspire a broader view of what's possible.

Visualizing a Better Future

Learning to think and live beyond what seems possible is akin to going to the gym to develop a new set of muscles. What do you consider impossible, that if it *were* possible, would change everything? Every day practice helps you overcome the resistance to making the impossible happen. Of the millions of ways to develop insight, my favorite method involves tapping right-brain thinking and creativity.

World-class athletes use guided imagery to picture their ideal record-breaking performances. Russian Olympians perfected the technique of visualization and successful people all over the world have adapted it as a standard practice for achieving greatness. With a background of soothing music, most visualizations start by suggesting that you relax your body, breathe deeply, let go of tension and explore your creative state. It doesn't take long to get into a relaxed state; most people easily shift from reality to imagination.

Visualization serves an important role in the *Tell Your Vision* process, to awaken people to their highest aspirations.

Let's take a little trip into the future right now. Imagine a future where you feel and act the way you've always wanted. Imagine that you walk into the place where you work in the future.

Look around. What do you see? Describe the people. How do they interact? Now imagine that you see your Highest Self. Take in the essence of your future. Notice what your Highest Self is doing.

Imagine that you have a discussion with your Highest Self 10 years from now. Imagine that everything feels perfect, just the way you always dreamed it would be. Get comfortable and ask your Highest Self a few questions:

- *What key do you hold for leading a great life?*

- *Which of your talents and gifts have served you well?*

- *What do you need?*

- *What do you envision for the future?*

- *Notice what's most compelling about your Highest Self's vision.*

- *What other questions do you most want to ask your Highest Self?*

- *What would you like to explore further?*

Discuss whatever you wish. When finished with your conversation, explore the many ways you can tap into the power of your Highest Self. With the help of your Highest Self, you can reinvent yourself. Why not exercise your own exquisite power of choice and manifest yourself as wise, radiant, empowering and compassionate? This feels far more satisfying than any negative self-images you might currently hold. Visualization helps you achieve mastery instead of feeling subject to circumstances beyond your control.

Your Highest Self represents an image of yourself fully realized, living your full potential. Why wait 10 or 20 years to become the person you've always aspired to become? Since you already embody your Highest Self, you can choose to take on the essence of this fully-realized being now. How? When you face a difficult situation, ask how your Highest Self would handle it. Know that you can relax anytime and imagine having a conversation with your Highest Self, and ask whatever questions come to mind.

Whenever you feel stuck, take a moment to visit your Highest Self and ask for assistance. How can you operate more fully from the perspective of your Highest Self? Compare your current physical and energetic feelings with those of your Highest Self. What needs to change?

Try "acting as if" you are your Highest Self for the duration of a meeting, a phone call, or an event. This is different from "fake it 'til you make it," because you don't have to fake anything. After identifying how you experience your Highest Self, you can choose to embody your best qualities right now. When you embody the qualities of your Highest Self, you live to your full potential.

Instead of waiting for your vision to manifest, you can choose to become your Highest Self right now. Start by practicing being your Highest Self for 20 minutes a day and extend the time frame until you live mindfully the life you choose. Since your Highest Self already resides within, embrace your desired attributes now. In that way, you become the kind of person who can achieve your vision.

Stimulating the Right Brain

In addition to intellect and analysis, human beings can choose from tremendous creative resources. To tap the creative aspects of your vision, right brain activities are great sources of inspiration. Traditionally we place a high value on left-brain activities because we value the practicality of math, logic, and language. Our left brain tends to dismiss anything coming from the "flaky" right side of the brain, including holistic thinking and artistic talent. Optimally we utilize both sides of the brain, blending reasoning with creativity and imagination. To spark the under-utilized right side of the brain, we consciously fill our minds with creative emotional and visual images.

Don't start the vision process by thinking about what's practical. Look at what's impossible. Think beyond contemporary limitations. If the questions that follow sound farfetched, that's intentional. Start by thinking big! You can always pare it down or tone it down, but get creative first. Get as outrageous as you dare! It's okay to be silly, wild, or absurd, since that's where many great ideas come from.

Start by drawing a picture of your ideal future. Consider using watercolor or markers or any other medium. Close your eyes and get in touch with your longing. What's missing? Explore who you wish to become. Write about your deepest yearnings. Count yourself fortunate to create the future consciously. You can ask yourself the following questions, but only answer the questions that speak to you:

1. *If all your dreams came true, what would the future look like?*

2. *If you could fix one social problem in the world, what would you fix?*

3. *When you picture the world 10 years from now, what excites you the most?*

4. *What metaphor describes the vision?*

5. *What juicy words or visual images excite you?*

6. *What part of your body longs for the future? Imagine that part of your body speaking. What message does it offer?*

7. *Get up and allow your body to respond to your vision. What dance helps you to feel your vision more deeply?*

8. *How does your vision bring out your core aliveness more fully?*

9. *What elements from nature (such as trees or flowers) represent your vision?*

10. *What animals symbolize your vision?*

11. *What talents and gifts do you have that support your vision?*

12. *What outrageous elements could you add to your vision?*

13. *Imagine people responding to your vision. What attracts them?*

14. *In what imaginary place would your best self emerge?*

15. *If you could choose anyone in the world, who would you trade places with for a week?*

16. *What would you do with an extra 100 million dollars?*

17. *If you put your vision to a piece of music, what music would you choose?*

18. *What famous artist would ideally paint your vision?*

19. *What feelings and colors do you associate with your vision?*

20. *What delicious foods do you associate with your vision?*

21. *If you expand your vision a million times, what would you see?*

22. *If you went a million times deeper with your vision, where would that take you?*

23. *What does your heart say about your vision?*

24. *What does your gut say about your vision?*

25. *How would a child describe your vision?*

26. *What bubbles up, just beneath the surface of your vision?*

27. *What if your vision knew no limits?*

28. *What if you had all the time in the world?*

29. *What if you had an unlimited amount of money to realize your vision?*

30. *What if you had all the enthusiastic help you need to implement your vision? Then what?*

31. *What kinds of people express excitement about your vision? What do you imagine about them?*

32. *What resources can you tap to create your vision?*

33. *Remember Dr. Martin Luther King Jr.'s "I have a dream" speech? What is your dream?*

34. *What themes do you notice as you've answered the preceding questions?*

Refining your vision takes a lifetime, so be patient if you don't have full answers to these questions. Revisit the questions from time to time.

Tapping Visual Imagery

The outpourings of intuition consist of a continuous, rapid flow of choice, choice, choice, choice. When we improvise with the whole heart, riding this flow, the choices and images open into each other so rapidly that we have no time to get scared and retreat from what intuition is telling us.

— Stephen Nachmanovitch

Tuning into your intuition means getting into the flow. So trust your intuition and collect powerful visual images that call out to you. Notice what images grab you—and grab them. Choose from multiple sources for inspirational pictures, such as magazines, photos or clip art on the web, your camera, mental pictures, drawings, postcards and greeting cards. Also, look for mementos, knick-knacks, and small or even large objects. Take advantage of nature's gifts. Look for intriguing seeds, feathers, rocks, leaves, or flowers that represent your desired future. Look for images of objects, activities, feelings, and the ambience you want to create.

Gather your favorite images and create a collage, mural, mobile, shrine, kite, meditation corner or terrarium. One of our clients uses an image basket where she randomly puts anything that catches her eye. Every month she sits down with her basket, handling the images and objects to see what they offer in the way of new ideas.

Mary Kuentz, who leads "Design Your Future" workshops with me, says, "I always thought that making a collage was a silly approach, but people really come alive during this activity."

Whatever medium you use to hold your images, trust your intuition and let go of your doubts. Don't stop to ask why you are attracted to some imagery more than others. You can add to your imagery collection indefinitely, but after a few days, stop and take time to reflect on your creation. Notice what themes stand out.

- *Which images call to you most powerfully?*

- *What do the images say about your desired future?*

- *How do your heart and soul respond to the images?*

Crafting a Powerful Vision

When there is a genuine vision (as opposed to the all-too-familiar "vision statement"), people excel and learn, not because they are told to, but because they want to.
                                                              — Peter Senge

An energized vision takes the form of a story instead of a dull lifeless statement. If you are acting as facilitator, here's a fast way to help a group craft their vision. Begin by asking each person to write their own version of the vision, spending five minutes writing and revising the story of their preferred future. Next, each person underlines the three most important words or phrases in their story. Then they write each of the three words on a separate piece of paper, in large bold letters so that people in the back of the room can easily see. With smaller groups, you can put the words on large post-it notes. With large groups, use a full sheet of paper and stick them to the wall so that everyone in the room can see the words.

While the visionaries work, write connecting words such as *which, the, with* and *to* on separate sheets. Next, divide the group so that about five people sit at each round table. Ask them to pool their top three words or phrases and take about five minutes to brainstorm additional key words. Give them about five minutes to visit other tables to discuss new ideas. Encourage them to stand up for this part of the process, rather than passively waiting for people to come to them. The benefits of this method:

- Time pressure sharpens the focus
- Small group discussions get more people involved

- Cross-fertilization between groups generates shared ownership of ideas

Each person chooses their most important word or phrase, and sends it forward to you. Place the words about six feet up on the wall, grouping similar words together. When the same word shows up more than once, instead of tossing it out unceremoniously, acknowledge the confirmation of ideas. Ask for their second and third most important words until you post all the words on the wall, and continue grouping similar words together.

Now the fun begins! The group collaborates to rearrange the words until they build consensus about the story. Participants repeatedly take a shot at word-smithing the vision until everyone can live with it, and most of the people express excitement about it.

- *What's your personal vision for the organization?*

- *What's your collective vision for the organization?*

Building Consensus

The process of creating a vision energizes a group. People usually get far more value from the process of alignment than in the final words on the page. To ensure alignment and ownership of the end result, check for group consensus.

The five levels of consensus:

1. I can say an unqualified "yes" to the vision; I believe it represents the shared wisdom of the group.
2. I find the vision perfectly acceptable.
3. I can live with the vision, but I don't feel especially enthusiastic about it.

4. I do not completely agree with the vision and need to express my view about it. However, I choose not to block the direction and I am willing to support the vision.
5. I do not agree with the vision and I think we need to do more work before we can achieve consensus.

To determine if the vision needs more work, ask people to write down which of the five preceding statements most closely represents their viewpoint. Next put a piece of masking tape on the floor and ask them to view it as a continuum, where one end of the tape represents "one" and the other a "five." Everyone stands on the continuum so that they get a visual sense of where the group stands.

While standing on the line, further dialogue ensues when you ask questions along the lines of, "What would it take to get you to move toward one?" When every member of the group stands between one and four, you've reached consensus, but the closer the group moves toward one, the more enthusiastically people implement the vision!

Most groups come up with an acceptable vision story within two or three hours, but some groups do it in half an hour. Others take up to a year. Occasionally the group selects a finish team to fine-tune the vision that they later share with the group.

To take the process one step further, tell the vision to all employees. Using a *Strongly Agree* to *Strongly Disagree* scale, take a simple survey:

- *Does this vision reflect your view of the desired future of the organization?*

- *Do you believe that we can collectively implement this vision?*

- *Can you endorse this vision in your daily actions?*

The vision helps bring into focus the essence of the organization and its direction, and a short survey inspires employees who identify with the vision and wish to contribute. Publish the shared story about the future, and more importantly, tell the vision story. Unlike a static vision statement, the vision in a story format expands and evolves continuously. The story of the future changes with each personalized telling, the same way as stories about the past.

Part II Realizing Your Vision

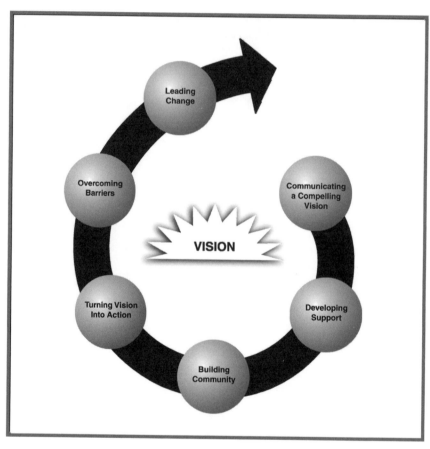

Realizing Your Vision

Chapter 9:
Communicating a Compelling Vision

Look, look, look to the rainbow. Follow the fellow who follows the dream.

— Song sung by Fred Astaire in the film Finian's Rainbow

All the imagination in the world takes you nowhere unless you learn to describe the vision compellingly, gain support, take action, overcome barriers and lead the people side of change. That's our focus in Part II as we work on realizing the vision. We begin this chapter by exploring the tools that help people communicate their vision. We start by looking at presence, passion, and authenticity, then discover the power of metaphors and stories, and end with communicating compelling visions that inspire people to take action.

According to *Leadership* magazine, communicating a vision is one of the most frustrating aspects of leading an organization. However, when we communicate a vision the same way we tell our favorite stories, the process is fun, fascinating, and uniting. Powerful stories fill our minds with visual imagery. Like an engaging movie, a vision uses the senses to engage people. Sights, sounds, feelings, tastes, and scents draw people in just like a good restaurant.

Radiating Presence and Connection

Maybe "journey" is not so much a journey ahead, or a journey into space, but a journey into presence. The farthest place on earth is the journey into the presence of the nearest person to you.

— Nelle Morton

Our imaginations have the capability to revise the past or invent the future. We can choose to live in a fantasy world, far from the now. However, we become most real and authentic when our bodies, feelings and thoughts stay in the present. People who radiate presence live their lives in the moment. If you've ever noticed politicians working a room, the naturals connect with each person, one at a time. Many say that Bill Clinton is especially good at this. After a group of five had an audience with the Dalai Lama, one asked, "Did you notice that he talked directly to *me*?" Another in the group said, "I thought he was talking directly to *me*." All five felt the same way.

Sharing your hopes with others allows you to test your ideas and find out how others connect to your message and your presence. In workshops, we ask listeners to use a response meter so that each participant gets immediate feedback. While one person describes a vision, listeners continuously change the pointer on their meter from 1 to 10 based on their level of engagement.

Reading body language gives you a sense of how your vision resonates with your audience. Using the metered approach gives you even more information and invites dialogue. People will tell you which parts they find compelling and which parts put them to sleep.

Consider video taping yourself while talking about your passion. Use a focus group of 8 to 10 people equipped with people meters who continuously rate your emotional impact. Don't plan your presentation, just get up and speak, trusting your passion and presence to shine through no matter what words come out of your mouth.

As you clarify your vision, dialogue with others to discover what attracts and what repels them from the picture you paint. When you ask powerful questions, you promote a deep level of sharing. Use the feedback to develop your fantasy into a source of inspiration and impact.

If you share your vision as an invitation, ask for an RSVP. Instead of wondering what reaction people have, ask! Ask what part they'd like to play in the drama, what contribution excites them, and how they can expand the view.

Communicating Passionate Energy

By focusing our efforts to a single point, we achieve the greatest results. The first rule of success, and the one that supersedes all others, is to have energy. It is important to know how to concentrate it, how to husband it, how to focus it on important things instead of frittering it away on trivia.

— *Michael Korda*

You can't develop passion by holding a pep rally and chanting, "Let's get passionate!" Passion develops through quiet exploration about what already excites you. Shared convictions that emerge from personal visions create the spark that lifts people out of the doldrums and helps them realize the extent of their courage.

Norman Vincent Peale held burning conviction and infectious enthusiasm as the most critical factors to leadership and successful living. He said, "Your enthusiasm will be infectious, stimulating and attractive to others. They will love you for it. They will go for you and with you."

Many people in positions of power do not know how to speak authentically, enthusiastically, or movingly. They may be physically attractive, mentally agile, have a stimulating voice, and still not reach their listeners if they do not know themselves.

If you know your audience you may connect at some level, but when you know yourself, you connect deeply. More than anything else, sharing personal experiences touches people. Opening up deepens relationships, which in turn expands the energy.

It took me a long time to realize that a group doesn't follow me because I know stories about famous people, or because I can tell a great joke. People follow me when I inspire commitment through personal authentic experience. What matters most is not the facts of the experience, but the heart and vulnerability of the experience, complete with hopes, fears, longings, and conclusions.

When I told a group of young high-potential leaders that when we ask for help, we develop the most important leadership skill of all, they nodded in agreement. When I told the following story about asking for help, and described my personal breakthrough, they became energized. They connected with me emotionally and could visualize the impact of what I was saying...

In the past, I rarely asked for help out of fear that people would say no. I loved my independent streak, and I assumed most people had better things to do than help me. So when the author of *Smart Speaking*, Marcia Yudkin, agreed to brainstorm some ideas with me, she helped me open new doors. Overnight I realized I could ask anyone for help! They don't always say yes, but taking the risk to ask, and ask again, helps me clarify what I really want. When I started presenting to groups, I made the mistake of trying to reach listeners by trying to act the part. I thought I had to give people a laugh a minute. Marcia taught me otherwise.

She advised that as long as I have valuable information to convey, expressing myself authentically would work. Marcia doesn't worry about whether people like her or not, or if she's putting on a good show. She says, "That would just get in the way." She even claims to have a mousy personality. People often thank her for showing them they don't have to change their personalities to become good speakers.

Personal stories inspire people far more movingly than a list of suggestions. Tips and rules rarely leave listeners with any lasting impression. The best communicators use stories, symbols, analogies, and metaphors. They understand the power of personal experience and know how to evoke emotion. They distill personal experiences into simple messages that listeners easily receive. Talking in sound bites or bumper stickers energizes listeners and leaves them with short simple messages.

As you learn to communicate with your whole body, you increase the depth and range of emotional expression. You gain a stronger command of language when you use the full range of your voice and truly feel your words. When you speak with passion you connect with people's hearts, which helps promote your ideas.

Self-exploration leads to discovering your passions. You connect with the underlying "why" of your communications. If you don't have a reason to communicate, stop talking. Breathe. Rest in silence. Wait until you have a purpose.

What you say and how you say it *are* important. *Why* you say it matters even more. Before you speak to any group, ask yourself a few questions:

- *Who is my audience?*

- *What impact do I want to have?*

- *How do I want listeners to react?*

- *What do I want them to think, say, or do?*

Journaling for Insight

I never travel without my diary. One should always have something sensational to read in the train.

— Oscar Wilde

Devoting half an hour each morning to writing makes a difference in your understanding of yourself and the world. Your journal is for you. When you write on a daily basis, not only your writing but also your thinking becomes clearer.

Stream-of-consciousness writing can get you started. As you write whatever comes to mind, you may start out whining, "I'd rather do something else. I have nothing to say. I am so stupid. I don't think I can write a single sentence today." Do it anyway. Don't think or edit, just write. A good way to cut through the fog is to notice the fog, and all its details. Brilliant insights can emerge from free-form writing.

If you are more of an evening writer, consider using learning statements in your journal. "I learned... I was surprised that... I relearned... I reaffirmed..."

A moving vision comes from deep reflection and introspection. Unless you invest time exploring the compelling nuances of your vision, your lack of conviction leads to lack of fruition. A deep wholehearted connection to your core helps you actualize the vision.

Asking Questions

Be patient toward all that is unsolved in your heart and try to love the questions themselves like locked rooms and like books that are written in a very foreign tongue. Do not now seek the answers, which cannot be given you because you would not be able to live them now . . . Live the questions now. Perhaps you will then gradually, without noticing it, live along some distant day into the answer.

— Rainer Maria Rilke

Embracing questions like a lover, the brilliant poet and mystic Rilke tells us how to live with our questions. If the answers do not come right away, steep yourself in the heart of the questions. The search for the answer is often more powerful than knowing the answer. Accept that the grail may remain out of reach. When the questioner is ready, the answer appears. Powerful questions help you discover, clarify, and hone your convictions. So if you're not sure what to journal about, consider answering the questions that speak to you:

- *What meaning do you make from your earliest memories?*

- *What do you truly need to make you happy?*

- *What makes you unique?*

- *When your closest friends talk about you, what do you hear them say?*

- *What do you want from your work?*

- *What do you want from your life?*

- *What do you feel most passionate about?*

- *What have you always dreamed about?*

- *Looking back on your life, what contributions have you made?*

Dreaming for Clarity

The future belongs to those who believe in the beauty of their dreams.
— Eleanor Roosevelt

When you ask both big and small questions before you sleep, and explore the possibilities in a dream state, often the answer awakens you. Withdrawing into your cocoon leads to self-transformation, allowing you to share your true colors with the world.

Albert Einstein claimed to get most of his inspiration from his dreams. Keeping a dream journal that you write in each morning helps you remember your dreams and mine them for inspiration. When I get stuck, my favorite remedy is to take a purposeful nap, allowing my subconscious to figure out the answers.

One way to work with your dreams is to review them in your mind's eye and draw the key images. Draw any visual impressions that stand out, whether you see people, places, symbols or feelings. Then "free-associate" by writing about the images you've drawn. How do you feel about each image? Allow your images to speak, and notice what emerges. What message does each image have for you? When your dreams seem fragmented, explore the images and discover what the symbols mean to you personally.

Create two columns, and describe the image in the left-hand column and provide your translation in the right-hand column. If you are not sure of the translation, make it up! The intention is to translate the subconscious dream story to your current situation. Highlight the key words on both sides and open yourself to the hidden messages.

Another way to work with your dreams is to tell the dream out loud, remembering as much as you can.

I dreamed that I ran through the forest leaping and flying above the snow until I came to a huge bird's nest where a red-tipped raven feather lay. Three rugged men joined me and they seemed friendly at first until I noticed the barbed wire fence and realized they had captured me. I got away by biting and fighting. I found a beautiful ancient basket, a mysterious gift from someone very old.

Tell the dream a second time, using the words "The (blank) part of me..." The second version sounds like:

I ran through the dark forest part of me, leaping and flying above the cold snowy part of me. I came to the big huge bird's nest part of me and found the red-tipped raven feather part of me, which reminded me of the unusual and beautiful part of me. I saw the rugged male part of me, which looked friendly on the outside, but I also saw an evil side of me. I noticed the barbed wire fence part of me, which felt scary because I knew I had fenced in or captured part of me. The biter and fighter part of me got free and I found a lot of solace in the beautiful mysterious basket part of me. I felt special because the ancient part of me has inner wisdom.

The value of the second version is in seeing the various parts of the whole self. In nightmares, we often think of evil as being outside ourselves, but looking within ourselves often offers new insights. In Denise Linn's book *The Hidden Power of Dreams*, she suggests that nightmares are a positive sign that our subconscious is finally ready to break through and face our demons.

If you awaken and find your dreams confusing, consider drifting back to sleep seeking clarification. Intentional lucid dreaming reveals the hidden meanings of your dreams.

Practicing Meditation

One of my favorite meditations is to breathe in all that the world has to offer, and breathe out all that I have to contribute to the world. Following the breath or repeating a phrase stills the mind and gives access to the wisdom within. Suspending judgment provides openings for new insights to bloom. A regular meditation practice invites inspiration. Theologian Matthew Fox defines prayer as a radical response to life and its mysteries.

I envy all my meditative friends and their quiet stillness. I used to feel annoyed with myself because I couldn't sit still, until I learned that not all meditation involves sitting. A walking meditation reaps great benefits.

If you pack your life full of action, take some time for personal reflection. Go for a walk that is just a little too long, which is where author Eudora Welty believes great ideas come from. Getting away from the daily noise opens up new channels of creativity.

My preference is to explore the inner landscape with people I love. We act as sounding boards to explore our hopes, failures, and learning. Listening and sharing my heart brings me to stillness.

The Wyalusing Rocks in the Endless Mountains of Pennsylvania is one of my favorite places to sit. The rock ledges jut out over the Susquehanna River, flowing by 500 feet below. It's the only place I know where I can look down and see hawks flying below me. Wyalusing means "where the old man sits." The old man refers to a medicine man, and the place is steeped with history and divine energy.

When John Woolman, a Quaker Abolitionist spoke to the natives in Wyalusing during the 18th century, he chose to forego the use of an interpreter because it might interfere with the "tendering of hearts." The meeting ended with a degree of divine love, and the chief of the Delaware Indians, Papunehang, said to one of the interpreters, "I love to feel where words come from." What we say is not nearly as important as what comes from our hearts.

Movement is often an effective way of opening our hearts and minds. My favorite dance meditation is the Dance of the Seven Directions taught by White Feather from the Native American Wolf Clan in New York. Starting with the East, the home of the eagle, I dance the simple steps that help me see the big picture and new growth. Facing the south, home of the otter, I replenish playfulness, warmth and the child within. Turning toward the west, home of the bear, the place of hibernation and introspection helps me reflect deeply. Toward the north, home of the raven, the ancestors give me a sense of historical perspective, and invite me to open up to the magic and mystery. The other three directions help me to gather energy from above, Father Sky; below, Mother Earth; and within, from my center. The dance helps me physically align with energy, truth, and gratitude.

Exploring Emotions to Uncover Passion

> *Every change, every burst of creativity, begins with the identification of a problem or opportunity that somebody finds meaningful... The simplest way to discover what's meaningful is to notice what people talk about and where they spend their energy.*
>
> *— Margaret Wheatley*

Our emotions give us powerful clues about what's meaningful. Thanks to Daniel Goleman, people have a heightened awareness of emotional intelligence, which can be even more important than IQ in predicting success in work and in life. In his book *Emotional Intelligence*, Goleman says that of the five dimensions of emotional intelligence, empathy is "the fundamental skill of management."

Although some people seem to be born with empathy, most of us have to learn the skill. Often confused with sympathy, empathy is a far cry from pity. When we empathize, we create a heart connection and share a deep understanding and appreciation of emotions and needs.

In many organizational cultures, feelings are never expressed, and in others, feelings are limited to happiness. Avoiding feelings may seem like the easiest route, especially when people have a low tolerance for emotional tension. The trade off is a steep price to pay because we abandon what we truly want. Emotions are the key to what we want, and when we lose touch with our desires, we abandon the vision and lose sight of our goals. When we willingly explore the causes of emotional tension, we gain a better understanding of what matters most. In organizations where people develop awareness of emotions, they shift from fault-finding to concern for one another, and they become grounded in compassion.

One of my favorite clients, Jana, a director in a small company complained, "He's the owner of the company; he's never going to change, and I'll just have to put up with the way he steps into my job, acts like he's helping me, but takes away all my authority."

After clarifying her emotions, she went to her boss to discuss their relationship. The gist of the conversation was, "When you hired the new sales manager without my input, I felt crushed, because I need autonomy and respect. Will you talk to me before hiring anyone new in my department?"

Pete, the owner, acted surprised and immediately said yes to the request. He seemed genuinely moved when he learned that "helping out" stimulated feelings of fear, and concerns about trust and confidence. Jana felt comforted when he said, "I value your input, couldn't run this business without you, and will do whatever it takes to create an environment where you can shine."

Unfortunately, his behavior didn't change one bit. You can imagine Jana's anger when he hired another new employee without consulting her. Instead of getting her work done, she spent the whole day revising her resume and connecting with her network. I worked with several people in the company, and they all had the same complaint: Pete usurped their authority, and it stung. They called him "The Big Spoon" because he would stir everybody up and leave. Exasperation levels were high, so Pete and several managers got together to discuss the deeper issues.

The managers translated their judgment of Pete into observations, feelings, needs, and requests. Gradually the judgmental language, "You make me feel worthless," shifted into higher awareness, along the lines of, "I feel disappointed because I need to contribute."

"But you *are* contributing!" countered Pete.

Frustrated because she needed to be heard, Jana stood up and said, "You are such a jerk. You don't hear anything we say!" Seeing Pete's hackles of defensiveness rise, Jana took a step backwards, closed her eyes and took a moment. She shifted into owning her feelings and spoke from the heart, "What I mean to say is, I feel deeply disappointed, because I need respect, understanding and camaraderie."

In the silence that followed, Pete felt her disappointment and with rare vulnerability, said, "I'm afraid that I'll lose my best people." The air thickened with emotion as they all tuned into their needs for connection, collaboration, and accomplishment. That's when the managers realized they needed to listen empathically to fully understand Pete's choices.

What they uncovered startled them. Pete had a gift for spotting talent. He'd put together a brilliant team. In his passion for excellence, he wanted to learn, jumped in, and felt disheartened because he wanted to contribute at their level. He sensed their dissatisfaction and worried that he didn't have the leadership skills to hold them all together, so he overcompensated by taking over. When the team reflected back the new information they just heard, Pete asked for their help in becoming a better leader.

Together they worked out a plan for Pete to maximize his contribution and at the same time, give full autonomy to the directors. The primary tool for getting autonomy was to speak up about observations, feelings, needs and requests, which Jana dubbed, "Let's get real." Whenever Pete stepped on anyone's toes, he heard about his impact. Just as important, the directors got to hear about Pete's hopes and fears. Moments of frustration evolved into opportunities for people to communicate their needs collaboratively to address those needs.

When we listen compassionately, we hear the connection between feelings and needs. Every emotion, every gut reaction relates to needs that are either met or unmet. Happiness and joy indicate that needs are met, but anger, fear, and sadness are the most common reactions to unmet needs.

The most powerful way to uncover passion is to build awareness of feelings and needs. To say, "I feel annoyed because I need trust," or "I feel afraid because I need camaraderie," unleashes the power of emotions and needs. When we focus on hearing each other's needs, we engage in the gutsiest form of communication.

Marshall Rosenberg's book *Non-Violent Communication*, is a resource for improving listening and facilitation skills. Practitioners all over the world use his simple but powerful compassionate communication model to build understanding and resolve conflict. Marshall works with volatile communities, gangs, war-torn countries, families and corporations to resolve conflict. Strong communication skills seem so elusive, but Rosenberg's methods make it easy for people to deepen their awareness using the OFNR model and distinctions:

- Observations
- Feelings
- Needs
- Requests

Observations differ from judgments.

- What you see and hear in a videotape vs. what you think about or evaluate

Feelings are not the same as what you are thinking.

- Your emotions or gut reactions vs. interpreting

Needs are not about figuring out what others should do.

- What you want for yourself vs. what you want from others

Requests are the strategies for getting needs met, and are very different from demands.

- Asking for what you want vs. insisting on what you want

For more details on these distinctions, visit the Center for Non-Violent Communication website at http://www.cnvc.org.

Try using the following formula until you develop a natural, fluent way to express yourself.

When you (observation)
I feel (emotion)
Because I need (unmet need)
Would you be willing to (request)?

For example,
When you read your newspaper as I talk,
I feel disappointed,
Because I need understanding.
Would you be willing to put the paper away and look at me while we have a five-minute discussion?

Rosenberg's simple but powerful model builds understanding and deepens communication. To develop compassion, make the shift from moralistic judgment to hearing and expressing *your* underlying needs. By noticing your judgments (without judging yourself), you can explore the passion and needs that bubble just beneath the surface.

Deepening Your Passion

I was passionate, consumed with longing.
I searched from horizon to horizon.
But the day the Truthful One found me, I was at home.
      — *Lal Ded, fourteenth century Kashmir poet*

Some leaders focus on the *what* and *how* of leading, however, it's more important to focus on the *why* or the underlying passion. Passion comes from your center and is based on what matters most to you, what moves you, excites you, and enlivens you. When your passion blossoms, you go through the process of awakening. Your ardor emits its own powerful energy that attracts people drawn to your enthusiasm, intensity, and devotion. They don't necessarily agree with your every word, but they're drawn to your passion.

When we pursue happiness, meaning, and passion, we find fulfillment in the journey. From an early age, we are taught to stifle our passion, to control it instead of letting it control us. Too often, well-meaning adults crush the spirit of a child by saying, "Sh... Be quiet. Be still. Stop wanting."

To reawaken your passion, to fuel your unique spark, notice what you care about most. Instead of stifling your desires, immerse yourself in your desires. To discover passion, tune into what excites you.

Many people avoid passion because they associate it with the tension of anger or sex. Afraid of the ramifications, they turn down the flame. The flickering pilot light seems safer than burning passion. But at what cost? Some desires do carry a negative charge. Usually your negative or shadow emotions want something intensely. For instance, the desire for revenge may indicate a need for fairness; lust could be about the need for connection; and greed may reveal the desire for security or comfort. Look into your heart for the positive intent underneath your negatively charged desires. Discover what lies just beneath the surface that you really hunger for.

- *Take a walk down memory lane. Think of all the times in your life when you expressed your passion fully. Look for exciting times and notice life's "wake up" calls. Make a list of all the times you felt deeply passionate. Then identify the three things you have felt most passionate about in your lifetime.*

- *What themes do you notice? How do you bring that kind of passion into the present? How do you apply your passion to other areas of your life?*

- *You can't develop passion by copying someone else, but think about the passionate people you know. Who expresses their passion in ways that you admire? List all the passionate people you admire and what attracts you.*

- *In all likelihood, you project your strengths on the people you admire. So turn the mirror around. What do you notice about their passion that you also see in yourself?*

Unleashing Natural Charisma

The creative process is a spiritual path. This adventure is about us, about the deep self, the composer in all of us, about originality, and meaning, not which is all new, but that which is fully and originally ourselves.

— Stephen Nachmanovitch

How do we define something as elusive as charisma? Charisma is that magnetic and magical quality of attraction. People follow charismatic politicians without knowing what they stand for or how their track records impact constituents. People with charisma attract others more because of their energy than their appearance.

Leaders rely on charisma to invite others to share their visions. But charisma often gets a bad rap. Organizations run by charismatic leaders often fall apart without them. Their less charismatic counterparts tend to leave long-term legacies that continue long after they retire. Churchill worried that his strong personality would deter people from confronting him with the brutal facts. Rightfully so. Exceptionally charismatic leaders can intimidate, so their views rarely get challenged. Some consider charisma more of a liability than an asset, but I believe that charisma is a positive, powerful force that anyone can develop.

When you hear the word charisma, whom do you think of? John F. Kennedy? Princess Di? Martin Luther King, Jr.? Margaret Thatcher? Like physical attraction, charisma is a subjective quality. People don't always agree on who has charisma, but they often hold strong opinions about who *doesn't*. I believe most people have charisma, but they rarely know how to access it; they simply don't know what makes them compelling.

Charisma is the key to our survival, a part of our genetic makeup. We're born with it. Babies exude charisma. Like a magnet, they draw people of all ages to them. People coo at them, feed them, nurture them, and love them. One reason babies attract so much attention is they don't hide their emotions. Everything they feel shows on their faces. As we grow older, most of us don't maintain our magnetism. More often than not, we allow fear to wrap its tentacles around us and we hide our true feelings. Through conscious effort, we can stay in touch with the power of our charisma.

The Greek word "Charis" is the name for the Graces, the three goddess sisters and daughters of Zeus. Brightfulness, Joyfulness, and Bloom represent the triple incarnation of grace and beauty. As the fertility goddesses, they "gave life its bloom." We can all nurture charisma, literally a gift from the Gods, until it blossoms.

Charisma is personal magic. To deepen your awareness of your unique qualities and develop them is your gift to the world. When you express your own truth in your own way, you reveal your hidden self, and the world benefits from your special expression of individuality.

To develop your own unique spark, actively focus on your strengths, not your weaknesses. Use your personal strengths as the starting place for your development. Pay attention to your dreams and gifts. Step into your charisma. Step into your light. Discover your unique strengths and use them to enrich the world. What a wonderful gift!

Tapping Authenticity

Many women today feel a sadness we cannot name. Though we accomplish much of what we set out to do, we sense that something is missing in our lives and — fruitlessly — search "out there" for the answers. What's often wrong is that we are disconnected from an authentic sense of self.

— Emily Hancock

To reconnect with an authentic sense of self, we must listen deeply, and speak courageously. Authenticity is *not* about polishing your presentation skills. In Ireland in 1963, when John Kennedy gave one of his last speeches, he became so emotional during the last few minutes that he looked down at the podium and folded his paper over and over again. But the crowd roared their approval as he left the stage. When Kennedy was elected President, his brother Bobby chewed gum as he spoke to the campaign committee and he couldn't complete a sentence without several ahs and ums, but he spoke excitedly and authentically.

Most people consider themselves genuine, honest, and real. But few are perceived that way. Rarely do we hear leaders admit that they lack integrity, but most of them have difficulty expressing themselves candidly and honestly. Why? Because they fear judgment. Or perhaps they want to protect others from harsh realities. Leaders who willingly risk disappointment and admit that they don't have all the answers invite people into the inner circle where they share their vulnerability.

Speaking authentically goes beyond telling the truth. When we speak from the heart of our experience, we create trust. Straight talk gives people a sense of connection and hope. Even when the truth is hard to hear, sharing real emotions creates an open space for new possibilities. When we align who we *are* with what we *do* and say, people sense our conviction.

When we withhold a tough message, or put a positive spin on a dire situation, we *think* we are contributing to ease and comfort, but in actuality, we breed fear and insecurity. No matter how stonily we hold a poker face, people intuitively know when we aren't being real. Instead of *knowing* what we're withholding, they *imagine* all kinds of explanations, most of which are far from the truth.

Listening authentically means we're open to the influence of others, calling forth their contribution to our learning rather than listening to judge or evaluate. Valuing diverse perspectives gives us a fuller understanding of the real issues and opens us to what's possible. When we listen appreciatively, we foster a culture that helps people bond.

Authentic listeners don't allow people to babble or go off on tangents that diminish the connection and dampen the energy. Instead of pretending to listen or making an excuse to leave, authentic listeners interrupt compassionately as soon as they've heard one more word than they want to hear. Rather than rudely cutting people off, they stick their necks out and share their desire to reconnect wholeheartedly. When you are the one speaking, when do you want listeners to let you know that their energy is waning? What would serve you and your listeners? When you become aware that your words are not having the desired impact, stop. Then start asking curious questions to reestablish the connection. Another element of authenticity comes from the desire to serve. When we acknowledge that our interdependence creates value, we connect emotionally and spiritually.

In our unpredictable, changing world, people long for strong, authentic leaders. Television and movies make great entertainment, but we seek real-life heroes and heroines as well. How tragic that many of our great leaders boost their heroic status with their death. Princess Diana's call to eliminate land mines made more headlines the week of her death than all during her short life.

With advanced technology emphasizing the visual, authenticity plays an important role in effectiveness. With so much footage deleted, television gives us reason to doubt anyone who stumbles, stutters, or lacks spontaneity. We expect leaders to have it all. All over the world, people yearn for connection. People hunger for authentic communication.

To connect genuinely with others, learn how to establish intimacy. For some people nothing comes easier, and for others, nothing feels more painful. When you share what feels most alive for you in the present moment, you fling open the doors to intimacy. To build awareness of authenticity, look for moments when you show up fully. Bask in the moment when you find yourself in the flow or when the energy of the group seems electrically charged.

Developing Influence

So who needs influence? You may enjoy working behind the scenes, greasing the wheel and have no desire to bask in the limelight. Whether you bag groceries at the supermarket or speak to audiences of thousands, you have many opportunities to influence others. Your vitality helps you in everyday life, from convincing a child to look both ways before crossing the street to encouraging an elderly neighbor to join the gym. Your ability to influence others positively has a snowball effect.

Most people want to follow, and they want to follow a decisive leader. In the book *Leaders*, Bennis and Nanus say, "The truth is that leadership opportunities are plentiful and within reach of most people."

Like everyone else, you are both a leader and a follower. Even self-proclaimed wallflowers influence thousands of people during a lifetime. They give opinions on where to go on vacation, which book to read, or what car to buy. When you think of the many different people who have influenced you in big and small ways, you begin to gain a sense of your own influence. As you compare your current impact with your desired impact, you become inspired to lead more effectively.

Jim Kouzes and Barry Posner say that the best leaders are the best followers. However, acting sheep-like doesn't make a good follower or a good leader. Many entrepreneurs are mavericks who push the envelope. It's not uncommon for them to have been fired early in their career or to have dropped out of school. Early failures can prompt people to take the road less traveled, which could lead to jail time, or it could inspire people to clean up their act, prove themselves, and accomplish greatness. The willingness and ability to change our own behavior, or influence *ourselves*, is the key to developing influence with others.

Honing Integrity

The very act of speech is courageous because no matter what we say, we are revealed.

— David Whyte

From the book *Profiles in Leadership* by Alan Axelrod, we learn how top business and government leaders answered the question, "What quality is most important to your success as a leader?" Almost unanimously they answered, "Integrity." People with integrity are consistent in word and deed. Fearless leaders have nothing to hide, and their lives read like an open book. Walking the talk, keeping promises, contributing to others, and speaking honestly are all components of integrity.

Anita Roddick took social responsibility to new heights when she dedicated her business, the Body Shop, to the pursuit of social and environmental change. She said, "This is not about one penny being spent on so-called cause-related marketing which is disingenuous. This is about having a passion to stand out and be persuasive about what you do." To live her values fully, Roddick stepped down from her position at the Body Shop so she could more effectively address global issues.

If you're like most people, you perceive your own integrity as nearly flawless, so why do some people see you so differently? The best way I know to clean up integrity is to get feedback, starting with self-feedback.

- *In what ways do I send mixed messages?*

- *How am I out of alignment?*

- *How can I live in full integrity?*

Linking Metaphors to Your Vision

Some metaphors are as dead as door nails, but original metaphors give us a jolt of creative energy. It is easier to understand a new idea when explained using a metaphor. Metaphors are vivid, sensual forms of communication, whether they're verbal, visual, musical, ceremonial, or ritual. You can use metaphors to give language to your emotions and create pictures in the minds of others. When you use a metaphor to describe your experience or your hopes for the future, you reveal something unique and deeply meaningful.

Metaphors are the tools of great communicators. To hone your skills, practice using metaphors to describe your vision.

Compare your vision to a:
- *Costume*
- *Adventure*
- *Boat*
- *Game*
- *Rescue*
- *Piece of Music*
- *Ceremony*

- *Famous Painting*
- *Sacred Object*
- *Sport*
- *Revolution*
- *Scene in Nature*
- *Dance*
- *Gift*

A few examples:
- I envision a three-piece band, a booming trombone, a swaying sax and a fired up fiddle that gets people to dance.

- I see the lightning that connects sky and earth, lighting the darkness, bringing energy to earth.
- I envision a pick-up game of basketball, hooping it up, in the zone with new players.
- In my canoe, I lead the exploration into new territory, one with the river, at home with the turbulence.

Now elaborate on your own metaphors. Notice that when your metaphors change, the way you think about your organization changes too.

- *What phrases, bumper stickers or slogans describe your future that excite you and others?*

Gathering Inspirational Stories

Making a list is good. It makes you start noticing material for writing in your daily life, and your writing comes out of a relationship with your life and its texture. In this way, the composting process is beginning. Your body is starting to digest and turn over your material, so even when you are not actually at the desk physically writing, there are parts of you raking, fertilizing, taking in the sun's heat, and making ready for the deep green plants of writing to grow.
— Natalie Goldberg

Known for the book she wrote with Judith Guest, *Writing Down the Bones*, Natalie Goldberg suggests that our lives are full of writing material. So that you can talk easily about your vision, write about it! Your vision may be an ember that you blow the ash off, or a raging bonfire that you learn to express through controlled writing.

Writing your story gets you grounded in the details, so consider writing several versions, depending on whom you hope to reach. Which part of yourself do you want to touch? One version might be what colleagues put on their website as a link to yours, and another for a feature-length article for a magazine. Design the article-length version to attract customers, collaborators, new employees, and anyone else who wonders what you *really* do.

Albert, a prolific writer of mysteries, appreciates the power of written stories.

> *Speech is temporary, transient. Spoken words rise like mist on a still pond, then evaporate, the idea often lost in the very instant of utterance and misunderstood even when we think we are being most clear. Written words are stronger, surer. If our told stories can sweep across our souls like a strong wind, our written stories have hurricane potential!*
>
> *— Susan Wittig Albert, Writing From Life*

Albert movingly builds a case for honing our writing skills in order to have greater impact. We all have something unique to say, based on our rich and varied past. A past peppered with problems adds spice to our personalities, our stories, and our unique contributions.

- *List your best stories — the ones that really engage people.*

- *What stories have you heard again and again, yet never get tired of?*

- *Create a notebook full of inspiring stories. List the stories and identify the highlights, especially looking for the moment when the story has the strongest emotional impact.*

Engaging People with Storytelling

> *If one is aware of storytelling as a way of being present in the world, one soon becomes aware of its opposite: not telling. If we can't tell our story, if it's caught in our throat, it seems to block our spirit's longing to participate in the world. At an extreme, we can't reach out at all. And everybody, I think, has a story or two caught in the throat.*
>
> *— Mary Rose O'Reilley*

To unblock your spirit's longing to participate in the world, open your throat and tell your story. Communicating a compelling vision means that we not only engage people's intellect, we engage their hearts and ours. To reach people at the core means we reach them emotionally, and stimulate their imagination. An enticing vision gets our attention the same way a good story holds us rapt or we're drawn to the scent coming from a cozy kitchen.

My mother used to read a variety of books to us at bedtime, but we always begged for the mouse family stories because they were about us! The thinly disguised identities of the mice gave us a peek at what new adventure might wait just around the corner. How do you include or involve listeners in *your* story?

Stories offer a wonderful way to connect. Here's a story I've told a few times:

> One of my favorite fun-loving people, Mary Kuentz, co-facilitates workshops with me often. The first time Mary and I worked together, a client called asking us to complete the project two weeks earlier than we'd originally agreed upon. I wanted to create a long-term relationship built on treating Mary well, right from the start. That seemed almost impossible based on the client's demands. We put in long hours, didn't stop to eat, and we both felt the crunch.
>
> We met the demands of the client, but didn't even take time to celebrate because the next day I went out of town to facilitate a customer service workshop. During the workshop, we made live calls to evaluate customer service. I thought it an opportune moment to call a flower shop and send Mary a dozen roses with a note that said, "I love you!"
>
> The following day, Mary told me that someone sent her a dozen roses but she didn't know who, and the flower shop wouldn't tell her. So I asked her, "Well, who do you *think* sent them?" expecting her to guess right away. She said, "Well, I don't think it was my boyfriend, because he wouldn't have sent yellow." Then she proceeded to name all the possible senders, an old flame, a guy she just met at the grocery store, a man

who looked like a stalker, but I didn't make the list. She announced, "I'm going to call them all and ask them. I really want to know who sent those flowers!"

That solution looked like a lot of work, so she decided to call the flower shop and tell them, "Whoever sent me those roses, send him a dozen roses with a card that says, "I love you, too." That's when I told her I sent the flowers, but she said, "No! I don't believe it!" and continued to imagine who might have sent the flowers, expanding her list and laughing.

Our stories reveal us. A memorable story helps people connect with what we care about.

- *What stories can you tell that reveal yourself?*

- *What stories can you share that clarify your vision?*

- *Who are the most engaging storytellers you know and how can you learn from them?*

- *What compelling stories have you told about your organization repeatedly?*

- *What new stories would you like to start telling?*

Taking a Stand

> *We never know how high we are*
> *Till we are called to rise;*
> *And then, if we are true to plan,*
> *Our statures touch the skies.*

> — *Emily Dickinson*

When we take a stand, we transform a possibility into a reality. By "putting a stake in the ground," we declare what we believe is possible. Declarations go beyond intent and add to our credibility.

Taking a stand involves courage, but it doesn't mean standing alone or without support.

If we stay open to challenge and improvement when we declare our intentions, we invite people to join us and help us shape our vision. So the trick is to stay open, but take a stand that comes from our center. Making a bold promise involves risk, but also generates a sense of certainty. Not that we know with surety the outcome, but that we feel certain of our persistence and capabilities. That means trusting that when we open ourselves to others, we accept that "not knowing how" is not a barrier.

Elliot Richardson, who held four federal cabinet positions in the 1970s, said, "And yet, on balance, affirmative action has, I think, been a qualified success." With all those hedging words, William Zinsser, author of *On Writing Well,* calls it the most wishy-washy sentence in modern public discourse. It gets worse. Richardson concluded an analysis of how to relieve boredom among assembly line workers by saying, "And so at last I come to the one firm conviction that I mentioned at the beginning. It is that the subject is too new for final judgments."

When you tap your own source of conviction, you maximize the possibility of commitment from others. People will follow you, not because you have all the right answers, but because you have experienced the same fear, hope, and confusion as they have.

- *What would get you up on a soapbox?*

- *Imagine that you will give a speech in five minutes. Prepare to share your outlook of the future including the most important change you foresee, and how you plan to make that change come about.*

Calling People to Action

The more people you involve in shaping your future, the more help you will get to carry it through. That doesn't mean you design your vision by following the consensus of other people's opinions.

However, their involvement leads to commitment and a willingness to implement the plan. An effective vision acts as a catalyst for other people to expand their goals.

Ask people to talk about the organization's vision in their own words, to test their collective understanding. Get them to discuss the implications and how they will apply the vision. The real test comes when you see whether their actions are congruent with the vision. When their behavior reflects the vision, you know you've reached them.

Whether you're talking to inspire a few people or many, why bother unless you leave them with something to take away, something to remember. How can you leave your listeners with a sense that their time was well spent? Among speechwriters, the gems, or morsels are known as "take aways" or "keepers." Your words can have a tremendous impact, often based on a simple message.

As you talk about your plans, look for ways to include people and make it easy for them to contribute. Don't just put your ideas out there and expect people to run with it; tell them exactly what you want them to do. Instead of considering this an imposition, consider the call to action an invitation or a gift. When you ask for action, you make an important request that others can choose to act on. Desire without a sense of urgency inspires no one. The need to get out of trouble or the desire to develop a major new opportunity or threat can inspire people to act now.

- *How do you convey a sense of urgency?*

- *What impact do you want to have?*

- *As a result of sharing your vision, how will people think or act differently?*

- *What do you want people to take away?*

- *What is your call to action?*

Repeating the Vision in all Mediums

How often do you communicate your vision? As often as you can. In every medium you can. Press releases, annual reports, meetings with the troops, brochures, website, email, the water cooler, social events, community events, the company newsletter— these are just a few of the places where you can communicate your vision. You can't just assume that people receive and understand your message; you have to enlist key players to reinforce the specific expectations.

Sharing the vision with everyone in the organization improves esprit de corps. Not just employees, but the board of directors, customers, friends, lenders, stockholders, members of the community, suppliers, and strategic partners need to hear about the vision.

- *What mediums do you choose as the best ways to communicate your vision?*

- *What has worked in the past and present? What will work in the future?*

Chapter 10:
Developing Support

There is no more powerful engine driving an organization toward excellence and long-range success than an attractive, worthwhile, and achievable vision of the future, widely shared.

— Burt Nanus

Picture your vision widely shared. When you gather support, miracles happen. In this chapter, we explore ways to assess and expand our support systems, give support and make requests. We also look at ways to find mentors, leverage networks, and get others on board.

Assessing Your Support System

People used to stay linked by family and close-knit communities, which had strong support systems built into them. In Western culture, we reluctantly ask for help, believing that rugged individualism equals strength. Attachment to independence brings less real support and makes getting help seem like a "weak" or "bad" thing. However, true strength comes from *inter*dependence.

It takes courage to choose interdependence and to know that you don't have to "go it alone." Caretaking, or doing things *for* people can be disempowering, but *caregiving* can be an empowering gift. Although many people need caretaking because they cannot physically take care of themselves, caretakers face the danger of making choices for others who are perfectly able to do so, fostering dependency that serves no one. In contrast, caregivers strive for full presence, and the receiver takes full responsibility for their goals. There's a big difference between giving because we think we "have to" and giving joyfully, because we want to contribute. Caretakers sometimes present themselves as an authority figure. They want to rescue others, and often have great difficulty receiving from others.

Take a look at your support system and make sure it works to relieve stress, not create stress. You have access to more resources in the world than you can ever tap and you probably have a lot more support to give than you think.

- *What has worked in the past when you've built support for yourself?*

- *How has your support system changed in the last five years?*

- *What do you most need to get from others?*

- *What do you most need to give to others?*

- *What themes do you notice about your support system?*

Have you seen the mural that shows the difference between Zen Heaven and Zen Hell? In hell all the spirits stand around a sumptuous banquet table, filled with the most tantalizing food you can imagine. They have a problem though. All the spirits have spoons so long that they cannot bring the food to their mouths. In heaven, they have the same spoons, but they feed each other.

Think of a time when you accomplished something that you would never have done without the support of others.

Think about what you need from the people in your life right now. Using the following list, check off the support you already have in your life, and put a star beside anything you want more of in your life. To have success both at home and at work, you may need people who:

❑ Remind you of personal strengths

❑ Challenge you or tell you the hard truth
❑ Listen, talk to you or share confidences with you
❑ Care for you when you are sick
❑ Provide emotional support or love or care
❑ Give tangible support like feeding the cat or giving you a ride
❑ Give you professional support
❑ Offer information, such as job opportunities or best restaurants
❑ Believe in you or celebrate your success
❑ Do things for you, or do things with you
❑ Motivate you or help you not to quit
❑ Have fun with you or bring out the best in you
❑ Act on their own dreams, or act as a role model
❑ Introduce you to new activities, ideas, or people
❑ Mentor you or share their knowledge

Read through the list again, crossing off the ones you don't need, and putting the initials of people who support you in each area. In what areas do you need support, but don't yet have it?

Expanding Your Support Team

Many people take pride in their individuality and fail to realize the power of support. You can find a support group for every addiction, every hobby, and every profession known to mankind. The twelve-step programs spawned by Alcoholics Anonymous offer wonderful opportunities for community and support. They have paved the way for recovering alcoholics, sex addicts, gamblers, cancer survivors, mental health consumers, and many others. Instead of focusing on problems, the best support groups focus on creating an ideal future. Writers, sales people, entrepreneurs, young mothers, veterans, and teenagers have multiple support opportunities. Some join because they're overwhelmed or they've hit bottom; others join in pursuit of a dream or of a supportive community. Virtual communities of every size, shape, and color permeate the Web, but also consider the multiple opportunities for face-to-face connections.

At "Design Your Future" workshops for highly successful professionals, I'm always surprised that so many of them have gotten as far as they have all by themselves. One executive in her forties told me she learned from her family never to ask for help because they saw it as a sign of weakness.

Ann's family believed in *giving* help, but not in *receiving* it. She embraced this norm so strongly that she began to shake when I asked her to think about who she could ask for help. "But I don't need any help!" she insisted.

So I asked her to think about all the people who have helped her so far this week. In the beginning, her list consisted of people paid to help her—her office manager, the gas pump attendant, the check out clerk, and her hair stylist. The unpaid help took a little longer to surface—the person who gave her directions, a colleague who offered advice on an investment firm, the friend who suggested a dinner theatre production. It took much longer to coax out all the other ways she could *get* help. For instance, never in a million years would Ann dream of asking anyone to take care of her if she became sick. If she couldn't take care of herself, she'd just go to the hospital, but she'd never ask a friend to bring over some soup just because she had the flu.

Ann cracked the code when she realized that it actually felt great to *give* support. Realizing that she deprives her network of all the great feelings that come from *giving* support, her resolve to do everything herself weakened. After all, if she helped them to feel happy about themselves because of their need to contribute, maybe she could muster the courage to ask for help. People who know how to ask for and receive help have mastered one of the essential skills of visionary leadership. To realize our hopes and dreams, we need lots of help.

A year later, Ann leads a richer and fuller personal and professional life because she asks for help. When a cancer survivor asked her to help raise a million dollars for the American Cancer Society, she said yes immediately. To raise that kind of money she asked everyone she knew for money, time, and advice. By embracing the spirit of both giving and receiving, she deepened her relationships and asked for help at home and at work. She exudes a deep awareness of all that she has to give, and all that she can receive.

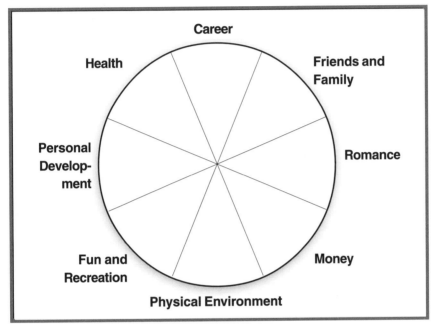

Support Circle

To develop a plan for building support in each of the eight areas, write your current allies in each section of the circle. Notice any gaps or holes in your support system, and with a different color ink, name the allies you would like in your life and list how they could support you. Where will you look for allies?

Reciprocity builds support systems faster than anything else. To achieve balance, we look for opportunities to both give and receive support. People who have had great mentors usually seek out opportunities to do the same for someone else.

The first woman president of the Harvard Law Review, Susan Estrich, paved the way for countless women to attain positions of leadership in politics. She mentors many women for free with the understanding that she will call in the favor by asking them to mentor someone in the future. We receive so much when we give.

Enlisting Your Allies

To enlist the allies you want in your life, first imagine the perfect support system. Imagine that you have unlimited resources to put together an ideal team of people to manifest your ideals. Don't limit yourself to people you know. Think big. Include people who lived in the past or exist only in your imagination. This might seem a little silly at first, but your fantasy support team helps you create the real support team. Since they aren't real, they don't help you mail out a newsletter, but they do help you develop your courage. You can talk yourself into courage, but your imaginary support team does a better job because they offer so many different perspectives. If you choose them well, they see your magnificence and they believe in you and your aspirations.

Many Native Americans use animal totems or animal spirits for guidance and support. The passage into adulthood often includes a vision quest where a young person spends three days alone in the wilderness. Part of the process includes connecting with animal spirits and inner power.

I had just read Brooke Medicine Eagle's inspirational book about vision quests, *Buffalo Woman Comes Singing,* when a Native American friend told me about his vision quest. He had hoped for a powerful name, an eagle or a hawk, but didn't feel disappointed when he received the name Singing Wolf. He drew hawks to him like a magnet, but as a teacher with a strong voice, his name fit. Wolves rarely visited him, but I wondered why hawks surrounded him, sometimes flying within a few feet or crying out loudly.

One day, he pointed to the sky and said, "Do you see those two hawks way up there?" I nodded, and he said, "Not everyone can see them." I looked at him quizzically and he said, "Spirit Animals." I laughed and thought, "Yeah, right," but when I looked up again the hawks had disappeared. Only a second had elapsed, and I felt eerily exposed. Intuitively I knew how much my doubt costs me, and remembered a time when a clairvoyant told me that my guides felt annoyed that I ignored them. Perplexed by lots of things I can't explain, and skeptical about hawks that "disappear," I still want to stay open to the great mysteries in life, including the possibility that guidance is available to me in many forms, in every moment.

Unsure of my intent, I mulled over the last paragraph and thought about deleting it, when I heard the unmistakable cry of a hawk. I got up from my desk, went outside, and looked up at three hawks flying above. One of the birds was red, a much brighter red than a red-tail hawk. They circled and one flew away toward the west. I watched the other two fly upward and vanish. The experience left me feeling unsure and mystified. But this time I felt less rattled, more at ease with not knowing. Appreciating my confusion, I steeped myself in awe and wonder. Adopting a Zen beginner's mind, I chose to trust that my allies would help me uncover the mystery over time.

In *Live the Life You Love*, Barbara Sher talks about choosing imaginary allies from historical figures, animals, heroes, fictional characters from movies or books, or people from your childhood. She suggests giving them a voice and place in your life. Here's a partial list of my imaginary allies and how they inspire me:

- Gandhi—mobilizes people
- my grandmother—multi-talented spiritedness
- the hummingbird—sees beauty and magnificence
- Scout from *To Kill a Mockingbird*—stands up for what matters
- the waterfall in the glen—the stillness of movement
- Maya Angelou—bold daring self-love
- Isak Dinesen—writes circles around me and lifts me up
- Babe Ruth—willingness to strike out inspires me
- Lightning—electrifying intensity energizes me
- child I met at the Taj Mahal—joyful asking
- my dog Benny—intuitive loving

Sher says, "There's another very wonderful reason for creating spirit allies: it will give you practice asking for help—and receiving it." Gathering my imaginary allies around me when I seek advice or solace helps me tap their courage and find the answers within. I have imaginary conversations with each, enjoying their creative responses to my questions.

For instance, when a learner in a class on Leveraging Workplace Diversity accused another of "playing the race card," I paused and silently asked, "Bobby Kennedy, what would you do in this situation?" Immediately Bobby suggested we discuss feelings and needs on both sides and encouraged me to share an article by Peggy McIntosh called "White Privilege: Unpacking the Invisible Knapsack." The dialog opened up and I give Bobby the credit.

The beauty of imaginary allies is that they believe in you. They encourage you, but they also *challenge* you. Instead of surrounding yourself exclusively with adoring fans, enlist people who question you and call you forth. When you ask imaginary allies for advice, you develop the beautiful habit of seeking and receiving help, which makes it much easier to attract real live allies, and much easier to enlist their help. After making a list of your imaginary allies and what they have to offer, work on building your team of *real* allies.

- *What kinds of people do you want in your life to give you the support you need?*

- *Who do you want to play a bigger part in your life? Often you already know them, but don't shy away from people you have not met yet.*

Giving Support

Appreciation is a wonderful thing; it makes what is excellent in others belong to us as well.

— Voltaire

Often the type of help or support we like to give to others mirrors what we hope to receive. What do you love about helping others? How does what you wish to *give* complement what you hope to *receive*? What are you giving that you would like to get?

To attract great allies into your life, become a great ally to others. You serve as an ally to others when you:

- Know their dreams and goals
- Understand their resistance to change
- Willingly risk the relationship
- Challenge them to go to the next level
- Take the conversation deeper
- Lighten things up
- Explore choices

Our presence is the greatest gift we can give. Witnessing another's experience connects people at the core, which is different from trying to fix things up.

- *Who would you like to support more fully?*

- *What do you have to offer?*

Making Requests

Peace activist Marshall Rosenberg tells a story about his mother, who grew up in an economically impoverished family:

> She recalled asking for things as a child and being admonished by her brothers and sisters, "You shouldn't ask for that! You know we're poor. Do you think you're the only person in the family?"
>
> Eventually she grew to fear that asking for what she needed would only lead to disapproval and judgment. She related a childhood anecdote about one of her sisters who had had an appendix operation and afterwards had been given a beauti-

ful little purse by another sister. My mother was 14 at the time. Oh, how she yearned to have an exquisitely beaded purse like her sister's but she dared not open her mouth. So guess what? She feigned a pain in her side and went the whole way with her story. Her family took her to several doctors. They were unable to produce a diagnosis and so opted for exploratory surgery. It had been a bold gamble on my mother's part, but it worked—she was given an identical little purse!

When she received the coveted purse, my mother was elated despite being in physical agony from the surgery. Two nurses came in and one stuck a thermometer in her mouth. My mother said, "Ummm, ummm," to show the purse to the second nurse, who answered, "Oh, for me? Why thank you" and took the purse! My mother was at a loss, and never figured out how to say, "I didn't mean to give it to you. Please return it to me."

We all know people who don't know how to ask for what they want. When my husband asked if he could skip giving me a birthday present one year, I took pride in making it clear that I'd feel really disappointed. "But I don't have a clue what to get you!" he agonized.

I said, "Well just get me something that you would like then!" I imagined artwork or jewelry, so I felt surprised when I ended up with a chainsaw. A chainsaw! When I gave him my "What the hell is this?" look, he said, "What? That's the best chainsaw on the market!" Since then we've made it a tradition to see who can top the list of most unwanted gifts. My father insisted he didn't want anything for his anniversary, so my mother gave him a bathroom scale, all in bad taste, but good fun.

When we're vague about what we want, we don't get what we want. When we ask for what we want, and make specific requests of each other, we develop one of the best ways to build support.

I did some team building work in an organization that attracts exceptionally bright people who complained about each other non-stop. When asked to examine their complaints for the underlying requests, they insisted they had no requests. It wasn't part of their culture to ask each other for anything. That all changed when they learned to listen to each other's needs.

Do you ever wonder why others don't seem to figure out what you want? Have you ever noticed that you don't ask for what you want? Perhaps you want to protect yourself from the pain of disappointment, so you stop asking for what you really want. My business partner, Virginia Kellogg, calls this the "broken wanter" syndrome. This syndrome gets reinforced when you label yourself as "selfish" for wanting anything at all.

Best known for his book, *The Path of Least Resistance*, Robert Fritz says that practically all of us have a "dominant belief that we are not able to fulfill our desires." When you change that deep-seated belief, you develop boundless creative capacity.

A lot of personal disappointment and professional ineffectiveness stems from implied requests and assumed agreements. For example, we expect people to perform actions, even though we never made a request, we never agreed to a deadline, and we never discussed the specifics of the task. Teams become far more effective when members start voicing their desires, which starts with making simple requests.

Requesting What You Want

Some young mothers in New York's Welfare to Work program did some work designing their future, and it became clear that in order to bring their visions into reality, they needed to create some support systems. But the director of the program found the idea of creating support systems ludicrous and said, "They hate each other. You can't create a support system amongst these unwed mothers! Most of the women in the program go out with each other's boyfriends. Their children have the same fathers, and you think you're going to get them to support each other? They'd rather kill each other." Getting past the stereotypes seemed insurmountable, but surprising things happened.

The participants who came to the workshop had very little experience with support. Beverly walked in with an attitude that seemed to uphold the director's stereotypes. She described herself as "a victim of the system," and she seemed proud that nobody could help her. Early in the workshop she stood up and said, "I don't need help from anyone, least of all from the people in this room." But she stayed.

Eventually tiny cracks in her armor showed as she mentioned that she could ask her daughter to help cook dinner. On the second day, Beverly revealed that she'd had a life long dream to become a professional photographer, but didn't think it possible because she hadn't graduated from high school.

She asked people in the class to tell her who took pictures. As her confidence grew, she decided to go talk to a professional photographer, who gave her a camera. She convinced a friend to develop her pictures for free, and started working on her GED, so she could go to photography school. At first, her aspirations looked completely unrealistic. Nothing looked possible or practical, but engaging in her dreams opened up new possibilities. On the last day of the workshop, she really started going after what she wanted. She stood up and said, "I need a bicycle for my son and a washing machine. Who's got one for me?" Although she didn't get a firm offer, she did get a lead.

When we make requests instead of demands, we invite real, meaningful dialogue because we're open to hearing either "yes" or "no" in response. We can tell the difference between a request and a demand, partly by the language and tone, but mostly by our willingness to hear other options. When we make requests without being attached to the answer, people are more likely to hear us. Afraid of getting a no, we avoid asking for what we want, so we use all kinds of weasel words to hope people will get the hint and figure out what we want them to do.

Requests come in all shapes and sizes, but typically start with:
- Will you…
- I request that you…
- Would you be willing to…

A request does *not* start with:
- Don't you think it's a good idea to...
- Wouldn't it be better if you...
- Have you considered...

When you use the phrases above to frame your question, people may approve of your way of thinking. You assume they'll act on it, but since you didn't make a specific request, you won't end up with an agreement. When you say, "I want this project finished by next week," your language is specific, but since you haven't made a request, you have no idea if you have an agreement. The listener nods in agreement, but thinks, "Yes, I can see it's important for you to finish the project by next week, but I have my own projects to work on."

A request includes these components:
1. A specific action
2. A time frame
3. Conditions of satisfaction

"Will you treat me with respect?" sounds like a request but it doesn't include a specific action or a time frame. Although the question seems linked to something missing, you have no idea what conditions will satisfy the requestor. So make sure your requests are doable. An example of a more specific request is, "Will you give me five minutes to explain why I think we need another programmer?"

You can make small or large requests, but if you only ask for things that you know you'll get a "yes" to, you aren't playing a big enough game. On the phone a teenager said, "Ask your Dad if we can take the car to Florida over spring break... When he says no, ask him if we can have it for the weekend to go to the concert in New York... When he says no to that, ask him if we can have the car for the school dance on Friday night, and I'm sure he'll say yes."

I don't recommend manipulation as a strategy for getting what you want, but the premise of going after what you *really* want produces far better results than asking for less than you want. Outrageous requests can surprise you, because you're likely to get a counter offer that's even better than you hoped for. No, they didn't go to Florida over spring break!

Getting a Response

Did you ever make a request and wonder why you didn't get an answer? You may have to ask more than once. When you expect an answer, you're more likely to get one. To get the most out of your requests, open yourself to a wide range of possible answers:
1. Yes—absolutely
2. No—absolutely not
3. Counter offer—I'll do something other than what you asked (which could be less than you expected or a whole lot more!)
4. Commitment to commit later—I'll get back to you on that

Avoid becoming attached to the outcome of your requests. Counter-offers usually result in win-win solutions, far preferable to the original outcome either party had in mind. Too often, people avoid responding to a request because they don't want to disappoint you, but it's better to get a "no" and know where you stand than to wonder or guess. Give people plenty of freedom to say no, so that you get the real answer instead of the one they think you want to hear.

People who over-commit, people who say yes to every request, usually lack self-confidence, or they simply want to be liked. They fear saying no, which makes them unreliable because others doubt their ability to fulfill their agreements.

Listen carefully to the response, particularly to the quality of the "yes." Some people have never learned to say no. Eager to please, they respond to every request with a "yes," and you won't hear the imbedded "no" unless you really pay attention to tone, body language, and words. You'll notice a big difference between

"I promise," or "I'll do it this week," and "No problem," or "I'll do it as soon as I can." When their words say something different from their tone or body language, ask for clarification. Get curious and ask, "Will you check with yourself and see if you really mean to say yes?"

An even more common tendency is to under-commit or never commit. Say you ask for a project completion date and you get evasive excuses or explanations. Explore the reluctance by asking, "What might keep you from completing the project by next month?" If you still don't have the clarity you want, consider asking, "Can I put you on my calendar for Thursday so that we can come up with a joint action plan?" Don't give up when people avoid responding to your request. Keep making the request until you hear a yes or a no. You can enjoy the no as much as the yes, because when people say no, they are really saying yes to something else that's even more important.

Making Agreements

When people agree to your request, they can agree at three different levels:
1. Fully intentional — I promise to finish the project in six months (doing the project is important to me).
2. Shallow — I will try to hire a few new people by next month (but I'll probably have more important things to do).
3. Deceitful — I will pay you the money on Friday (but I don't have the money).

Shallow agreements often mean we don't have the courage to say no. Listen for the language. "I'll try" implies expected failure. Freedom and dignity come from daring to decline. In many organizations, the culture dictates that people can only say "yes." That only leaves us guessing which agreements people fully intend to honor.

On the flip side, many organizational cultures consist of excessive no's. When most requests receive "no" as a response, possibilities cease to exist, which dampens creativity and sucks the life force out of morale.

Breaking Agreements

Making an agreement or a promise always involves risk. As soon as you make a promise, you know that you might not fulfill it. A truck could hit you just as you speak the promise. A promise is not an absolute guarantee, but it does mean that you have every intention of fulfilling the agreement.

What happens when you make a promise and then find out you can't fulfill it? You promised to finish the job by Friday. On Monday, you find out that a vendor has failed to provide a part you need to finish the job. You might find a new vendor in time, but after assessing all the options, you have only a 25 percent chance of completing the job by Friday.

So what do you do? You could choose to revoke your promise, which has the potential to damage trust. Trust takes a long time to build, but you can destroy it in a moment.

Perhaps you feel reluctant to bring bad news to the person you promised. So you hang on to the hope of the new vendor coming through, and you don't share that you can't finish the job until Friday at 4:55. Or worse, you let the deadline go by without mentioning the unfulfilled agreement. When you break a promise, the longer you wait to retract or revise the promise, the more likely that you will damage trust. The sooner you alter the promise, the more likely that you can build trust.

Regretting Broken Agreements

Expressing regret when we break an agreement, followed by the making of a more realistic agreement, will go a long way toward rebuilding trust. We often do not share our disappointment in breaking a promise because we did the best we could or we blame someone else for the problem. Unable to ask for understanding, we spend huge amounts of energy avoiding relationships with people we've hurt or disappointed. When we're the victim of a broken promise or injustice, we stop trusting without ever making the effort to understand the others' side. Carrying resentment leaves us feeling trapped, but the act of expressing regret frees us, especially when we don't blame ourselves or others.

Both at home and at work, we often *think* we have an agreement, but we do not. Typically, we make way too many assumptions. A great deal of personal suffering stems from "apparent" agreements that don't get fulfilled. Here's an example: I told Nicole the client would come on Tuesday, so I expected her to have her presentation ready by then. When Tuesday rolled around, I felt disappointed that she did not prepare. Looking back, I realized that we never had an agreement. So it's my job to express my regret for judging Nicole's actions based on an agreement that we never made.

We often find it difficult to ask for help and difficult to forgive. Then we have private conversations with ourselves, judging the other person, or beating ourselves up for our role in the lack of clarity. Cleaning it up means surfacing the judgment, mourning the loss of understanding and making new agreements based on what we learn. Ideally, what we say in public and what we say in private are the same, and that includes the private talks we have with ourselves!

Don't forget to celebrate fulfilled agreements. Just because we have a promise doesn't mean we should take the fulfillment of that promise for granted. All kinds of new priorities arise, so when people fulfill their promises, what a wonderful time to celebrate! To reinforce effective communication skills, make it a point to acknowledge the ability of your friends and colleagues to make, keep, and revise agreements!

Request Guidelines

To summarize, use these guidelines for effective communications between team members:
1. Become aware of what you want.

2. Ask for what you want by making requests, not demands.
3. Get a response to your request (yes, no or counter-offer).
4. Check for shared understanding of the agreement.
5. When you break an agreement, express your regret as soon as possible and work together to revise the agreement.
6. Voice your regret for judging others when you only "thought" you had an agreement.
7. Celebrate and acknowledge fulfillment of agreements.

Our ability to make, accept and decline requests allows us to deepen our understanding, generate new possibilities and coordinate activities. Team spirit depends greatly on our ability to communicate what we want!

• *What requests will you make this week?*

Finding your Teachers and Mentors

The fragrance always remains in the hand that gives the rose.
— Mahatma Gandhi

Nine years after the Chinese invasion of Tibet, many of the Tibetan Buddhists escaped to India where their spiritual leader, the Dalai Lama, still lives today. When the Dalai Lama was asked, "Of all your teachers, who was the greatest?" he replied, Chairman Mao. He learned patience from Chairman Mao.

Our apparent enemies reveal themselves as our most powerful teachers, but rarely do we go looking for this kind of teacher. Rarely do we go looking for mentors at all. Instead of waiting for your teachers or mentors to come knocking on your door, know what qualities you seek in a mentor and ask for the help you need. Lots of people love working with protégés, so let them know your interest. Typically, mentors value the relationship as much as the protégé. When we have people in our lives who believe in us and encourage us, we set aside our self doubts and raise our expectations.

Choose a teacher or mentor who is actively growing, changing and learning. Don't choose a mentor who has already arrived, unless you want to model yourself after someone who has stopped growing. If your mentor does not share what she's learning, it's probably because the inner critic has taken over. Next she will unleash the harsh critic on you. Some people say they learn best in an environment of criticism, but profound learning takes root in a challenging but supportive culture. Too much wind, rain, or sun can destroy, but a balance nourishes the seedling.

- *Name your favorite teachers and mentors you've had over the years. Which teachers have had the greatest impact on you in the past? In the present?*

- *What qualities do your ideal mentors possess? How do you hope to change as a result of your interactions?*

- *What teachers do you seek? Who will you ask to mentor you?*

Leveraging Your Network

Power in organizations is the capacity generated by relationships.
— Margaret Wheatley

Your approach to networking reveals your attitude. If you've ever gone to a networking event, then you've probably seen the three types of people who show up. The first walks into the room with the attitude of "I hope nobody notices me." The second walks into the room with the attitude of "Here I am!" And the third walks into the room with the attitude of "There you are!" followed by, "Come with me. I want you to meet someone!"

A lot of people make the mistake of viewing networking opportunities as a chance to sell themselves, their company, or their ideas. The most successful networkers bring people together. They serve as the elbow joint of the plumbing connection, the glue that brings two pipes together and allows new opportunities to flow.

Creating a great network takes time. Like building a wardrobe, it takes a while to find people who fit together, but eventually with your extensive network, you can recommend the right person for almost every opportunity. When you develop a powerful network, people connect with you not just because you might have the answer to their problem, but because you might know someone who does.

As a California contractor, Iris Harrell brings people together. She chooses the best players, lifts her magic wand as if she's leading an orchestra, and keeps directing until the standing ovation. She learned the art of networking in a farm town in North Carolina, where her divorced mother supported her family as a hairdresser. Networking was a game and her mother took her business cards everywhere she went. From her roots in farm country, Iris grew up believing that artwork had to be functional. Instead of limiting herself to quilting, she chose remodeling as an uplifting form of artistic expression. With a spiritual understanding of why she's in business, Iris does the work because her calling is to offer guidance about function, beauty, architectural integrity, and holding value. Her clients want a contractor who hears their concerns, can both design *and* build, to help them realize their dreams. When sales reached $350,000, she had done everything she knew to work efficiently, including keeping her checkbook in the truck so that she could pay subcontractors on the spot.

Wanting more knowledge, Iris joined Networks. Twelve companies met for a three-day weekend twice a year to share business systems and learn from other contractors. Each of these young companies had less than ten employees and less than a half million dollars in revenue. They shared their financial statements, which one contractor said, "Really opened the kimono." From there, the trust built quickly, allowing them to discuss the undiscussables and explore the competitive aspects of their network.

Each contractor worked in a different area of the country so they weren't true competitors, but they all vied for the honor of most profitable company in the network. At the same time, they eagerly shared their successes and failures and learned from each other. Each session, one company took the spotlight. In preparation, members of the network interviewed several employees and clients of the company in the spotlight. They shared new ways to improve their businesses.

Ten of the twelve companies grew to $5 million in sales within three years of joining the network, and most of them regarded the network as the single most important cause of their growth.

Iris repeatedly had the highest sales in her Network, and after ten years, she left to learn from bigger players. She joined TEC, a networking group of local CEOs from various industries which meets her needs for sharing best practices. Although not a big joiner, she yearned to network with people in construction. Recently she joined the Remodelers Advantage Roundtables where she learns from larger contractors, who experience the same problems and opportunities as she does. She calls her networking experiences incredibly valuable, and often wonders, "How did they get a hold of my diary?" Because Iris has been in business for 20 years, the other contractors value her expertise in marketing. They marvel at her ability to grow the business without losing market share, despite the severity of the recession.

Iris says that networking is all about choosing what events you show up for and helping each other network. A feminist who would like to see more women in the trades, Iris helps Girl Scouts earn their Ms. Fixit badge. Sure, she might connect with a mother whose home needs work, but more important, she enjoys empowering young girls. She also helps frame houses for Habitat for Humanity each year. Many of the volunteers who show up have never held a hammer, so her employees get a kick out of teaching their trade. Her volunteer efforts honor her values and her beliefs that home ownership should be something that working class people should be able to enjoy.

She wants to leave a legacy greater than building beautiful homes, so she looks for the impact she can have beyond retirement. A leader in the industry, her employees have 401K retirement plans, employee stock ownership plans, and profit sharing, all unheard of in construction ten years ago. What inspires her most are thrilled clients, but she also enjoys developing employees who will someday run the business without her.

Putting yourself at the hub of any network involves outreach, pulling people into the circle, and banding people together. A strong networker doesn't keep score of who owes favors, but isn't afraid to give or ask for favors, knowing that "what goes around comes around."

Another passionate networker, Maya Balle knows how to bring people together. Once she sent me a note during a meeting that said, "Harry just came in. I want you two to meet before you leave. He's on your wavelength." On her recommendation alone, I sought him out. Whenever I spend time with her, she tells me about other people and arranges for us to meet. A professional matchmaker who helps people connect, Maya suggests, "When you bring people together, later ask about the outcome." She believes in tracking the results, not because she gets a commission or needs appreciation, but because she can verify her intuition and explore new options for bringing people together.

- *Describe your ideal network.*

- *What networking opportunities will you pursue?*

- *What do you have to offer your network?*

- *What would you like to receive from your network?*

Choosing the People Who Surround You

Over time, you are likely to become like the people who surround you, so choose the people in your work and life well. To become rich, surround yourself with rich people. To become smarter or more adventuresome, or calmer, seek out the people who naturally exude the traits you want to embody.

Choosing the people who help you create the future is even more important than the vision itself. Jim Collins, who wrote *Good to Great,* believes that great leaders begin the transformation by getting the right people on the bus and getting the wrong people off the bus, *before* they figure out where to drive it. He says, "For no matter what we achieve, if we don't spend the vast majority of our time with people we love and respect, we cannot possibly have a great life." Since members of great teams often become friends for life, it makes sense to choose the people we work with as carefully as we choose our mates and inner circle of friends.

Ever hear the old adage, "You can't choose your family"? I assert that you *can* choose your family, although your "real" family, the people who truly support you, may not be related by birth or marriage. What about the workplace? Even if you have ultimate hiring and firing responsibilities, you may still spend time with people you'd rather avoid. You did not choose the one bad apple on the board of directors, the customer who threatens you, or a stranger who runs you off the road, but you *can* choose how you interact with them.

When people in your life drain your energy, redesign the relationship. It helps to have their agreement, but even if you don't work *together* to improve the relationship, you can choose your attitude and your behavior. You can choose to confront them, learn from them, practice compassion, use them as a mirror, or avoid them altogether.

- *Which people in your life drain your energy and how do you choose to interact or change your relationship?*

- *Which people bring out the best in you, and how can you spend more time with them?*

Getting Others on Board

The practice of shared vision involves the skills of unearthing shared "pictures of the future" that foster genuine commitment and enroll-

ment rather than compliance. In mastering this discipline, leaders learn the counter-productiveness of trying to dictate a vision, no matter how heartfelt.

— Peter Senge

Visionary leaders don't live in a vacuum. They realize they can't go it alone, that they need people to help them shape and implement their plans. The vision process awakens new ideas, new behaviors, and new opportunities. In Peter Senge's *Fifth Discipline Field Book*, Charlotte Roberts describes a senior executive who said that his newly energized team was like, "trying to steer seven wild horses instead of beating seven dead horses to move." Leaders find it more difficult to lead an alive workforce when they don't have the skills to channel the new energy. Instead of the command, coercion and control model, they need new skills in listening deeply, coaching for success, and aligning a diverse workforce.

Ten-year-old Caylin Brahaney knows something about getting people on board. She loves her home. So when she met some homeless children, she decided to do something about it. She grew sunflowers and sold them for a dollar apiece to raise money for the homeless. Before summer was out, she recruited seven friends to help. As young as five and as old as ten, the children sold seven hundred sunflowers. Next year, she and her crew plan to expand. Their goal is to sell more than 2,000 sunflowers.

How did she get so many kids to take part? Caylin says, "They all think it's cool to help the homeless. If *we* were homeless, we would want people to help *us*." She cares deeply about the cause and she creates a party-like atmosphere. "You can make the signs! I'll make the lemonade. Let's flag down some cars!" The best part for Caylin is that when people stop in their cars to buy flowers, they want to help too, and some of them give extra money.

James Kouzes and Barry Posner say, "To get a feel for the true essence of leadership, assume everyone who works for you is a volunteer." Who do you want on your dream team? Forget about whether they really exist. Just imagine the perfect team. What skills do they have? What stake do they have in the outcome? How do their personal desires complement your vision? What new elements do they bring to the mix? Do they adore you or challenge you?

The Maharaji from India used to pack 20,000 people into stadiums. They all wanted to hear the young guru speak, but what happened? Among his entourage of followers, no one challenged his megabuck lifestyle, which became part of his downfall. At one time as leader of the Divine Light Mission, he had 96 Rolls Royces, but today his ex-followers maintain hundreds of pages of disparaging stories about him on the Web.

Suppose you only surrounded yourself with people who like you just the way you are? Great supporters willingly challenge you, even when it puts the relationship at risk. That's why family and close friends are not always the best people to help you change your life. The desire for continued relationships often leads to complacency. While it's great to have family and friends who commit to your developmental process, unattached advocates can do even more to help you become a powerful leader.

To pull together a powerful team, invite people who make their own commitment and add value to your pursuits. Ultimately, you determine the success of the process by the extent to which leaders at all levels live and grow the vision.

As an ally, you learn to model the kind of support you wish to receive. Requesting change of each other, offering challenges, and sharing high expectations all require an element of risk. Invite each individual on your dream team to make a commitment to personal growth, and a commitment to the personal development of the other members of the group.

When you communicate high expectations of others, you set the tone for what you want the group to expect from you. Taking risks and making bold requests of others encourages them to do the same for you.

- *Who already supports your vision?*

- *Who do you need to get on board?*

Chapter 11:
Building Community

Call it a clan, call it a network, call it a tribe, call it a family. What-
ever you call it, whoever you are, you need one.

— *Jane Howard*

Everywhere people yearn for community: a place where they belong and feel accepted, where they can express themselves authentically, and live comfortably in their own skin. In this chapter we explore practices that build community, including acknowledging contribution, leveraging diversity, and developing leaders at all levels. We also look at ways to cultivate fun, learning, creativity, and spirituality. We end the chapter by looking at new ways to leverage power and develop high performance teams.

Today the workplace serves as the old neighborhood or community. When we support each other in the workplace, we unleash a source of magic where hidden talents emerge and the spirit of opportunity comes alive. The former president of Meredith Corporation's magazine group suggests, "If you're not creating community, you're not managing." But how do we create community? How do we invite people to care about each other's well-being and still get the work done? Far too many leaders believe socializing shouldn't be done on company time and want their people to have only one focus, to produce. But production is contingent on relationships, and a sense of community provides the encouragement where people test their wings, learn to fly, and produce at ever-higher levels.

Acknowledging People for Their Contributions

People... do better work and put forth greater effort under a spirit of approval than under a spirit of criticism. Encouragement is oxygen to the soul.

—*John Maxwell*

One of the most enjoyable ways to build community in the workplace is to affirm people for their contributions. In survey after survey, people cite "feeling appreciated" as the number one intangible reward in the workplace. At all levels employees want acknowledgment that what they do matters.

People are hungry for compliments and praise, but they are even more starved for genuine appreciation. People seem delighted when they hear, "Way to go," "Great job," or a simple, "Thank you." What people *really* want is deep appreciation for who they are and for what they contribute.

To acknowledge people deeply, we listen for their core values, and go beyond empty compliments. We share what we see about them that they might not see about themselves. We notice their courage, their generosity, and their gifts. To foster a connection, we express appreciation by telling people how they have contributed to our learning, inspired us to take action, or helped us become more authentic.

Think of someone you would like to acknowledge. Consider some phrases that help the listener receive the depth of your appreciation:

- I believe in you because...
- Here's how you contribute to my life...
- You inspire me to...
- I like being around you because you encourage me to...
- You have changed the way I think about ...

Naturally, we each have to come up with our own language, but the more specific we are in our acknowledgment, the more valuable the gift.

Storytelling enhances the quality of our appreciation. When we share our appreciation in groups, we tap the life-giving energy that transforms people and organizations. Stories are far more memorable than raw data because the visual descriptions give us a taste of the actual experience and we learn what people truly appreciate in each other.

To thank people in meaningful ways takes practice, but eventually we spread the habit of expressing true appreciation throughout our organizations and in other areas of our lives. It may take a little longer to thank someone from the heart, but true gratitude becomes a habit. Since we get what we give, the benefits ripple inward and outward.

We can take this a step further. When people give us perfunctory compliments, we can teach them to thank us from their heart by asking them to be more specific. Some phrases we can use to turn compliments into genuine appreciation:

- Good job: I could enjoy that compliment even more if you told me what you value about my contribution.
- You are great: Would you be willing to tell me specifically what moved you to say that?
- Way to go: Which means you are happy because…?
- Life is special when you're around: Can you tell me what I do that makes your life more special?

Whenever we think that others are not appreciating us enough, and we are aware that we want acknowledgment for our contributions, there are two ways to get what we want. The first and most direct route to receiving appreciation is to ask for it. This almost always works in the short term. In the long term we can increase both the quantity and the quality of the appreciation we receive, when we can step up the appreciation we *give* to others. When we take time to appreciate the big and small contributions that others make, we model an approach to life that will increase the appreciation we receive from those around us.

- *How would you like others to acknowledge you?*

- *In what ways can you acknowledge others?*

Leveraging Diversity

When we acknowledge people, energies shift because we help them open up to their full potential and passion. To maximize the impact of passionate energy in the workplace, we need to create cultures of inclusion. Leveraging diversity goes way beyond race, gender, sexual orientation, age, and culture to maximize individual potential. When an organization cultivates diversity, people create innovative solutions continuously, just because different people see the world differently, think differently, act differently and do things differently.

How do you create an environment where every person feels a high level of trust and confidence? How do you receive supportive energy and commitment from others so that you all do your best work? How do you create a workplace that feels vibrant and spirited, where diverse people want to join, contribute, and continue to grow together?

One way to foster an appreciative culture is to form diversity dialogue groups. Dialogue groups typically meet weekly for a year or longer to engage in open discussions about assumptions, stereotypes, and individual perceptions about differences. With a shared understanding that there are no right or wrong, or good or bad perspectives, members of the group encourage each other to talk openly and take risks. As people build awareness of personal bias and the incoherence in their thinking, they learn to suspend their assumptions. By willingly challenging their own thinking, they let go of certainty and open to new truths. They explore discomfort and defensiveness by inviting a joint inquiry into the underlying causes. By challenging each other, they venture into new territory and learn ruthless compassion.

In dialogue groups where we listen curiously and eagerly to diverse perspectives, we explore the flow of meaning and discover shared unity. We give voice to our hunger to connect. When we truly hear each other at the core, we recognize shared injustice, shared dreams, and a shared desire to work together on meaningful issues. Instead of defending our personal viewpoint, we dialogue as a means to discover new views. As members of the group test their ideas, a sense of playfulness and trust emerges. Highly avoided "hot topics" become discussable, leading to new insight and awareness. Dialogue groups help individuals maximize their contribution.

Even though people are aware of the business case for diversity, we need to nurture a diverse culture vigilantly so inclusion becomes a way of life. Visionary leaders don't just introduce a diversity program from the top; they build grass-roots initiatives because people fully support what they've helped to create.

- *What is your organization doing that makes it worthy of its people?*

- *How do you attract talent, engage people in new ways of thinking, invite diverse perspectives, and invest in the people who contribute to your ideal future?*

Developing Visionary Leaders

Sometimes our light goes out but is blown into flame by another human being. Each of us owes deepest thanks to those who have rekindled this light.

— Albert Schweitzer

Good leaders do not simply look for meek followers. Rather, they draw out and articulate the best aspects of a collective wisdom, combining it with their own evolving map of the future. Then they work with like-minded colleagues to inspire and mobilize other leaders who wish to join the cause. Together, they develop leaders who often step out of defined roles to pursue the extraordinary.

In traditional organizations, only the managers develop their subordinates, but in progressive organizations, 360° development encourages an atmosphere of trust and growth. True mentoring transcends boundaries of position and age. When you put a stake in the ground for development at every level, you awaken the opportunities for mutual growth and contribution.

When we develop others, we create fabulous opportunities to develop ourselves. Richard Bach says, "He teaches that which he most needs to learn." We bring excitement to developing others when their experience enriches our own learning.

I worked with Lindsay, a gifted manager who intellectually knew the value of developing subordinates, but feared they'd usurp her authority. She'd invested a lot in one of her star employees, but as he won awards and outperformed everyone else, she began to worry, "I'm losing control. Tyler accomplishes so much and I'm afraid that he makes me look bad. Everybody adores him! I'm not as outgoing and I'm worried."

Disappointed that their relationship was deteriorating, Tyler approached his manager about exploring the issues. He had such a winning personality, that eventually Lindsay told him the truth about her fears. Touched by her honesty, Tyler became just as vulnerable about his hopes and fears. He shared that his obsession to excel in the workplace stemmed from his parent's rejection when they learned he was gay. He wanted full acceptance at work and he planned every action to win approval. Lindsay and Tyler chose to support each other's dreams by championing each other, and they both earned promotions. When Tyler leapfrogged ahead to a senior executive level in another city, Lindsay threw a party in his honor. There wasn't a dry eye in the room when she talked about how much she would miss the intimacy of their relationship, his humor, and the camaraderie. Only a phone call away, she knew she would always have his undying support.

Every participant in succession planning can choose his or her attitude. Succession planning can be steeped in fear or filled with hope. According to a McKinsey study, the war for top talent will be fierce, affecting companies and industries new and old. Since their 1997 study, the economy has faltered and many have assumed the battle is over. It's not. McKinsey believes the war for talent will persist for at least another 20 years.

Early retirements, downsizing, and short-term maximization of profits have dire side effects — there aren't enough middle managers in the wings ready to take the lead. Many companies who face the decision of whether to "make or buy" their next generation of leaders, can't find a lot of ready-made leaders on the market at any price. Before top talent gets recruited away from our organizations, we have to develop raw talent.

Without succession planning, production suffers because key positions take too long to fill, and high-potential candidates often leave the organization. Matt Paese, practice leader of executive development at Development Dimensions International says, "Seventy-five percent of executives are currently marketing themselves in some active way." In times of downsizing, mergers and acquisitions, the risk of losing top talent rises. Companies with foresight prepare their next cadre of leaders, which keeps morale high, reduces turnover, preserves excellent performance, and assures continuity of leadership.

The Gallup Organization and the Harvard Business Review claim that people leave managers, not companies. Too often people view succession planning as the "flavor of the month" unless leaders carefully design the process. Well-designed succession plans weave in an ongoing coaching and mentoring program. They recognize that challenge and exciting work are still the leading factors for engaging and retaining top talent.

What Kills Succession Planning?

Andrea Sigetich, my long-time coach from Bend, Oregon, helped me create this list of ways that organizations kill succession planning:

- Promising promotions before decisions have been made
- Arbitrary identification of high potential candidates
- Subjective feedback that damages someone's reputation or potential
- Failure of current leaders to develop the competencies themselves
- Promotions of individuals who clearly do not reflect the competencies
- Promotions that support the company but not the candidates themselves (I know you aspire to job X but we need you in job Y for the next seven years)
- Broken confidences
- No development for individuals outside the program (non-succession planning candidates need development opportunities too)
- Exclusivity - the program must include diverse candidates or it will lose support
- Inability to express the hard truth when it comes to giving feedback
- Secretive process that drives talented people away because they don't know where they stand
- Inadequate development budget
- Unexplained outside hires

Making Succession Planning Work

Fortunately, you can avoid failure by paying attention to all the ways that successful organizations make succession planning work. Highly respected benchmarked firms:

- Get top management support
- Focus on developing competencies aligned with the future strategy and culture
- Utilize objective multiple assessment methods
- Develop a pool of high potential leaders, not a queue
- Commit time and resources to leadership development, not just selection
- Empower individuals to drive the process using leadership development plans
- Foster a feedback culture to accelerate leadership development
- Update succession plan annually at a minimum

Developing Future Leaders Begins at Home

We can apply the principles of succession planning in corporations, communities, and families. Whether you are a leader in an organization or in a family, there's no more powerful example to set than living wholeheartedly.

The Belfiore family knows how to set a powerful example. A big believer in learning from her children, Susan does a lot of research, but listens to her heart and follows her intuition when she determines which vitamins and anti-viral cocktails to give her HIV positive children. She only gave one child AZT and stopped after a couple of weeks because she "just didn't feel good about it." Later research showed that infected children given AZT die faster than infected children without AZT.

The thriving, energetic Belfiore teenagers are among the few survivors from the Romanian orphanage featured on 60 Minutes in the early 90s. Daughter Mihaela, an avid horseback rider, was given an AIDS cocktail that had never been tested on children, so the doctor could only guess and gave her half the adult dosage. Later another doctor determined that she should have received twice the adult dosage; at such low dosage, Mihaela only built up immunity to the most promising drugs available. Susan raves about the care given by their doctors, but with inadequate research, their hands are tied.

That's why the Belfiores became proponents of the Food and Drug Administration's Pediatric Rule, which will provide an essential protection that requires drug companies to test their products for use in children. Currently about 75 percent of medications for children have only been tested on adults. When asked to speak about the rule at a press conference with four senators in Washington, Susan said, "The last thing we wanted to do was drag our whole family to Washington, but this issue is too important." The press conference took place the day before the war with Iraq started, and the children seemed worried and didn't want to leave school.

In school, two of the Belfiore children were in the midst of studying how Congress makes laws, so now they had two reasons to make the trip, to learn more about how laws were made and to influence the passing of new legislation that would impact their family directly. Bill Belfiore spoke movingly during the press conference, and they all gained a better understanding of how one person or one family can make a difference.

Susan's friends describe her as "an angel who loves to laugh." A family friend admires Susan and says that Bill doesn't get enough credit. Full of fun, he spends a lot of one-on-one time with each of his five children. At the press conference he said, "As a parent, there is nothing more difficult than knowing your child is sick. You feel scared, frustrated, terrified, helpless... I can tell you that our family believes in miracles. But miracles won't happen without the correct medication and the correct dosing—which can only be established through pediatric testing."

Although the legislation is still pending, the Belfiores have nothing on hold. They live each day to the fullest, enjoying life's miracles.

- *What can you do to develop leaders at home, in your community, and in your workplace?*

Cultivating a Fun Culture

*Leaders everywhere, no matter what their culture or tradition, are
pressured to focus on numeric measures of efficiency and narrow
measures of success, i.e. growth and profit-making. These practices
are not sufficient to create a healthy and robust workplace or planet.*
— *Margaret Wheatley*

So how do we create a healthy and robust workplace and
planet? Children provide clues for healthy living. Fun, laughter,
and joy are an important part of creating a healthy workplace.
Taking the time to have fun or relax allows ideas to incubate and
creativity to flow. During the heyday of the dotcoms, fun flourished
until the bubble burst, and many firms returned to a nose-to-the-
grindstone culture. Although few companies regulate bathroom
breaks, many work cultures expect employees to save the fun and
games for weekends.

Linda Naiman, author of *Boost Creativity in the Workplace*, says,
"Our childhood passions are the key to our genius. In the midst of
play we experience unlimited possibilities." She asserts that children
who are allowed to daydream develop a higher IQ. More than a
few firms cultivate an atmosphere where both fun and play
permeate the culture. Alan Webber, founding editor of *Fast
Company* magazine says, "There are a lot of companies that either
got it from the get-go or gradually discovered that there was a lot
of value to creating a workplace where people are genuinely
engaged."

One successful entrepreneur says that when interviewing job
candidates he only asks one question, "What's the most fun you've
ever had?" Although every candidate answers the question
differently, and some can't answer it at all, he says that this question
works for him. He's put together a team of people who work hard,
have fun and exude team spirit.

Anything that gets endorphins flowing helps stimulate creativity
and productivity. Lots of people disagree with me, claiming that

fun is frivolous. Many textbooks say there is no evidence that a happy workforce is a productive workforce. A business professor who once mentored me insisted, "Work shouldn't be fun. That's why we call it work." He advised me not to crack a smile until the third week of class. Fortunately for the learners, I ignored his advice. I didn't believe I could do that or that it would positively affect the learning environment.

The Seattle-based Pike Place Fish Market has built a business around making work fun. One of their goals is to "make people's day." They sell a lot of fish, in part because their fun-loving approach engages customers. All of their employees get an invitation to buy into and expand on the vision, to "see companies all over the world make it their business to improve the quality of life for people everywhere." Although they've never spent a dime on advertising, they've become "world famous" by serving and appreciating people, and influencing the way they experience life.

The company serves as living proof that integrating fun into the workday doesn't need to detract from productivity or cost more. Like other companies who advocate fun at work, their employees radiate innovation and productivity. They don't just think outside the box; they live outside the box. With every employee and every customer fully engaged in the success of the organization, Pike Place broke away from the pack. Their contagious energy inspires men in business suits to stop by in the morning to shovel ice and say, "I would love to work here!"

People also love to work at Southwest Airlines. CEO Herb Kelleher once settled a legal dispute with a rival airline in an arm wrestling contest. Having fun permeates the culture at Southwest where they spend far more time planning parties than writing policies. One of their recruiting ads said, "Work at a place where wearing pants is optional." They believe that customers come second to employees, which fosters employee loyalty and creativity.

Partying and playing games aren't the only way to develop a fun atmosphere. For a lot of people, nothing is more fun than hard work. When one team had a near impossible deadline to meet, they worked four weeks straight without a day off. The entire team agreed to forgo vacations for the summer. Sound like a fun place to work? Not to me! But every time I walked into their cramped workspace, I felt awe-struck by the joy, the level of camaraderie, and the fierce dedication.

In the midst of burning the midnight oil, they got together to talk about phase two. The manager of client services said, "I'm having way too much fun." A team mate joked, "We could change that." Right away, the manager said, "I'm not so sure that you could." He went on to explain, "I was in over my head when I joined the team, but after several setbacks, I know I am now at the top of my game and *I am not alone.*"

The folks at IDEO had a great time creating the Palm V, the first laptop computer and stand-up toothpaste. Tom Kelly, general manager of IDEO and author of *The Art of Innovation*, emphasizes an open, collaborative, and sometimes wacky atmosphere. High levels of trust, risk taking, and fun support a creative culture.

An organizational development practitioner from Mumbai, India, Sushma Sharma, shared a story about fun that she heard at an Appreciative Inquiry summit:

> Toward the end of a grueling day full of emotional ups and downs, a young man began drumming on his desk. His neighbor tapped on a glass and another played the spoons. The boss turned over his waste can and joined the band. Within minutes the entire office took part in music making, singing and dancing. The music became a passionate celebration of their spirited camaraderie, and a release of the day's tension. After twenty minutes or so, the cathartic music suddenly stopped. No one said a word, but their wide eyes said it all. In stunned silence, one by one, they left to go home for the evening.

Spontaneous or planned, celebrations generate team spirit. Whether you celebrate simply or extravagantly, quietly or flamboyantly, your celebrations build esprit de corps and meet the basic human need of belonging. Both planning celebrations and participating in celebrations give people the opportunity to nurture relationships and build community.

One office has a celebration board, a place where people celebrate accomplishments, brag about their children, or post a compliment from a customer. Instead of thanking someone privately, the celebration board is a place to recognize peers publicly, which builds connection.

A few people complain that celebrations are costly and detract from the real work of the organization, but these critics ignore the opportunity to reinforce values, generate team spirit, and share the collective accomplishments of all the players.

Opportunities to celebrate include:

- special events, milestones
- expansions, reorganizations, mergers and acquisitions
- promotions, awards, new markets, financial success
- learning from failure, lost opportunities
- birthdays, marriages, anniversaries, holidays
- contributions of individuals, teams

In most work cultures, we hold a tradition of celebrating when employees leave an organization, whether they retire or move on. What about their arrival? How do we celebrate a new employee's decision to join our organizations?

- *How can you cultivate a fun culture at home and at work?*

Fostering Learning in Organizations

We build community in organizations when we create opportunities for life-long learning. The love of learning lies innate in all of us. At the heart of the desire to learn is the desire to be generative or creative. Outstanding organizations shift from focusing on adaptive learning to generative learning; instead of coping, they learn to create.

According to revolutionary thinker Peter Senge, learning organizations are "...organizations where people continually expand their capacity to create the results they truly desire, where new and expansive patterns of thinking are nurtured, where collective aspiration is set free, and where people are continually learning to see the whole together." In a rapidly changing world, leaders who foster learning environments discover new ways to tap internal motivation and commitment.

Aire De Geus, from Royal Dutch Shell said, "The ability to learn faster than your competitors may be the only sustainable competitive advantage."

Instead of reacting to the past, people in learning organizations actively create the future. They create a graphic, life-like mental image that they hold in their hearts. Shared vision begins with individuals, and an organizational vision is built on a common evolving direction. The difference between current reality and the shared vision produces creative tension. Organizations that continually expand their capacity to learn are able to create a more desirable future.

Organizations only learn when individuals learn. As leaders, we create profound organizational shifts when we adapt from the role of teacher or advisor to designer of learning opportunities. Instead of imposing learning on others, we create openings for mutual learning and deeper understanding. Mandates from the top don't produce learning. Informal networks create opportunities for real learning that goes way beyond absorbing knowledge, to changing behaviors and perspectives. When we model life-long learning, we stay open to changing our actions and continuously recreate ourselves.

- *In your organization, how do you learn from careful reflection and apply new knowledge to the future?*

- *How do people learn from failure as well as success?*

- *In what ways do you encourage creative thinking and experimentation?*

- *What structures can you put in place that would make it easy for people to share their learning?*

Tuning into Creativity and Inspiration

I could use a hundred people who don't know there is such a word as impossible.

— Henry Ford

The business sector provides marvelous opportunities for innovation and creativity. Driven by the bottom-line, businesses experiment, stretch, and continuously recreate themselves.

Changing a mature, policy-driven culture to one that's conducive to creativity presents a few challenges. To nurture new ideas we need to encourage impromptu brainstorming sessions where off-the-wall ideas are entertained and spun out rather than crushed. A creative work environment gives people the chance to express fully who they are and what they care about. To build on creative potential, we need new ways to encourage autonomy, tune into intrinsic motivators, give people the freedom to fail and embrace personal idiosyncrasies.

Laughter and humor release endorphins to the brain, which stimulates creativity. Starting the day with a joke or an inspirational thought or story uplifts us and keeps our minds open. Educated in public school systems, most of us approach challenges habitually, even when we need new flexible ways of doing things.

We each have our unique sources of inspiration, a favorite chair, the ideal time of day, the clothing we wore when we had a creative breakthrough, a piece of music, a special pen, a babbling brook, or a sensual meal. Inspiration also comes from dreaming, dancing, meditation, affirmations, mentors, high adventure, and workshops.

When I'm writing, my favorite inspiration comes from hats. Lots of hats! Not ordinary thinking caps either. When I'm longing for new insights, I pull out a wizard hat and a magic wand. I put on a jester hat to awaken humor, a tiara for making proclamations, my cat-in-the-hat stove pipe hat to invoke a sense of mischief, and a fiery top hat for tapping passion. Another way that I find my voice is through puppets. Angel, Doc the horse, Mother Theresa, and a knight puppet come to my rescue when I'm lost for words. Do hats and puppets really work? Of course not! They *play*. They change my perspective. Anyway, they're a lot more fun to be around than the hatless squinty-eyed editor who usually does the writing.

To unleash creativity at work, anything out of the ordinary has potential. Breaking the rules, jumping the gun, opening Pandora's Box, acting child-like, and pulling pranks all have merit. Every workplace ought to have a creativity box full of toys, hats, balls, props, frisbees, poetry, magic wands, puzzles, soap bubbles, jokes, and gifts. Surely you can come up with better ideas about what goes in your box. Even buttoned-down firms can pull out their koosh balls after a tense meeting.

Whenever I talk about unleashing passion in the workplace, I inevitably get some flack because some people equate passion with sex or anger. Talking about sexual energy generates a lot of laughter and fear simply because people don't know what to do with it. Discussing the undiscussables feels a bit like wearing fiberglass underwear and longing for silk. In the workplace, we've been asked to shut down sexual energy to the point where most work cultures have written or unwritten policies that romance, sexual innuendo, jokes, touching, and even looking are off-limits.

The problem with those policies is that creativity and sexual energy are often interconnected. The lower abdomen is the energy center for both creativity and sexuality. This energy center is where projects germinate and babies are conceived, the highest form of creativity. When we open ourselves to the boundless creative energy of the universe, we activate our passion, paving the way for fresh ideas. Sexual innuendo almost always finds its way into creative brainstorming sessions, just because people are thinking way outside the box, with no holds barred.

So how do we create a safe environment where the flow of creative energy isn't hampered by discomfort and fear? The solution is in developing an appreciative culture where individual energy is honored, and we aspire to full *transparency* and *integrity* in all our relationships. We practice radical vulnerability and choice. Energized by personal passion and creative forces, we can collectively reach new heights.

- *When it comes to your unique brand of creativity, what awakens your best ideas? What calls you forth?*

- *What are your favorite sources of creativity?*

Fostering Spirituality in the Workplace

When you ask people about what it is like being part of a great team, what is most striking is the meaningfulness of the experience. People talk about being part of something larger than themselves, of being connected, of being generative.

— Peter Senge

To support visionary goals we need to create opportunities for connection, shared meaning, and generating new ways to contribute. Some organizations support meaningful projects by lending employees to non-profits, or by contributing funds for community and charitable projects.

Mention the word "spirituality" in the workplace and you can expect a wide range of responses from discomfort to yearning for integration of spirit and work. Talking about spirituality sometimes stimulates touchy emotions, even when you make the distinction between religion and spirituality clear.

People often question the definition of spirituality and the appropriateness in the workplace. Some share their fear that religious beliefs or practices could be imposed on employees. Despite these concerns, awakening the soul at work helps people connect with whatever they find meaningful, something greater than self. Spirit transcends religion and connects people in a greater world.

Some view spirituality at work as a fad, but others see spirituality as fundamental to personal and organizational prosperity, just as vital as environmental stewardship, quality improvement, and financial profitability. The word "spirituality" from the Latin word "spirare" means breath. "Breathing life into our being" and "connecting with a spirit larger than ourselves" comprise the essence of spirituality.

A recent Gallup poll shows that 65 percent of Americans don't like their jobs. Even when work feels life draining, many people stick with the job because it provides a livelihood. Yet they long for a transformed workplace that nourishes the soul. Integrating life-giving forces with livelihood helps people connect what they do with what gives meaning. Some companies openly discuss their desire to be led by spirit. In others, people feel more comfortable and inclusive using euphemisms like "building team spirit."

Spirituality and profitability are *not* mutually exclusive. As part of a project to revolutionize product development, Xerox executives went on weeklong retreats where they practiced a Native American model of council meetings and went on vision quests to explore the meaning of their work. The result? The struggling copier company designed and produced Xerox's bestseller, the 265DC, an environmentally friendly, 97 percent recyclable product.

The poet David Whyte facilitated a series of week-long trainings where 600 Boeing executives learned to unleash feelings, take risks, and explore their reactions to change. They shifted from terror to excitement.

Spiritual study groups at noon called "Higher Power Lunches" have replaced the usual "power lunches" in some organizations. Many people want to connect their work with a deeper meaning and purpose, and no longer find it acceptable to check their spirituality at the door. In supportive cultures, commitment levels rise, productivity increases, and behavior becomes more ethical.

Author of *Spirituality@Work*, Gregory Pierce says that spirituality should not be confused with religion or piety. He calls for a new way of connecting to the sacred, "If a spirituality of work is going to be successful, it cannot be based on exercises that take us away from the daily grind," he says, "but rather must allow the daily grind to be grist for our spiritual mills."

Tom Heuerman, author of *Transformational Change*, believes that organizational change is a spiritual process. He says, "Spirit at work represents the expression of our deepest authenticity as inspired by our sense of purpose and guided by our values, we step into the unknown and move courageously together toward a bold vision feeling the aliveness of life experienced completely and humanity realized more fully."

As we connect with life-giving forces, we awaken to new possibilities. Gail Straub and David Gershon coined the term "growing edge" in their book *Empowerment*. Your growing edge serves as your spiritual compass, the point that your ever-evolving self magnetically moves toward. When you experience your growing edge, you engage energetically with life. Invariably you notice some internal discomfort, but you also experience exhilaration as you push yourself to break through barriers.

- *What is your growing edge?*

- *Where is your spiritual compass pointing?*

- *How can you awaken spirit in your work and in your life?*

Leveraging Power in the Workplace

We all need power. Without it, we can do nothing. The scholar Kenneth Boulding said that power is "the ability to change the future." All over the world people strive to get power, in order to do some good in the world. We use power to build community in the workplace and to create a better future. However, most of us have had negative experiences, and associate power with abuse, corruption, and violence. Boulding said that power comes in three forms: threat, exchange, and love.

When you use power to violate, stifle, or oppress, you amplify life-draining forces. But when you use power to generate, create, and liberate, you amplify life-giving forces.

I define "power" as the ability to get needs fulfilled. There are three kinds of power:

- Power-over
- Power-within
- Power-with

As individuals, we choose how we use each form of power. In our culture, the most prevalent form of power is *power-over*. When we dominate others, we have power over them, or have the ability to make them do what we want. The obvious forms of *power-over* are violence, force, or threats, but there are much more subtle forms of *power-over*, including rewards. We have power over others when we hire, fire, and control salaries. Whenever we force others to submit, regardless of their wishes, we have power over them, which usually leads to estrangement.

Power-within refers to the true strength associated with courage, faith, and self-discipline. Self-confidence comes from knowing ourselves intimately and being grounded in our power within. *Power-within* arises from deep connections: to ourselves, to others, and to the environment. While *power-over* promotes fear and aggression, *power-within* awakens love, peace, and contentment. Reclaiming personal power is a life-sustaining process.

One way to multiply our *power-within* is to develop *power-with*. When we rely on empowerment to develop *power-with*, we express our faith that people are able. *Power-within* and *power-with* augment each other. We experience exhilaration in our own unfolding and in the unfolding of others.

Power-with reflects the ability to work with others to accomplish results through collaboration. Our ability to listen, empathize with, and understand others helps us to cooperate with others to achieve shared ends. When we have *power-with*, we're aware of both our own interests and others' interests — their feelings, hopes and needs. By seeking the inherent power in any relationship, the whole is greater than the parts. Synergy is achieved when we recognize every stakeholder's interests — everyone's needs are important.

Power is inherently fragile. When people lead through *power-over*, they tend to hide their weaknesses, ashamed to reveal their shadow side. People who lead through *power-with* explore their darkness and embrace their aliveness and truth. By sharing their vulnerability, they reveal the source of their inner power — their willingness to grow and change. A *power-with* style of leadership recognizes every person's unique gifts, which uplifts and inspires people, helping them to become the best they can be.

Shifting from a *power-over* to a *power-with* culture takes a tremendous amount of fortitude because norms are deeply imbedded in power relationships. Gregg Kendrick, the president of a small technology training company in Charlottesville, Virginia, lives and breathes the *power-with* philosophy. RRTC established a life-giving structure, where each work group chooses its own manager, and they're all empowered to change their leader at any time. Not only do they have an open-book policy, where every employee has access to the financials of the company, but employees collectively determine their salaries.

When the technology industry went through a downturn, RRTC employees explored how to handle layoffs compassionately, some of the toughest work any of them had ever done. They all enjoyed the *power-with* culture, and wanted to continue working for the company, but they knew their revenue streams couldn't support everyone at the same salary levels. Kendrick asked those who remained to re-determine new salaries, not by asking them, what's the least amount you'd be willing to accept, but by asking, "What salary are you joyfully willing to work for here?" To survive as a company, each employee did some soul searching and examined their financial needs. Back around the table, they looked at company needs and individual needs to determine who would stay, and at what salary.

During a break, one employee went to Kendrick and said, "Don't make me do this." Hearing her *power-over* language, she realized she didn't *have* to do anything. She said, "It's hard. Painful. But I'd rather do it this way." She returned to the table to make the tough choices. Today the company is enjoying a comeback and they're exploring the options of becoming an employee-owned company.

Margaret Wheatley, president of the global-reaching Berkana Institute, describes a life-affirming leader as "someone who knows how to bring out the best in us, who knows how to nourish and sustain us for our great human creativity, our great human hearts, and our great human desire to do good in the world." Life-affirming leaders know the value of shared power because they believe in the resourcefulness of people.

Developing High Performance Teams

We would all like to belong to high-performance teams, but sometimes we get frustrated on the way to the peak. Most teams don't start out sharing power and leadership; they start out feeling both hopeful and fearful as members jockey to get their needs met.

Some teams have a strong desire to start out in 5th gear, but they come to understand the value of each phase of group development. Team members seem more relaxed about their process when they share an understanding of the beauty of group dynamics, and the value of appreciating each stage of a team's growth. From Ohio State University, professor Bruce Tuckman created the stages of group development model:

1. Forming
2. Storming
3. Norming
4. Performing
5. Adjourning

Often the process through the stages is subconscious, but when team members understand the value of each of the five stages, they reach effectiveness less painfully.

When people get together during the first stage, *forming*, they share important elements of their lives, and they express their humanity and connectivity using an emotional process that builds community. The team needs direction, and individuals wonder how they fit in and what's expected of them. Driven by the desire for acceptance, people avoid conflict. They focus on routines, gather information about the task, and form impressions about each other. Most people enjoy this stage, but because they avoid the threat of conflict, not much gets accomplished.

During the *storming* stage, transparency builds community. When people get past being overly polite they test the waters by sharing their shadow emotions. Typically, people question leadership and express conflict about roles. As minor confrontations arise, the group glosses over them quickly, but as they start to address important issues, conflicts rise to the surface. Some group members are eager to address the real issues, but others revert to the comfort and security of stage one. Contrary to popular belief, great teams don't aspire to an absence of conflict; they seek the learning that comes from surfacing conflict.

During the *norming* stage, the team discovers how to work together, leadership is more consultative, and they develop a process to follow. They establish guidelines for engagement and become part of a cohesive, effective group. In this stage, people listen to each other and offer genuine appreciation and support. Since they've worked hard to get to this stage, they resist pressure to change, especially if they fear that the group will revert to the *storming* stage.

Not all groups reach the fourth stage, *performing*, where continuous improvement is the norm, leadership is shared, and trust levels are high. Attuned to the needs of the group, roles and responsibilities change almost seamlessly. Group identity, loyalty, and team spirit are all high, which means that people can focus on completing their tasks. In high functioning teams, people recognize the value of learning, interdependence, and flexibility. They give each other the freedom to loop back and return to any of the previous stages.

During the *adjourning* stage, the group recognizes its accomplishments, consciously completes its work together, and disengages from both the tasks and the group members. They share pride in their work, celebrate their successes, and mourn the demise of the group. Some call this stage "deforming and mourning" to recognize the sense of loss that often accompanies this stage.

During each of the five stages, the team needs a balance between people-orientation and task-orientation. To build a strong community, we build people; we don't just use people to make our dreams come true. People have to come first. The more people we develop, the bigger we can dream.

Author of *The Road Less Traveled*, Scott Peck says, "To lead people into community a true leader must discourage their dependency, and there may be no way to do this except to refuse to lead. Paradoxically, the strong leader in these instances is she or he who is willing to risk — even welcome — the accusation of failing to lead."

- *What risks are you willing to take to build community in your workplace?*

Chapter 12:
Turning Vision into Action

The future is not a result of choice among alternative paths offered by the present, but a place that is created, first in mind and will, created next in activity. The future is not some place we are going to, but one we are creating. The paths are not to be found, but made, and the activity of making them changes both the maker and the destination.

—John Scharr

A powerful vision generates the energy needed to overcome the gap between the current reality and the idealized future. Grounding your vision by connecting it with reality prevents time-wasting daydreams and foolish illusions. Daring to dream and shaping yearning into a clear vision lead to solid goals and objectives that stretch you far beyond your present capacity. Having a vision is special, but it doesn't eliminate the need for hard work. Allowing your mind and heart to soar while putting one foot in front of the other allows you to contribute to the good of all.

In this chapter we'll explore planning, setting stretch goals, breaking goals into manageable steps, choosing actions, and developing commitment. We'll also look at tackling procrastination, delegating, and celebrating milestones.

Planning the Future

The greatest thing in this world is not so much where you stand as in what direction you are moving.

— Goethe

Most people spend more time planning their vacation than planning their future. Or they get all excited about planning their children's future, but neglect to plan their own. An educator explained that she couldn't spend $400 on a professional development workshop for herself because she was paying more than $120,000 to send her son to college. What's wrong with this picture? Why do we hold so much hope for our children, but lose touch with our own potential? One of the best ways to inspire our children to lead outstanding lives is to model the way by planning and choosing a life that is exciting and fulfilling.

Once you've determined your *raison d'être*, or reason for being, then planning your future and identifying your major goals comes easily. Too many goals can feel intimidating, so focus on your top five or six goals. Clearly prioritize your daily actions so that you reach your top goals. Narrowing your scope to include only what you truly value leads to greater accomplishments. Allowing yourself to become overwhelmed can destroy inspiring plans. Fortunately, you can avoid feeling overwhelmed when you focus and break things down into manageable steps.

Walt Disney said, "If you can dream it, you can do it." Starting with the end in mind, and working backwards to the first step inspires planning and action. It helps to remind yourself of the value of the goal, anticipate barriers, and get the support you need so that you can celebrate the outcome.

Seeing the Big Picture

All the talk about the future and all the good intentions mean nothing unless you deliver. To see the big picture, draw a mind map, breaking down your vision into the main components and action steps. Draw your mind map freehand, or consider using mind map software. Inspiration and Mindjet offer visual tools for brainstorming and planning, and you can download a free demo version at www.inspiration.com or www.mindjet.com. Your mind map might be free flowing like the first example or linear, like the second. Either way, you can use mind maps to create a sense of the big picture.

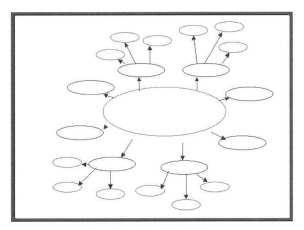

Free Flowing Mind Map

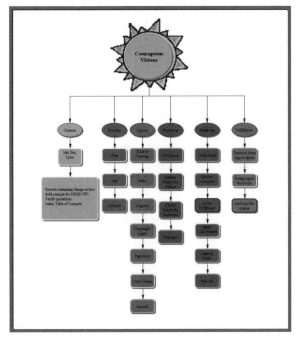

Linear Mind Map

Exploring the Future Using Multiple Scenarios

Planning used to mean figuring out how to go from the present to the preferred future. When we're uncertain about how the future might unfold, meeting the goals and deadlines of the strategic plan becomes difficult. Sometimes we box ourselves in and continue to implement the plan without responding to the changes in the external or internal environment. Even when our strategic plans consider a variety of future scenarios, we still need to prepare for the unexpected so that we can respond quickly to unforeseen threats or take advantage of undreamed of opportunities.

We can explore multiple scenarios by looking at wild cards, which are events that are unlikely to occur, but have the potential to impact the way we operate. Some of the wild cards to consider are technological breakthroughs, changes in demographics, economic crisis, socio-political upheaval, natural disasters, or new opportunities. When we explore low-probability scenarios, we exercise our brains and expand our options in order to prepare for unanticipated possibilities. Multiple scenarios help us work with an eye toward the future, so that we are better prepared to course correct.

In small groups write down the answers to these questions:

- *Think about your future and the future of your organization. What two questions would you most want to ask an oracle?*

- *What answer would you hope to hear? Imagine that everything goes perfectly. What answer does the oracle give to your two questions?*

- *What answer do you hope you do not hear? In your worst nightmare, how does the oracle answer your question?*

Developing Goals that Matter

Leaders manage the dream. All leaders have the capacity to create a compelling vision, one that takes people to a new place, and then to translate that vision into reality.

—Warren Bennis

Goal setting helps us translate daydreams into reality. One of the most important purposes of setting a goal is to get us moving with passionate energy. When we set goals that are connected to our values, we take charge of our lives, feel more alive, and boost our self-esteem.

Consider the goals you hold in your personal or professional life.

1. *What goal matters most? What does the end result look like?*

2. *Why does this goal matter to you or to others? What values does the goal honor?*

3. *What will you do by when? List the do-ables in manageable steps. Which step comes first?*

4. *Who can support you? What resources can you tap?*

5. *What roadblocks do you anticipate? How can you remove the roadblocks?*

6. *What milestones will you celebrate along the way? How will you build in small wins that propel you forward?*

Start by defining your outcomes. Have you heard the story of the traveler who noticed two workers, one grim, the other whistling and smiling? The traveler asked, "What are you doing?" The first said, "Laying stone." The second said, "Building a cathedral!"

Having a vision changes our outlook and our attitude. Starting with the end in mind makes it easier to determine our path and our goals. Breaking down the vision into small units or goals inspires us to act. To set efficient goals, we use the SMART acronym:

S   Specific
M   Measurable
A   Attainable
R   Relevant
T   Timebound

Specific: The more specific your goal, the more easily you will enlist others in the dream. The clearer you state what you want, the more powerful the goal. Start by asking, "What do you want?" Then move into the details so that you have a clear end in mind.

Measurable: Measurable goals define the desired outcomes. You know when you have completed your goal. You know when to celebrate your accomplishments because you don't ascribe to illusive goals like, "Become a better leader." What does the end result look like?

Attainable: Set goals with high expectations. Unrealistic goals don't inspire anyone, so set lofty but attainable goals.

Relevant: Without a sense of what makes the goal important, people rarely commit to or realize their goals. What values does the goal honor? What will the goal get you?

Time-Bound: Reluctance to date your goal usually means you lack commitment to the goal. A goal of increasing sales by 5 percent seems meaningless without a date attached to it. "Let's have lunch some day," sounds very different from, "Let's have lunch on Friday."

Sharing your goals with others vocalizes your commitment, and takes you one step closer to fulfillment. When procrastination becomes repetitive, identify and overcome resistance by asking, "Do you really want this goal, or do you have another more important goal?"

I recently worked with a man who talked about starting a business, but something was holding him back. After a lot of discussion about *why* he wanted his own business, we discussed the losses he'd incur... the familiarity of his old job, great friends at work, the stability of a regular paycheck.

He kept saying he wanted to write a business plan, but week after week, he didn't take action.

"You want to, but will you?" I asked. After a deep breath, he answered, "Yes."

"When?"

"Next week."

"And finished by...?"

"You are tough! In one month the plan will be finished."

I pushed a bit further. "How will I know you have finished?"

"I'll send it to you."

"By when?"

"October 31st."

Sensing his hesitation, I asked, "Is that reasonable?"

"Yes. I mean, No. November 15th. Definitely."

"I'm writing that down. Are you writing it down?"

"Yes. It's on my calendar."

"How will you reward yourself for this accomplishment?"

"I'll make a birthday cake to celebrate the birth of my business."

"Will you call me on November 15 to tell me about the cake? "

He did some more work about letting go of the past before he was able to step into the new business plan fully. We practice the art of perseverance when we turn dreams into plans into reality. Effective goal planning becomes the crux of the process. Making sure that our goals are SMART helps us get where we want to go faster. Harvey Mackay says, "A goal is a dream with a deadline."

The first time Ron Renaud saw an Ironman contest on TV, he *wanted* it. Although he'd never swam except to cool off or biked except around the neighborhood, he acted on his emotions and signed up for a triathlon. *Then* he started training. On his last leg of his first triathlon, a spectator called out, "Great work, Ironman!" Ron felt a surge go through him. After the race, he excitedly told people that he wanted to participate in an Ironman, which consists of a 2.4 mile swim, 112 mile bike ride and 26.2 mile run. Someone asked him, "Have you ever done a marathon?" No. "Well you have to do several marathons. Then you do a half-Ironman, and then you do the Ironman," veterans told him. He didn't take their advice. Ron completed his first Ironman in the middle of the pack, and has since signed up for more.

Signing up is one way to commit to your goals. Dreams in your mind constitute elusive wishes. When you commit your dreams to paper, they take shape. Personal commitment to your goals brings them into reality, but when you tell people about your goals, that's when you really become invested.

So write it down. Written goals have a way of transforming wishes into wants; can'ts into cans; dreams into plans; and plans into reality. The wish lists that you keep in your head feel more like fantasies compared to the goals you put on paper. Then announce your goals. Tell five people. Now your written goals become even more real.

- *List your five most important SMART goals.*

- *Which five people will you tell?*

Setting Stretch Goals

Shoot for the moon. Even if you miss it, you will land among the stars.

— Les Brown

To set stretch goals, start with a practical goal that you are sure you can achieve. Notice what makes your goals compelling, and become deeply aware of their importance. Tune into your feelings and then honor your intuition. Search for a growth opportunity by expanding the goal. What would make the goal outrageous? What would you do if you knew you couldn't fail? What if you had unlimited people, money, or time to realize your dream? What if you had a magic wand? How can you play a

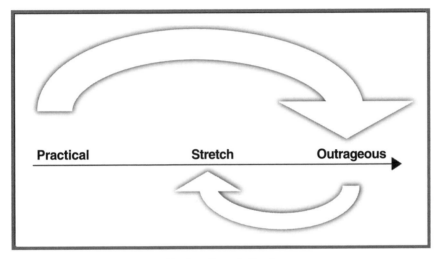

Setting Stretch Goals

bigger game? Go way out beyond what's practical, beyond your wildest dreams. At this stage, don't worry about whether you can afford it, or whether it's even possible to achieve, just dream big.

After looking at the practical left side, and looking at the outrageous right side, come back to the middle, to the stretch point. An example comes from a young music lover who wanted to become president of a fan club for an up-and-coming country singer. He was pretty sure he could get the job, but in looking at his wildest dreams, what he really wanted was to be a famous singer and songwriter himself. Although he didn't think he had the talent or money to promote himself, he set some stretch goals that included voice lessons, cutting a CD, and getting a job in the music industry.

- *What are your practical goals?*

- *What are your outrageous goals?*

- *What are your stretch goals?*

In tenth grade my sister Janet made a list entitled, "Things I want to accomplish before I die." Many years later when she found out she had a terminal illness, she made a videotape of things she wanted to say to her children as they grew up. Going through her personal belongings and thinking about who should get what, she came across the list of goals she made as a teenager. As she began reading through the list, she became distressed that she may have already accomplished each item on her list. That would mean her life was complete, based on her tenth grade viewpoint anyway. The list didn't say anything about sticking around to raise her two young children, her biggest concern. Finally she came to the last goal on her list, the only one she hadn't accomplished—to be on the cover of *Time* magazine. She felt delighted that she still had something to shoot for!

About a week later, *Time* magazine called and wanted to do a story about her business. A building contractor, she'd just won the New Jersey Small Business of the Year Award, and they wanted to write a short article about small business retirement plans. The caller offered her a dream come true, but she felt a sense of alarm and said, "I'll have to call you back," and hung up the phone immediately.

She thought it over for a day, called them back and said, "Okay, I'll allow you to do the article, but you can't put me on the cover." We laughed and laughed because there wasn't a chance in a million that she'd be on the cover.

My sweet sister is a shameless publicity hound. She's been on television several times, including Oprah, and she's been in many magazines. Years ago she was on the cover of Dun & Bradstreet magazine, but even if she lives until she's 100, it's unlikely that she'll make the cover of *Time*. I wouldn't put anything past her though.

Even if you don't regularly read over your written goals, you tap the power of your subconscious when you strive to accomplish something that is just barely out of reach.

Creating Big Hairy Audacious Goals

In the 1995 business bestseller *Built to Last: Successful Habits of Visionary Companies,* Jim Collins and Jerry Porras assert that most enduring great companies set and pursue BHAGs (pronounced BEE-hags), which is an acronym for big, hairy, audacious goals.

There are three key characteristics of a good BHAG:
1. It has a long time frame, from 10-30 years or even more.
2. It is clear, compelling, and easy to grasp.
3. It connects to the core values and purpose of the organization.

Another way to discover your organization's BHAG is to ask three questions posed by Collins:

- What are you deeply passionate about?
- What drives your economic engine?
- What can you be the best in the world at?

Examples of BHAGs are when the founding fathers wrote the Declaration of Independence and when President Kennedy declared that we would land a man on the moon during the next decade.

Jim Collins tells the story of his conversation with Princeton professor Marvin Bressler, who said, "Those who leave the biggest footprints, have thousands calling after them, 'Good idea, but you went too far!'"

- *What can you do that gets people to shake their heads and say, "Good idea, but you went too far..."?*

- *What's your Big Hairy Audacious Goal?*

Setting Short-Term and Long-Term Organizational Goals

Vision without action is a dream. Action without vision is drudgery. Vision with action is leadership.
— *Filomena Warihay*

A powerful vision sets the stage for creating short and long-term strategies. Goal setting helps us bridge the learning from the past with the high road of the future. Inspirational goals provide compelling reasons for focusing our actions. Southern Baptist preacher Vance Havner says, "The vision must be followed by the venture. It is not enough to stare up the steps—we must step up the stairs." The goals and the action plan bring the vision back down to earth, so that you take the steps to make it real. Collectively setting stretch goals helps us leapfrog outside the usual parameters.

When setting stretch goals, look at both the short term and the long term.

- *What will you do in the next 10 years, and what will you do this week to start realizing your vision?*

- *What five critical actions would get your organization headed in a new direction?*

Breaking Goals Down Into Manageable Steps

The secret of getting ahead is getting started. The secret of getting started is breaking your complex overwhelming tasks into small manageable tasks, and then starting on the first one.

— Mark Twain

A master of making great use of her time, Tink Bolster, a long-time friend and the mother of 14 children, used to lock herself in the bathroom for five minutes a day so that she could read a book. That's how she kept her sanity. As her children grew up and left home, she carved out time for other pursuits. When only five children remained at home, she immersed herself in studying Greek, exercised, and traveled. I'll never forget the day I took my son to a triathlon, and I saw Tink Bolster, in her seventies, coming across the finish line. Although surprised to see her, I wasn't at all surprised that a woman who reads a book five minutes at a stretch could complete a triathlon in her seventies. She knows how to break down her goals into doable steps.

By breaking the whole into manageable chunks, and tackling one step at a time, you develop increased confidence in tackling the next. Checking off lots of smaller items on your to-do list provides visible proof that you can accomplish what you wish.

Big goals sit on the back burner until we identify the smaller actions steps. Spending as little as 15 minutes a day on accomplishing your goals is a fine way to achieve your vision. Novels get written that way. So put it on your calendar!

Doing the Do-Ables

When you commit to daily action, your vision becomes tangible. Taking baby steps, pushing yourself out of your comfort zone, and focusing on the do-ables gets results. Here's a way to help you visualize the do-ables: create an action map using post-it notes on a large open wall. Starting with the end in mind, break the outcome into do-able components, and put each step on a note. Ask yourself what has to happen before the last step. Move them around as you go, adding dates, or breaking each component down into smaller do-ables or sub-steps. Make your action map colorful,

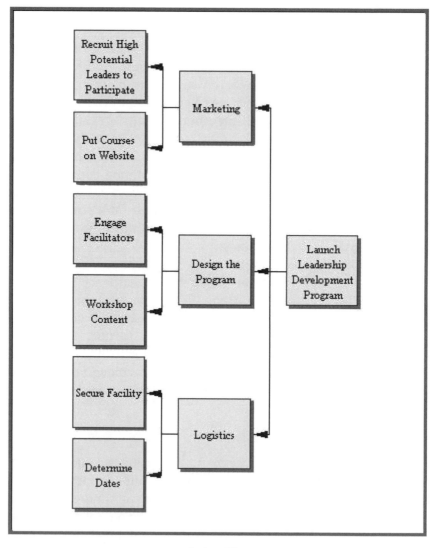

Action Map

adding celebratory stickers as you complete each task, or find another way to highlight your accomplishments.

The start of an action map is illustrated on the previous page. Although creating an action map on the computer is quick and easy, when you use a large wall, you can engage the whole team in the process to capture the collective wisdom of the group.

Choosing Your Attitude

We who lived in the concentration camps can remember those who walked through the huts comforting others, giving away their last piece of bread. They may have been few in number, but they offer sufficient proof that everything can be taken from a person but one thing: the last of human freedoms – to choose one's attitude in any given set of circumstances – choose one's own way.

— Victor Frankl

Ah choice! We always have a choice. Perhaps we can't always choose what happens to us, but we can certainly choose how we react. While too much freedom leads to chaos, too much rigidity stifles possibility. Taking responsibility means to be responsive, and to stand behind our actions. We can eliminate words like "have to," "should," and "can't" from our vocabulary and replace them with "I choose to." When we take responsibility, we act with discipline and integrity, recognizing that every action is a choice. As we honor our own nature and rhythm, we face life directly and act from a sense of purpose.

A few companies look at attitude as the most important criterion for hiring new employees. We can teach skills easily, but we find it far more difficult to teach people to change their attitudes. An airline found that 95 percent of its complaints involved five percent of its employees. The company began hiring through the group interview process, asking why each prospect wanted to work for the airline. Most of the people thought they were judged by their answers, but in fact, they were chosen based on their behavior while others were being interviewed. Those who showed the most eye contact, smiles, and support received the highest rating, while those who paid little or no attention did not get hired. The company's complaint rate dropped over 80 percent as a result.

Although changing other's attitudes is nearly impossible, changing your own is merely difficult. To change *your* attitude, notice the attitudes of people you admire and make the commitment to take on their traits. Name one person you admire. What do you most admire about this person?

What do you admire most: an attitude, a skill or physical appearance? When John Maxwell, author of *Developing the Leader Within You*, conducts this exercise, he finds that 95 percent of the descriptive words represent attitudes. As a leader, your attitude defines your experience and reveals your most important asset.

To develop a plan for changing your attitude:

- *Write down your desired attitude and why it's important to you*

- *Make a public commitment to change — tell five people about it*

- *Measure and acknowledge your progress daily*

- *Find someone to give you feedback and hold you accountable*

- *Ask for help from people who have the attitude you desire*

Deciding How You Spend Your Time

We all sorely complain of the shortness of time, and yet have much more than we know what to do with. Our lives are either spent in doing nothing to the purpose, or in doing nothing that we ought to do. We are always complaining that our days are few, and yet we act as though there would be no end to them.

— Seneca

Many people tell me they don't have time in their lives to do what they really want to do. Whenever I hear anyone say, "I don't have time," my gut reaction is, "Surely everyone has seven days a week—lots of time!" Even if you have a terminal illness, you can still live each moment fully. To have enough time to do what you wish, eliminate the unfulfilling parts of your life.

The Tappet brothers, Tom and Ray, also known as Click and Clack, host "Car Talk" on National Public Radio. They give car advice and their infectious laughter fills our living room every weekend. One of their callers, Allen, started pouring a lot of money, about $1 a mile by his estimation, into his Mercedes, which had 110,000 miles on it. He asked, "When do you decide to get rid of it and when do you decide to keep putting repairs into the vehicle?"

To this age-old question, instead of doing a cost-benefit analysis, figuring in down time and comparing the present situation to new car payments, Tom and Ray gave some fine-tuned philosophical advice. "You know when to get rid of your car? When you fall out of love with the car, then it's time to dump it." The caller hesitated, so Tom asked, "Are you already looking around?"

Allen said, "Yes. I'm looking at a Toyota."

Ray shot back, "You've been cheating! This is like having a little affair."

The caller said, "I'm trying to keep an open mind."

"No you're not. If you're looking around, then you're cheating on your car!"

As I laughed at their analogy, I wondered what would change if we listened to our hearts, not just about trading in cars, but for all aspects of leading our lives. Have you ever heard the old adage, "If you haven't used it in a year, get rid of it?" We'd get rid of our stuff a lot sooner by asking, "Am I still in love with those shoes?"

I'm not advocating over-consumption, but the opposite. It would simplify my life to keep everything I love and get rid of the rest. Tom and Ray remind me that I want great relationships with all the people in my life, all my possessions, and all my activities. And I get to choose.

Clearing out the clutter in your closets sets the tone for clearing out the clutter in your mind. Then you can clear out the clutter on your calendar. Do you love what you do? When do you trade in what you are doing for something new? How do you spend your days? Maybe you love the people in your life, but do you love your work, your leisure activities, your family time, and your alone time? What has to change so that you love your *whole* life?

The question isn't just about what you have or what you do, but how you feel and how you define your experience. Is envy creeping into your life? Would you rather trade places with someone else?

The big question is, "Are you cheating on yourself?" Do the outer characteristics of your personality represent the inner landscape?

We know our own authenticity when we see it because the outer mask is aligned with the inner aliveness. When our outer persona lives in harmony with our inner feelings, we are true to ourselves. What characteristics do you want to have? If you haven't fallen in love with yourself recently, it's time to start shopping — for a new you. Go for a test drive, try out new ways of living, and say good-bye to anything that doesn't serve you or the world! You can choose.

We fill our lives with all kinds of activities, but we often fail to spend time doing things we truly care about. As we rush from solving the latest crisis to the next soccer game, we notice how full our lives are. How often do we take the time to notice what fills our lives? Why not try journaling? A daily journal reveals whether we spend time doing what we love. We can do away with time ill spent by first noticing, then eliminating anything that does not nurture our souls. Any activities that do not honor our values represent a window of opportunity. When people keep a daily journal for a week, they're often startled to find out how much time they spend on email or other unimportant tasks. By refusing to look at email for large parts of the day, we can spend more time on the big picture activities. Looking for the best ways to spend our time sheds light on our values and passions.

Before you can manage your time well, it's important to know what your priorities and goals are, which direction you are headed, and your ultimate destination. In a world where on a good night, dinner is pizza, we get caught up in how fast we're going, confusing urgency with what is really important. Nothing wastes time (or life) like becoming more efficient at doing things that don't matter.

Is your time spent with people you love, admire, and want to nurture? Do you surround yourself with people who help you to live wholeheartedly?

You are responsible for the eventual outcome of your life. You have been given the greatest power in the world — the power to choose.
— Denis Waitley

As the author of your life, each day you have the opportunity to make many choices. Part of choosing well, means thoughtfully choosing what you say yes to, and what you say no to. I often start group work sessions by asking participants to rate their intentions for the day. Example:

On a scale of 1-10, rate yourself...
_____ How engaged do you plan on being today?
_____ How much risk do you plan to take today?
_____ How surprised do you want to be?
_____ How much responsibility will you take for your own learning?
_____ How much do you intend to contribute to others' learning?

- *What intentions do you hold for yourself today?*

Saying No!

In response to any question, request, or decision, we have a whole range of possible answers from "no" to "maybe" to "Yeah, I guess" to "OK, I know I should," to "YES! Of course, no question!" All the answers from "no" all the way up to "Yes!" constitute an absolute "no." Unless we are totally experiencing a "YES," we should always answer "no." To use this powerful tool in your life requires that you begin to truly experience your own feeling experience. Without that, you will answer "yes" by rote, thinking you mean it, and then wonder why you suddenly dislike your favorite old aunt, who has always needed your help. Begin to rely on your own experience, and live the life of a warrior — seeing the truth of your experience and living from the heart of it.

— Brooke Medicine Eagle

Saying "No!" always means that you are saying yes to something else. If your plate looks way too full, consider scraping it off completely. I'm not talking about just the desserts; I mean everything. When you go to the banquet table take only what you truly hunger for, one delicious morsel at a time. Look at all the options on the table you can say "no" to and celebrate your choices. Living fully means stepping into choice. That means mindfully choosing your experience and your actions.

If you have trouble saying no, spend the day with a two-year-old. They are experts at honoring the internal NO! The author of *Intrapreneuring,* Gifford Pinchot said, "A vision is not a vision unless it says yes to some ideas and no to others, inspires people and is a reason to get out of bed in the morning and come to work."

- *List five things you will say "no" to doing.*

- *Instead of making a habitual "To do" list, jump start your day with a "Stop Doing" list.*

Tackling Procrastination

The method of the enterprising is to plan with audacity and execute with vigor.

— Christian Bovee

One of the most common obstacles to realizing a vision is that we "can't find the time." If we can't make the time for the vision, then in all likelihood, we've chosen the wrong vision. Instead of judging ourselves for not getting around to it, we can renew our search for what really matters.

Goethe said, "One never goes as far as when one doesn't know where one is going." What a delicate balance between knowing where we are going, and remaining open to possibility! If we limit ourselves to what the mind can imagine, we miss out on huge possibilities.

Procrastination kills more time than anything else. Use it or lose it. Like a snowflake, time melts away while we consider our options. On the other end of the spectrum, we must learn to pause, or we miss everything worthwhile. Finding the balance point becomes a life-long quest.

A researcher who considers herself a big procrastinator takes an hour a week to do absolutely nothing. She calls this "white space," a sacred time when she gives herself full permission to do nothing. The purpose of white space is to explore what she is dying to do. If you are plagued by procrastination, consider posting a gentle reminder in the form of a note at your desk, "How can I best use my time right now?"

Instead of beating yourself up for inaction, notice how procrastination serves you. Do you need time to analyze? Do you need to get people on board? Are you using your down time well? Are you preparing for action? Explore the needs you are meeting when you procrastinate.

- *List a few things you have been procrastinating on.*

- *How does procrastinating serve you?*

- *What are five things you're procrastinating on that you're ready to take action on?*

Gaining Commitment

There is only one success — To be able to spend your life in your own way.

— Christopher Morley

The Polish concert pianist Ignace Paderewski demonstrated his commitment every time he played. After a concert, a fan said to him, "Sir, I would give my life to play like you." Paderewski answered, "I have."

Commitment means transforming intention and desire into action. Shifting from wishful thinking into full commitment feels marvelous. Very different from saying, "I really *should* do it," commitment serves as the driving force that transforms dreamers into doers. With commitment, you grow to believe in yourself and your ability to make your dreams happen.

We often "forget" to commit to our goals, and settle for lukewarm positive intentions. When we find ourselves unwilling to commit, usually that's because we've chosen the wrong goal. When we tell people about our goal we voice our commitment, which we experience very differently from just thinking about our commitment.

If people don't form their own commitments, you get compliance, not the flow that comes from awakening passionate energy. People don't commit if they don't think they will keep their promises. They fear dishonor if they don't keep their word.

You can choose. You can commit to a direction you feel passionate about, even if failure seems likely. Or you can take the cautious, predictable route where success is assured and life is dull.

Until one is committed there is hesitancy, the chance to draw back, always ineffectiveness. Concerning all acts of initiative (and creation), there is one elemental truth, the ignorance of which kills countless ideas and splendid plans: that the moment one definitely commits oneself, then providence moves too.

All sorts of things occur to help one that would never have otherwise occurred. A whole stream of events issues from the decision, raising in one's favor all manner of unforeseen incidents and meetings and material assistance, which no man could have dreamt would have come his way. I have learned a deep respect of one of Goethe's couplets: Whatever you can do, or dream you can, begin it. Boldness has genius, power and magic in it.

— W. H. Murray

If you easily keep all your commitments, check to see if your commitments have boldness in them. If you set your sights so low that you know with certainty that you will succeed, you know exactly what to expect — boredom. People who keep all their promises don't make very big promises.

To get moving, go public with your values and commitments. When you tell others about your commitments, you set up an accountability structure that pulls you forward. Telling five people what you commit to strengthens your sense of intention, the same way that saying marriage vows in front of witnesses provides a community of support to honor the commitment.

What game would you play if you knew you could not fail? Now ask yourself an even more telling question. Would you play this new game even if you knew you would fail? If you answer no, then go home. Don't play. Because you can't guarantee the outcome. You might fail. Playing wholeheartedly to win always includes accepting the possibility of failure. That knowledge nourishes a deep inner confidence. Accepting failure, knowing that you might fail to deliver, actually deepens your engagement in your passion.

Write your personal commitment statement. You can look over the following example for ideas:

- I commit to a bold new marketing plan that brings in strategic partners by the end of the year.
- This quarter I commit to finding a mentor who challenges me.

- I commit to knowing my Higher Self through daily meditation.
- I commit to spending fun time with my children every day.
- I commit to writing a book by the end of the year.

Now go to your center to find your own personal commitments.

- *What do you commit to?*

Celebrating Milestones

Building in small wins and successes along the way provides the momentum for moving forward. Instead of waiting to celebrate major accomplishments, create stepping-stones along the way. Give yourself plenty of reasons to celebrate your journey. Make a wish list for yourself and plan how you will celebrate each milestone, small or large. Acknowledge yourself for your successes and for learning from failure.

We can choose rewards as simple as a juicy peach or a wild flower. Consider a trip or a new car when you reach major milestones. The rewards don't have to be self-indulgent; giving gifts to others is a great way to share your success or acknowledge a friend's contribution to your work.

The R&D department of a software company celebrates every time they release a new version. They take a whole day for fun and games that include golf, go-cart racing, water balloons and ice cream. They come back rejuvenated and ready to begin the next version. Another company celebrates with a big breakfast where the managers cook the French toast and serve all the people who have contributed to the success of the team.

Some think of the celebration as, "the change is over," but we can use celebration as the opportunity to communicate the new changes on the horizon. Our celebrations help uplift and energize the team for the next phase.

Delegating What Matters

In honor of doing what you love, spend time on your priorities. If someone can do the job 70 percent as well as you can, delegate. When leaders hear this guideline, they often react strongly. "Our customers won't accept 70 percent!" or "Are you crazy? We'd go out of business in a week."

Once people start putting this guideline to work, it doesn't take long for them to convert. Reluctance to delegate implies an expectation of incompetence that leaves staff members feeling discouraged. As managers become better at delegating, they hover less and build a more trusting environment.

When managers let go of the "if you want the job done right, do it yourself" mentality, they begin to notice lots of changes. Most staff members appreciate development opportunities and they perform at higher levels than expected. Good managers aren't surprised that others can do parts of the job better than they can.

Empowered employees bring new perspectives and add value to the vision. They bring creativity, an eye for detail, or they offer fresh excitement that invigorates others.

Seven key points to remember when you delegate:

- Establish power with, not power over
- Stress the results of the vision, not details
- Don't take over or give solutions to problems
- Turn questions around; ask others what they think
- Collaboratively establish specific, measurable objectives
- Develop an inspiring but attainable schedule
- Develop a feedback system to acknowledge contributions

Too many managers make the mistake of giving away the "easy" parts of their job and keeping the parts they despise or aren't particularly good at. With a little foresight, delegators can create the perfect job for themselves and for others. That's no small feat. Today, six out of ten people don't like their jobs. It breaks my heart to find people who believe that working means doing what they don't like.

The prolific writer Elbert Hubbard said, "It is a fine thing to have ability, but the ability to discover abilities in others is the true test." Mastery is nothing compared to helping others become great. Growing from 70 percent competence to beyond 100 percent has a power all its own.

- *What part of your vision would you like to delegate?*

- *To whom? By when?*

Chapter 13:
Overcoming Barriers

The important thing is this: to be ready at any moment to sacrifice what you are for what you could become.

— *Charles Dubois*

Barriers are those frightful obstacles that keep us from becoming all that we dream of. Most of the obstacles between the current reality and our ideal future are self-imposed limitations. In this chapter we look at ways to tap courage, take risks, learn from failure, and step out of our comfort zone. We explore fear, the inner critic, and ways to break through barriers. We also look at resistance, managing transitions, and how to use the *Fired Up* model to help people collectively overcome barriers.

Everyone has their own style and their own pace for dealing with obstacles, but we all can learn to appreciate adversity as our teacher and friend. As a young man, Walt Disney was fired for "lack of creativity." Henry Ford dreamed of a car for every family. Steven Jobs dreamed of a computer in every classroom. At the time, skeptics thought their dreams were impossible. In the face of adversity, their persistence changed the world.

Another persistent dreamer, Steven Gates, moved to a new city, started a new career, and bought a new house all within a month. Nothing seemed to get in his way. A month later, he and his wife adopted a child. Usually it takes years to adopt a child, but the opportunity came and they jumped on it. After a series of rapid changes, he settled into a stable life centered on family and contribution.

Not everyone moves so quickly or overcomes barriers so easily. A finance director struggled to get in shape. After a brainstorming session where he explored lots of options, he realized that all he could muster was to climb a flight of stairs once a day.

What looks like baby steps to some looks like big changes for others. Why do some people change everything all at once while others feel hopeless or don't even believe that change is possible? Where does the courage to change come from?

Developing Courage

Courage is not the absence of fear, but the harnessing of fear. When people talk about courage, they almost never point to their heads. They point to their chests. The word "courage" comes from the French word for heart, "coeur," and means the ability to stand by one's heart or to stand by one's core. To develop courage we explore the possibilities, face fear, and take action.

Eudora Welty says, "All serious daring starts from within." People with courage tend toward restlessness and act brazenly. They trust their intuition and stay open to the magic of the universe. People see them as unconventional or mysterious. Some act with quiet courage; others act outrageously, bravely, and daringly. Always open to the possibilities, courageous people are bright, creative, and winsome. They respond to ever-changing situations with innovation, and their great ideas draw people to them.

Great courage means "being present." Real. Not faking it. As a result, courageous people readily access their gifts.Living on the brink of change is never easy. Ideas on the cutting edge excite controversy. What attracts some repels others. Just like a magnet. People with courage subject themselves to ridicule from others. That is the price of leadership. Leaders who are loved by the masses can also be hated. Look what happened to John Kennedy, Gandhi, Martin Luther King, Jr., and Jesus Christ. Courageous people evoke fear in some, but deep inspiration in others.

Here are five steps you can take to develop courage:

- Face fear
- Explore vulnerability
- Celebrate the learning from success and failure
- Lean toward the risk
- Take action—again, and again, and again

Facing Fear

We develop courage by facing our fears and tackling the big questions. When we label fear as bad or something to avoid, we create resistance that magnifies fear disproportionately. Our unconscious suppression numbs and deadens us and keeps us from living fully in the moment.

When we are afraid of fear itself, we come across as inauthentic and we deprive others of our truth. Resisting an emotion in ourselves, whether it's fear, anger, or sadness, keeps us from facing it in others. Whenever we resist an emotion, we give the feeling a lot of power over us.

It's natural to be afraid of following our hearts or baring our souls. Fear shows up in the things that we want most. When we admit our heart's desire, we take an emotional risk. And that's the heart's challenge—to explore our deepest desires, despite the risk of being misunderstood, ridiculed, or disliked. When we willingly take greater and greater risks by expressing our passion, we continually unfold our true selves, revealing our inner core.

Sometimes we choose caution. Or we're afraid of appearing too conservative. We preserve our reputations, but at what price? The price we pay is that we appear passionless, mediocre, and unmemorable. We're afraid to take a risk, because we wonder, "What will people think?" If we don't take a risk, they will think nothing. If we refuse to take a stand, we go unnoticed. We get no response. We do not stand out in a crowd. It's a courageous act to take a stand. When we edit our thoughts, rehearse our emotions, and act as we think we *should*, we hide our true selves. The unwillingness to give voice to what we see feeds the false self. The more we pretend, perform or withhold, the more we abandon our true self.

Exploring Vulnerability

Give me a fruitful error any time, full of seeds, bursting with its own corrections.

— Vilfredo Pareto

You can live your life in fear of making mistakes, or you can take risks that can turn errors into fruitful learning opportunities. When you take advantage of opportunity and follow your inner bliss, you choose to honor your spirit and courage. Too often, I go into organizations where the leader takes the stance, "I have it all together." Imitating the CEO's behavior, the key players take the same stance, which trickles down throughout the organization. On the surface, everyone has stopped growing, and while they often point the finger at others who need to change, the desire to change *myself* is nonexistent. The difference in growing organizations is that people at all levels share their vulnerability and learning in an open, supportive environment.

We follow influential leaders when we find them trustworthy. To earn trust, we encourage openness in others, but we also have to *share* openly with others. Self disclosure starts with sharing our hopes and dreams, but it also includes sharing our disappointments and fears. By taking risks, we encourage others to do the same, which builds connection and trust.

When we express our fears, others feel our experience—deeply. We project richness when we share our experiences of trial and error. There's no sense in pretending infallibility, because people see right through it. Instead of futilely trying to cover our weaknesses, we build our confidence by not holding back and letting others see us as human. Like a rose unfolding, no fragrance is as refreshing as the scent of vulnerability.

We all have a sensitive core. Don't make the mistake of equating vulnerability with softness or weakness. Strength does not mean petrified hardness but mental flexibility and emotional agility. When we put a shell over emotional conflict, our bodies stiffen or get twisted. When we let go of the facade, it shows up in our eyes and our voices. When we share our vulnerable side, we expose our true selves—without apology.

Celebrating the Learning from Failure

Last night as I was sleeping
I dreamt—marvelous error!—
that I had a beehive
here inside my heart.
And the golden bees
were making white combs
and sweet honey
from my old failures.

—Antonio Machado

One of the biggest fears to face is the fear of failure. Fear of making a mistake or appearing foolish can stop us cold. The desire to "look good" actually keeps us from greatness. As we learn to reveal our inner spark, we give ourselves full permission to take chances and make mistakes. Our willingness to fail has a power all its own. We learn far less from success than we learn from failure. After going through bankruptcy, one entrepreneur said he learned far more from the experience than getting his master's degree in business.

Imperfection and failure pave the way to greatness. As we find ways to appreciate our failures, we learn from them and increase our chances for success.

The challenge is to take calculated risks, and celebrate the learning from mistakes. Mistakes are a gift because we recognize our humanity. We get to relax the same way that a baseball team that loses its first game never has to worry about maintaining an undefeated season.

Likewise, a good carpenter is not the one who makes no mistakes, but the one who knows how to fix mistakes. Over and over again, people say that they learn more from their failures than their successes.

Would you like me to give you a formula for ... success? It's quite simple, really. Double your rate of failure. You're thinking of failure as the enemy of success. But it isn't at all... You can feel discouraged by failure – or you can learn from it. So go ahead and make mistakes. Make all you can. Because, remember that's where you'll find success. On the far side.
— Thomas J. Watson, IBM

Although IBM has a history of many successes, the IBM PC Junior, which introduced the chiclet style keyboard in 1983 was one of IBM's biggest failures, often called the "Edsel of computers." They dropped the product a few years later due to slow sales. The story goes that Don Estridge, the head of the division that produced the PC Junior, expected to be fired, and asked the CEO if he should clean out his desk. According to legend, the CEO replied, "You must be kidding. We just invested 10 million dollars in your education. Why would we want to fire you?" Although the archivist at IBM says she has no documentation to substantiate the story, she did confirm that Don Estridge became head of IBM Corporate Manufacturing in 1985.

I've heard and read variations of this story several times, and sometimes the dollar amount of the investment runs as high as 50 million. Whatever the price tag, the value of the legend is that it gives employees full permission to take risk, fail, and learn.

Not only do past triumphs shape our future, but our failures, our losses, and our traumas play important roles. Using mistakes to our advantage unleashes our potential. When we trust our instincts, we take a more adventurous stance. Taking chances enables us to embrace our fear as fuel for continuous growth. When we savor the pain of failure, we appreciate the learning we extract.

We recognize the hidden gift of renewal it offers—the permission to begin again and again and again.

Leaning Toward Risk

And the day came when the risk to remain tight in the bud was more painful than the risk it took to blossom.

—*Anaïs Nin*

Courageous leaders want to break new ground and do things just because they haven't been done before. Controversial thinking means taking the opposite view, pushing the envelope, thinking the unthinkable, or courting danger. Fueled by adrenaline, courageous leaders paint risk with the broad brush of the romantic. Some lead the seductive life of the gambler. Others calculate the certainty of the outcome.

Martin Luther King, Jr. seemed to know his time on earth would be short when he said, "I have seen the promised land. I may not get there with you." He risked climbing the mountain so that the rest of us might live more fully, more freely, more compassionately.

When you take risks, you take the surest route to self-confidence, which invites the confidence of others. A few may reject you. So what? The people who appreciate your vitality outnumber those who disapprove. Taking risks helps you become more genuine and more courageous. You develop courage when you face the big questions. So stand up and be counted!

Kirk Haller, an innovative director in a progressive firm, uses the metaphor, "My hand is on the downspout," as a reminder that he's about to take a risk. As a child, he and his rat pack of friends would jump off the roof of a local church. Some would climb up but could not face the jump. For Kirk, putting his hand on the downspout was the scary part, because he knew that once he began the climb, he would jump. On one excursion, a couple of kids decided to climb to the steeple. Kirk didn't join them because he knew that he would not make it down. The local fire department rescued them with a ladder truck.

Kirk says that the steeple climbers did not act from bravery, since in ascending they did not consider the scarier descent. Courage means that we evaluate the risks before we act. For Kirk, placing his hand on the downspout is the moment of courage, when there is no turning back. He has weighed the risk and has made his choice.

If you knew you would not fail, what risks would you take? Make a fantasy list of a series of risks you will take. Start small; go large. The greater the risk, the greater the reward. What five actions could you take that involve risk? Look at each item on your list, and ask:

1. *What's the best thing that could happen if you decide to take a risk?*

2. *What's the worst that could happen?*

3. *How will you prepare for both the best and worst?*

4. *If you decide to take action, what support do you need?*

5. *How long will you commit to this decision before you allow yourself to change your mind?*

6. *Who do you know who has already taken the risks you're considering?*

Moving Outside Your Comfort Zone

Life shrinks or expands in proportion to one's courage.
—Anaïs Nin

Your comfort zone has the familiarity of an old couch. But everything now in your comfort zone was once unfamiliar. Life is full of choices. We can live our lives in fear of making mistakes or we can choose to act in alignment with our deepest values. Acting boldly and truthfully unleashes our personal magic.

It would be foolish to suggest that every courageous act will earn a wide endorsement. American journalist Mignon McLaughlin said, "Every society loves its alive conformists and its dead troublemakers." Politicians know that changing things for the better doesn't always win followers. Usually rebellion, or doing things differently from the norm, takes an act of self-sacrifice. Someone brave paves the way for the good of all. Rebels are a necessity in a free society for identifying unmet needs and planting the seeds of change.

A word of caution, however—rebels often have trouble becoming effective leaders until they learn to empower rather than diminish others. When revolutionaries gain power, they struggle with the shift of power. Their habit of criticizing prevents them from getting people on board. When the common enemy is gone, who will they find fault with?

As people act on their courage, they don't eradicate fear from their lives. As leaders evolve, their fears change shape, vacillating between sharp barbs that paralyze and gentle prods that keep them moving in the right direction. Courageous people learn to use fear as the foundation for leadership. Fear serves as your personal invitation from life to develop your courage, character, and your own personal code of honor. You learn to take action even when it isn't always popular, safe, or certain to do so.

I knew I had an adventurous daughter when I woke up one morning to find her at the top of the ladder, near the peak of our roof. Almost two years old, Corynna could easily get out of her crib, but I had no idea that she'd venture outside without us, and I certainly never dreamed that she'd climb a 24 foot ladder. At age three she climbed into the UPS truck while I signed for a package, so that she could see the world. By age four, she insisted on high heels so she could meet the height requirement for the scariest rides at the amusement park. Throughout her life, she has pushed the envelope looking for opportunities, and I've found it hard not to project my heart palpitations on her. She taught me a few things

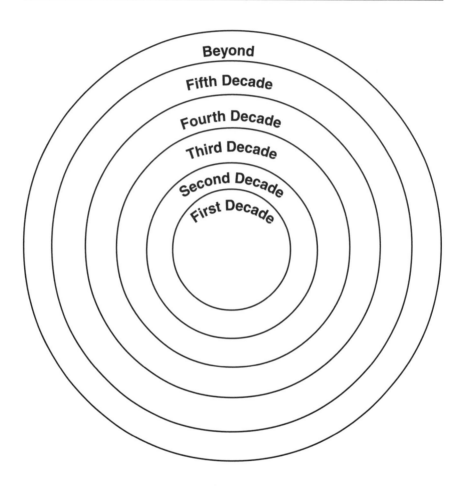

Stepping Out of Your Comfort Zone

Recall each time you stepped out of your comfort zone and write each event in the decade it occurred. In the first decade, you might include going to school, riding a bike, or diving off a diving board. In the second decade, riding a horse, going on a date, leaving home, or getting a job are examples of stepping out of your comfort zone. Marriage, asking for a raise, having children, going skydiving might show up in the third decade. Changing careers, living in a new country, running for political office... Keep going, filling in each decade, including the ones you haven't lived yet.

about stretching my comfort zone, and somehow she survived all the smothering. Today she designs recreation programs, working with youth and adults, helping them to stretch themselves and have fun!

- *Notice what it feels like to step out of your comfort zone.*

- *What happens when you expand or contract your comfort zone?*

- *To accept life's invitation to act with courage, what actions will you take?*

Discovering the Source of Fear

Most of us have a habit of treating our fear with disdain. When we expect to feel afraid, we avoid what we fear. We base most of our fears on old past experiences, ones we've already lived through and pose no real danger to us in the present. We perceive lots of danger, even when very little real danger exists. We don't always know how to tell the difference.

For instance, if you are afraid of public speaking, what real dangers do you face when you decide to speak to a group? You might do a poor job or feel embarrassed. Your voice might crack or you might feel panic, but that's not life threatening.

Use fear as a signpost for your next growth opportunity. Look at what you are afraid of. Decide to go there. Visit your fear and recognize the underlying positive intent. Fear serves as a protection mechanism, so explore what your fear really wants for you.

Sometimes your fear wants security, protection, familiarity, love, belonging, oneness, or gentle quietude. Ask yourself, how you can get all those things, and still go after what you really want in your life.

As a young adult, I got a thrill from public speaking, but it took me a long time to give up the jitters and become comfortable in front of an audience. So it came as a surprise that mild queasiness turned to feeling worried sick one morning before a presentation.

Exploring my fear, I realized I felt apprehensive because I needed reassurance that I could speak to a group of 1,500 people. My prior public speaking experience was mostly with groups of less than 40 people. Since my speaking style is highly interactive, I depend on the group to explore our collective thinking. I felt worried that talking "at" people would put them to sleep. My topic, board development and facilitating great meetings, had potential boredom written all over it.

I had heard that groups that size often refuse to interact with the speaker, which I could relate to, since I did not want to speak in front of 1,500 people either. Instead of believing that story, I decided to try an interactive approach anyway. Stealing an idea from an old friend, I offered a "kiss" to anyone who volunteered. I gave Hershey chocolate kisses to volunteers, reminding them that I'm from Pennsylvania. Virginia is for lovers. Pennsylvania is for kissers. A few people laughed, but more importantly, they volunteered and interacted. I spoke with passion so no wonder a good ole southern boy, who volunteered more than once, drawled "Can I have another kiss?" I crooned, " I love it when people ask me that. My goal is that everybody here gets a kiss before they leave."

My real surprise came afterwards, when many people stopped me in the hallway to tell me how inspired they felt, calling me sweet and precious. No one had ever called me precious. Sweet is another word that doesn't quite fit my self-concept. I'm more likely to hear myself described as pit bull or lightning rod, so this crowd really softened my sense of self. The next day in the airport, a group of participants spotted me and said, "We were just talking about you!" They shared the ideas they planned to implement and I left with the satisfaction that our interaction had planted the seeds of change.

Instead of basing your actions on avoiding what you are afraid of, listen to your heart, and base your decisions on what you want in your life. Anytime you take on a new challenge that scares you, your own resistance to change can stop you. To avoid fear, you can limit yourself to choices that don't scare you, but that translates into a dull life. One tactic for overcoming resistance to change is to decide to stick with your decision for a specified length of time, regardless of how you feel about it. That keeps you on track and keeps your fear from derailing you. Or get support from people who believe in you and who will remind you that your original decision will get you what you want.

Embracing Fear as Fuel for Growth

We can make a conscious choice between fear and love, instead of allowing love or fear to choose us. We can choose between:

- feeling closed or open
- sitting in judgment or curiosity
- expressing doubt or wonder
- experiencing distrust or trust
- seeing scarcity or abundance
- needing control or surrendering
- cultivating anxiety or peace
- focusing on problems or possibilities
- feeling disappointment or gratitude

When we choose love, we open ourselves to multiple possibilities. Fear of failure or fear of looking bad produces anxiety. Some people appreciate the impact of fear because it motivates them to achieve their goals. But who wants to live in a state of fear?

We actually have two more choices besides love or fear — fearing love and loving fear. We all know people who fear love, but how many people love their fear? Accepting, understanding, and even loving fear is ultimately a loving choice that allows us to live even more fully. Instead of judging fear, or wanting to eradicate it from our lives, we can embrace fear as a friend. By noticing the positive intent underneath the fear, we explore new ways to love the fear within.

I encourage you to explore the value of loving your fear—as in using fear as fuel for growth, a compass point that shows you your heart's desire, an indicator that you've hit on something important. There is no courage without fear, so look for new ways to harness it. Exploring doubt leads to a delightful path of trust and openness. When you hold fear gently, you open to appreciating the underlying needs.

On the verge of starting a new partnership, an entrepreneur tensed when his new partner didn't show up for two meetings in a row. He began to doubt the viability of the relationship. Unable to connect by phone, he sent an email voicing his disappointment, his need for communication, and a request about how to make and break agreements. He went into shock when he didn't hear from his potential partner immediately, but several days later, he received a long email filled with doubts about their potential partnership. After a lot of discussion, they both learned that their self-doubt was much larger than their doubt in each other. Only after they'd explored their fears could they share their hopefulness, high expectations, and intense desire to work together.

In all likelihood, you will never completely let go of fear. Ideally, you continue to confront bigger fears as you grow so that you can take even bigger risks. Fear helps you take life's stage with enthusiasm—helping you to make the most of your life.

If you show people your true nature, you might fear that you will be unworthy, unlovable, or unacceptable. Trying to get people to like you by hiding your fear does you more harm than good. Instead of wallowing in anticipated rejection, welcome your awareness as evidence of your power. When you face what disturbs you, you can seek ever-bigger challenges. That means shining the light on darkness and discovering new ways to live boldly.

Japanese Samurai warriors used the phrase "Die before going into battle," as a reminder of the inevitability of loss. By accepting death ahead of time, the warrior enters combat without fear of death. That way he completely frees himself to risk everything, increasing the likelihood of victory.

Instead of pushing fear away or allowing fear to roll off your back, capture it for your use. Treat fear like the grit in the oyster, the seed that starts the pearl. Your awareness of opposition strengthens your resolve and contributes to your success.

Too often fear of rejection and a history of pain become excuses to close your heart to others. One of the things that keeps you from revealing your spark is your own fear. Fear of judgment immobilizes people before they get started.

Elizabeth Cady Stanton, a 19th century advocate of women's rights, said, "Better, far, suffer occasional insults or die outright, than live the life of a coward, or never move without a protector. The best protector any woman can have, one that will serve her at all times and in all places is courage; this she must get by her own experience, and experience comes by exposure."

Exposure. It takes courage to share your heart—that part of you that has depth and substance and connects you intimately with other people. It takes courage to share your soul—that part of you that transcends the boundaries of space and time. The words "heart and soul" are easily trivialized, but they are powerfully, spiritually significant. The heart and soul glow like rubies, lighting a clear way to your ecstatic center. Together, heart and soul help you envision a better future and bring light to your vision.

For a long time, nothing had the same allure for me as the rich intimacy and boundlessness of women's talk. Fear of rejection kept me from sharing my innermost thoughts with people outside my familiar long-time friends. What a stretch for me to go beyond the safe confines of my closest friends, and share my dreams with people who don't know my history. The worst that can happen is that I will be misunderstood. More often, I find that when I take risks with people who don't know me, some part of me gets appreciated, and it's worth it even if the response is lukewarm, doubtful or hostile. Eventually people will get to know me, so why prolong the inevitable? Either we'll hit it off or we won't. Sometimes the relationship unfolds gradually or we know instantly that we're destined for life-long friendship.

Honoring the Inner Critic

People are like stained glass windows. They sparkle and shine when the sun is out, but when darkness sets in, their true beauty is revealed only if there is a light from within.

— *Elisabeth Kubler-Ross*

"I'm lazy. I love food. And I hate to exercise," said Bob, who was pushing 300 pounds. He'd quit smoking, a major milestone. Our discussions about his next goal, to lose weight, felt flat and lifeless. He complained about being a compulsive overeater, so I told him about the time I put a note on my refrigerator that said, "You won't find it in here."

"That must mean that you have a weight problem too. Let's have a contest!" He took off running, but I took off for the land of lame excuses. Soon afterwards a friend asked me to go cross-country skiing, but I said, "Oh no. My toes feel sore."

She said, "Who crowned you dairy queen? Don't you think you've been milking those broken toes long enough?" My toes had had two months to heal, so I acquiesced and off we went. The whole time I muttered to myself, "I'm too old for this crap... I don't have the right clothes... I'm thirsty... I need a character transplant... I have no gumption... I'm such a lard ass..." and on and on. I decided to pick up each of those raspy rats by the tail, dangle them over a pail of water, drop each one in and let them drown each other. That day my headspace had no room for animal rights activists — too many rats living there rent free, not contributing a dime to my well–being.

I never could take the advice of Sam Goldwyn who once said about a chronic critic, "Don't pay any attention to him; don't even ignore him." Like most people, I suffer from being my own worst critic. To quell the inner critic, I notice that my groaning inner voice serves as a dark angel offering insight. When I share my self-doubt and pain, instead of letting sadness and loss isolate me, it releases anguish and opens me to new levels of awareness.

Do you banish fear by eliminating the source? Or do you pay no attention to fear at all? You won't find much comfort in formulas that try to quell fear or eliminate anxiety. Instead, consider embracing fear like an old friend, and welcoming it as a source of energy that helps you convey your passion. Fear nags at you because you *know* something is missing and you want to make a change. An inner voice calls and you feel compelled to listen.

I lost some weight, but I didn't win the contest. Bob still sends a note every month or so to fill me in on his continuing progress. It seems his success earns him the right to reverse roles, and he gets a kick out of coaching me about my health.

Acknowledging the Positive Intent of Your Monkey Mind

Your monkey mind is the nasty inner voice that keeps you small. The louder the voice, the closer you are to what matters most. The message varies, but the inner critic usually reinforces cowardliness with lines like, "You aren't smart enough." "They won't like you if you do that," or "You'll never succeed." Also known as "the committee," "head trash," "old tapes," or "gremlins," your inner critic feeds you the same familiar refrain. When the monkey mind tells you that your work is awful, it's only a test. She's asking, "Are you willing to stand tall and face your inner critic?"

Instead of ignoring, silencing, or banishing your inner critic, begin to understand the inner judgments, not by agreeing with them, but by getting curious, by seeking their positive intent. Often your inner critic wants something for you: familiarity, comfort, or calm. Or mastery, security, or confidence. Working with your monkey mind to understand its underlying good will deepens your awareness. For instance, when you take risks, you don't have to abandon your inner desire for security. Risk and security aren't as mutually exclusive as a gremlin would have us believe. So why not have both?

If your inner critic won't leave you alone, imagine the voice is a real person in your life, sitting next to you right now. Tell the person about your vision and imagine the response. If you hear,

"You aren't good enough to achieve that," how do you respond? Do you agree or do you object vehemently? Get your gremlins on your side by winning them over to a new way of seeing you, by honoring the voice of your unmet needs.

Author and psychologist Marshall Rosenberg says, "Judgment is the tragic expression of an unmet need." The inner critic evokes anger, sadness, and fear, the emotions that point to unmet needs. The basic human needs are called different names by different people, but are universal:

- Connection
- Expression
- Adventure
- Freedom
- Security
- Belonging

- Justice
- Meaning
- Choice
- Community
- Play
- Contribution

Identify the unmet needs of your inner critic and you'll be able to appreciate the loving nature of your fear.

Releasing Fear

I'm the heavyweight champion of fearing that I'm coming on too strong, but lots of people compete for the title. When I'm not careful, I can crush people with a look or a line, and yet it's when I'm not careful that I'm "on," beautiful and powerful. Still, I often mistake "coming on too strong," for courage. The paradox is that when I'm holding back, nobody gets to see my fierceness or my spark. I have to learn how to come on strong before I can come to temperance.

For instance, as a group facilitator, I often ask those who dominate the conversation to share the airtime. I've done interventions poorly and I've done them well, but I'm not always able to maintain my neutrality when I see people feeling distraught. It's not uncommon for the facilitator to become the lightning rod, or the recipient of group frustration and anger. Holding back doesn't serve the group or me, and often reduces trust. Doing the clean up work after a poor intervention is always better than withdrawing or stepping over the issues.

Fear of judgment is the big wet blanket that dampens my spark. My fear keeps me small, but my own judgment feels even more debilitating. When my judgment kicks in, the committee in my head chatters about all my inadequacies and the things that might go wrong. I can either allow the committee to immobilize me or I can notice my fear and leap into action anyway.

Once I recognize my fear, I consciously choose to act from a place of love. When I notice self-judgment or judgment of others, the best way I've found to let go of it is to honor it when it comes up. Without judging myself, I look for the unmet need, and let go of the judgment. Ultimately, all judgment stems from self-judgment. Inability to forgive others comes from inability to forgive myself. If the judgment is recurrent, it helps to get really curious.

- *What's the source of my judgment?*

- *What's the positive intent?*

- *What's the underlying want or need?*

Breaking Through Barriers

Courageous leaders love the race of their own heartbeat. The thrill is in the risk-taking. They drink fear for breakfast. Audacity for lunch. Rejection for dinner. They run on pure adrenaline.

When my youngest son Woody graduated from high school, he wanted to pay for his college tuition himself without going into debt. When he told me his goal, to earn enough money to pay for his tuition over the summer by painting and doing yard work, I laughed! I feel embarrassed about it now, but I said, "You live in a farm community where people don't even believe in paying minimum wage for summer help. How do you think you can make that kind of money in three months?" My work includes helping people realize their dreams, so why didn't I apply these skills in my own family?

There's nothing more humbling yet inspiring than learning a lesson from a child. Even though Woody turned 18 that summer, I still thought of him as a child. In Tom Sawyer-like fashion, he got six friends to work for him, painting houses, landscaping yards and building stone walls. He paid them well, giving out $20 bonuses on good days, and still he managed to save enough money to cover his tuition. He made up business cards that said, Woody's Worldwide Works – painting, landscape design, stonework. At the end of the summer when he told me that he wanted to build a website that would attract customers worldwide, I wanted to say, "People don't buy landscaping or painting on the web—they buy locally." I checked my impulse to laugh at him, since he'd proven me wrong before.

When my brother David was five, a family friend asked him what he wanted to be when he grew up, and he said, "A mother." We sisters laughed and laughed. Pretty soon he changed his aspirations to a more male-dominated profession, Santa Claus, and we laughed some more. What if we'd encouraged his innate desire to give?

In fifth grade, my son Jake had an assignment to write about what he wanted to be when he grew up. His best friend, Scott, wanted to be the richest engineer in the world, but Jake wanted to play baseball in the major leagues. His teacher announced to the class that Scott had a much greater chance of reaching his goal than Jake. She meant well. Jake didn't score any points with her by arguing that there is only one richest engineer in the world, but more than 2,000 major league players.

Teachers, parents, and friends often seek to protect people from failure by encouraging them to stick to a career choice they consider attainable. I'm learning to stop focusing on the impossible, and my children continue to teach me what it means to think beyond what I see as realistic.

When you take chances, you face the big questions and embrace fear as fuel for growth. So why not learn to savor your pain, kiss your failures, and take risks boldly? Also look for opportunities for quiet, calm, decisive action.

Overcoming Personal Resistance to Change

When Sandy Tillotson co-founded NuSkin International, almost everyone around her said it was a dumb idea. Sandy calls these people "dream stealers" or people who say your dreams cannot come true. Some do it out of envy, of course, but many do it in a misguided effort to protect women like Sandy from disappointment.
— J. Farinelli

Not only mothers and well-meaning friends protect us from the fear of change. Most of us inherently resist change. Internal resistance has a language all its own, but it's easily recognizable:
"I'm too busy to do this."
"It will take too much hard work to pull this off."
"Maybe I don't want it badly enough."
"I'm lazy."
"This is boring."
"I have more important things to do."
"This is the wrong goal."
"What goal?"
"I'll get around to it eventually."
"I've tried this before."

Recognizing the language of self sabotage is the first step for overcoming personal resistance to change. When you find yourself stuck half-way between wanting to work toward your vision and resisting the change, choose from several steps to take to get moving again.

1. Remember that resistance is natural and not a reflection on your character. Accept your resistance and explore the underlying positive intent of resistance.

2. Remind yourself of the intrinsic value of the change. Consult with your heart and focus on what you truly want, not on what you should do.

3. If you feel overwhelmed by the enormity of your plan, break it down into manageable steps, and start with the smallest step.

4. Ask for help. Set up a support system or accountability structure with a partner to get yourself moving again.

5. Decide to keep working toward your vision anyway. Commit to a reasonable length of time and move forward, without second-guessing yourself.

Courage is personal. You might think of courage as taking advantage of your freedom, or taking responsibility, or accepting rejection willingly.

When you face what disturbs you, you are able to seek ever-bigger challenges. Shine the light on darkness and discover new ways to live boldly. Taking chances is the surest route to developing confidence, plus you invite the confidence of others. The bigger the risk, the bigger the reward. Your willingness to fail or make a mistake has a power all its own.

The Greek playwright Aeschylus said, "When a man's willing and eager, the gods join in." Attitude is power. If you find yourself resisting change, first determine whether the risk is worth taking. A list with the potential positives and negatives can reveal attraction and resistance.

Identify three things to build awareness of your resistance to change:

*   *Identify your personal values that the change would honor more fully.*

*   *Identify new behaviors you will need to implement the change.*

• *Identify new attitudes that you choose as you begin the change.*

Managing Personal Transitions

To be on this journey one must have an attitude toward loss and being lost...Loss, every loss one's mind can conceive of, creates a vacuum into which will come (if allowed) something new and fresh and beautiful, something unforeseen...
— *Robert K. Greenleaf*

In her book *On Death and Dying*, Elisabeth Kubler-Ross identifies the five stages that people experience when dealing with loss.

Stages of Dealing with Loss

1. *Denial*
   This will all blow over...
2. *Anger*
   It's not fair...
3. *Bargaining*
   I can make up for it if only...
4. *Depression*
   There's nothing I can do about it...
5. *Acceptance*
   I can deal with it...

Since dealing with change almost always involves loss, people in organizations go through similar stages whenever change is introduced. Losing a loved one feels far more painful than going through closing a plant. People who have experienced profound loss can help us transfer the learning to dealing with smaller losses.

Which losses frighten you the most?
- ❏ Job or role
- ❏ Relationships
- ❏ Contribution
- ❏ Reputation

- ❑ Income
- ❑ Security
- ❑ Control
- ❑ Responsibility

- ❑ Familiar routine
- ❑ Unmet goals
- ❑ Sense of competence
- ❑ Other

Exploring the fear of loss bring groups to a shared sense of new possibilities. Effective leaders manage the stages of loss in organizations in the following ways:

1. *Denial*
   Share information
2. *Anger*
   Encourage venting
3. *Bargaining*
   Reinforce the change that will happen
4. *Depression*
   Listen without giving advice
5. *Acceptance*
   Celebrate new opportunities

Make your "let go of" list. Write down everything from your past that you no longer want to carry with you. One way to rid yourself of old habits is to write down everything you want to let go of, and ceremoniously burn them, or tie them to a helium balloon and let them float away, literally or figuratively. Go ahead. Write down regrets, "shouldas," "couldas," "wouldas," disappointments, and mistakes. Seal them. Burn them with ceremony. This healing ritual releases you from the past.

But don't just leave an empty hole in your life. Decide how you'll replace your old ways. Getting rid of old aspirations frees your soul and awakens new possibilities.

What I aspired to be
And was not, comforts me.

— Robert Browning

- *What aspirations will you stop clinging to?*

- *What will you get rid of?*

- *What are you making room for?*

Moving When You Get Stuck

If the definition of insanity is to keep doing things the way we've always done them and expect different results, then getting stuck feels really crazy. One way to identify the insanity when you get stuck is to notice the patterns you fall into.

When you get stuck, what do you do? Check all that apply.

❑ Give up and live with it
❑ Ask for help
❑ Justify your position
❑ Look for someone to blame
❑ Take a step, any step
❑ Take a break and think about it
❑ Imagine the alternatives
❑ Fake it 'til you make it
❑ Buckle down and figure it out
❑ Create a reward system
❑ Break projects down into doable steps

❑ Eat chocolate
❑ Sleep on it
❑ Find a mentor
❑ Research the answer
❑ Enjoy the confusion for awhile
❑ Complain
❑ Yell or cry
❑ Take it easy and rest a lot
❑ Plan
❑ Withdraw
❑ Flee
❑ Other

Out of all the possibilities, including ones that aren't on this list, what's your default behavior when you get stuck?

Reread the list, and this time look for the one you'd never choose. Try it on the way you'd try on a new pair of shoes. Notice how it feels to try a different approach. How could this perspective serve you the next time you get stuck?

When I get really, really stuck, giving into being stuck is the only way out, the same way I would get out of a pair of Chinese handcuffs. Instead of trying to pull my fingers out of the handcuffs, I have to push into the restraint in order to get out. Or another strategy is to take a step backwards, because at least I'm doing something different, at least I'm moving. For instance, if I feel stuck and can't seem to create the time for a social life, I can do the opposite of going out; I can lock myself in my room, which is something I never do. It sounds counterintuitive, but changing any behavior, even if it means going in the wrong direction, gives us a sense that change is possible. Once I'm locked in my room, I eventually pick up the phone and invite people over, and in that way, I circle around and start heading in a new direction.

• *What's a new way to deal with an impasse that you will try next time you get stuck?*

Choosing Your Behaviors

We have met the enemy and he is us.

— Pogo

Many managers make the mistake of putting their energies into motivating others. Visionary leaders know the best way to move forward is to examine their own behaviors and choose the behaviors that will take them where they want to be.

• *Make a two-column list of behaviors, putting the behaviors that don't serve your vision in the left-hand column and the new replacement behaviors in the right-hand column. This is not an exercise about looking at other's behaviors; it's about looking at my behaviors.*

In an experiment, a scientist put some fleas in a glass jar. They quickly jumped out. He then put the fleas back into the jar and placed a glass plate across the top opening. The fleas began jumping and hitting the glass plate, falling back down into the jar. After a while, the fleas, conditioned to the presence of the glass plate, began jumping slightly below the glass plate, so as not to hit it. The scientist then removed the glass plate, and the fleas stayed in the jar without it.

You too probably have a "self-imposed lid" that prevents you from achieving new heights. To pursue self-development, take a look at how you contribute to your own problems. Instead of pushing for growth, remove the lids that limit growth.

- *What thoughts or "glass ceiling" keeps you from stepping into your personal power? How can you smash through the glass ceiling?*

Facing External Threats

External threats can be even more debilitating than internal threats. We can't control the economy, competitors, or the political environment. Technology and globalization often wreak havoc and destabilize organizations.

But you can prepare for threatening situations by exploring worst-case scenarios. For instance, imagine that your competitor has unlimited funds for putting you out of business. Step into the shoes of your competitor. How would you go about eliminating your organization? What will you do with this information?

You can also prepare for the future by exploring best-case scenarios. Imagine that your competitor exists purely to serve you. Perhaps their presence in the market place makes you less complacent. Maybe you can take advantage of their research or new product development. Or maybe they've neglected a niche market.

Seth Goldman and Barry Nalebuff started Honest Tea because they were thirsty. They wanted a drink that wasn't super-sweet. Entering an industry dominated by two international beverage companies that control 90 percent of the distribution, they knew they had their work cut out for them. "Beverage distributors weren't interested, so we'd work with anyone—a cheese distributor, a charcoal distributor, even a corned beef distributor," says Seth. "As long as they were going to the stores, we'd have them transport our product."

In the early days, Seth became so excited about closing a big sale that he started to believe, "This is going to work. We're going to be able to do everything!" That day he was driving a rented van full of Honest Tea, and came to an 8' height limit. Seth knew the van was 10', but he said, "I think we're going to make it!" They didn't.

He laughs about it now, but the experience helped him to accept certain limits. "Most of the time, it's about *not* accepting limits." It's been a bumpy ride, but after five years, they're still passionate about providing quality organic teas. Social responsibility is the driving force behind their work, and creating opportunities for economically disadvantaged communities is a labor of love.

At first, the Crow Nation was not interested in entering a relationship with a company that would commercially exploit their Native American culture. Together they created a partnership. Native Americans designed the labels and named the tea "First Nation" which recognizes the sovereignty of Native American people in the United States. They also chose to give part of the profits to an organization that addresses the needs of foster and homeless Native American children.

Despite major obstacles and fierce competition, Honest Tea is sold in all 50 states and they envision distributing internationally. Visa Business and Inc. magazine have named Honest Tea winner of the 2003 Dream Big contest. Their fierce competition inspired them to dream big.

- *What benefits do you receive from your competitor's existence?*

- *What other external threats and opportunities do you face and how will you address them?*

Getting Fired Up!

You must be the change you wish to see in the world.
— *Mahatma Gandhi*

To help people talk about barriers, issues, and concerns, I use the FIRED UP! model. The purpose is to create a safe space for dialogue. Each step ensures that everyone hears each other, so that we awaken creativity, make wise decisions, and unleash passion.

The FIRED UP! process works in groups, but you can also use it to unleash personal passion and personal wisdom. Sitting in a circle, we start with the facts, and move through importance, reactions, exploration, and decisions.

Facts — Objective Observations, Information, Sensory Impressions

- What happened?
- What did you see/hear?
- What words or phrases caught your attention?
- What events do you remember?
- What's going on right now?

Importance — Needs, Values, Inquiry, Interpretation, Deeper Implications, Underlying Meaning, Significance, Purpose

- What do you need?
- What values matter here?
- What insights and implications do you see?
- What is at stake here?
- What meaning do you make?

Reactions — Feelings, Emotions, Reflections, Personal Impact, Associations, Images

- What was your first response?

- How did you feel?
- What excited you, frustrated you?
- What internal images come to mind?
- What's your gut reaction?

Exploration—Creativity, Ideas, Possibilities, Options, Alternatives, Visions

- What are our options for meeting our needs?
- Five years from now, what do you envision?
- If you had a magic wand, what would you do?
- What ideas excite you?
- What alternatives would you consider?

Decision—Direction, Resolution, Action, Next Steps

- What change do you need?
- What's the consensus of the group?
- What actions or steps will you take?
- What requests will you make?
- What do you commit to?

UP!—Unleashing Passion

- What is most alive in you?
- What do you feel strongly about?
- Where do you see evidence of passion?
- How will you sustain the energy?

The FIRED UP! model accesses the wisdom of the body, starting with the head, and moving downward. Each of the five steps of the FIRED UP! process correlates with the body. Most groups who face a barrier, start with the last step, asking themselves, "What are we going to do about it?" because they imagine it's the fastest route to overcoming the barrier. Collectively discussing each of the steps gets people moving faster because they get to explore their observations, feelings, needs and options, *before* making their decisions.

To walk a group through the process, ask them to tune into the wisdom of their bodies, and explore the issue with the following questions:

Process	Body	Inquiry
Facts	Head	What do you notice?
Importance	Heart	What do you need?
Reaction	Gut	What's your reaction?
Exploration	Pelvis	What options can you imagine?
Decision	Legs	What action steps do you choose?
Unleashing Passion	Whole	How will you sustain the energy?

Why unleash passion? Isn't it safer to keep emotions and passion inside where they belong? Many people believe they need to "control their emotions," but when they build awareness of their feelings they can tune into what's missing, which leads to more options and better strategies for meeting everyone's needs.

- *Use the FIRED UP! model to address a personal barrier, asking questions about the facts, importance, reaction, exploration, and decision.*

- *Once you've used the model to address a personal barrier, use it with a group. What issue would you like to explore?*

Chapter 14:
Leading the People Side of Change

With the world in constant flux, change is inevitable. Change often leads to apprehension, conflicts arise and morale suffers. That shifts when we manage the people side of change proactively. In this chapter we start by assessing readiness for change and then look at building a case for change, enlisting change agents, and developing a communication plan. We also explore ways to manage resistance to change, build momentum, and sustain a culture that embraces receptivity to change.

We can learn a lot about change from the horse whisperer, Monty Roberts, who can get a green horse to accept a saddle and rider without fear in 30 minutes. Breaking a wild horse usually takes weeks, and causes a lot of pain. Sometimes horses get injured or even die. Roberts spent years studying horses in the wild and uses a different method to win a horse's trust. He simply honors the horse's natural instincts.

Out of fear, the horse's first instinct is to run away from Roberts, and he encourages this, sending non-verbal messages to drive the horse calmly away. He pays attention to changes in body language, looking for the cocked ear, chewing motion, and nose to the ground that indicates the horse is ready for negotiation, agreement, and trust. When the horse signals that it's ready to join up, Roberts turns away at a 45° angle. Following its herding extinct, and its desire to belong, the horse initiates the first contact by putting its chin on Robert's shoulder. When the horse whisperer walks away slowly, the horse follows. The horse refuses to follow if Roberts walks without self-assurance or direction, but follows curiously when the leader exudes confidence and walks with a sense of purpose. Afterwards the horse easily accepts the bridle, saddle, and rider because both sides have built trust.

Imagine using this approach with people who don't want to change. How do you show respect for a resister's natural instincts? How do you honor the positive intent of someone who does not want to change? Essentially, we give people the freedom to *opt out*, but at the same time, we give them the confidence to *opt in* and be part of an exciting, ideal future.

Organizational renewal takes time. The process goes smoothly when we give people a chance to adjust to each phase. To facilitate the change process, take your team through the Seven Steps for Leading the People Side of Change. You can skip some of the steps, but typically that would extend the process and reverse early successes.

Although *Leading the People Side of Change* is the last chapter of the book, leading change does not occur only at the end of the vision process. We lead change from the start, and each step works in tandem with the *Courageous Visions* process.

Seven Steps for Leading the People Side of Change

1. *Assess readiness for change.*
    Take the long view and explore your organization's history of change. Find out what made past changes successful and look for evidence that the organization can handle more change. If necessary, develop additional capacity for change.

2. *Build a case for change.*
    Discover the urgent crises and opportunities that get people's attention. Study the market and competitive forces that drive the change process. Explore the implications to the bottom line. Imagine what happens if you don't make the change.

3. *Enlist a team of change agents.*
    Start by finding your highest-level change sponsors. Look for other key influencers from all levels of the organization to enlist.

Recruit people who have the power to lead the change initiative and get others on board.

4. *Develop a change communication plan.*
   Design the best ways to communicate the benefits and the drawbacks of the change. Describe your vision so that you empower others to contribute. Incorporate the vision of how the change serves the highest good and helps the organization thrive.

5. *Manage resistance to change.*
   Identify the people most likely to oppose the change and determine how you will address their needs. Anticipate the obstacles and create a plan to overcome resistance to change.

6. *Build momentum.*
   Pay attention to the pace and tone so that people can easily absorb the changes. Build short-term wins into the process. Define the milestones you will celebrate along the way.

7. *Sustain a culture that is receptive to change.*
   Manage your continuous personal change process and model openness. Establish expectations, desired behaviors, and competencies that people need to develop to support the desired changes. Sustain a culture of continuous improvement and keep the energy alive to ensure future success.

Assessing Readiness for Change

Assessing readiness for change starts with self. Change is an inside out process. If I'm not willing to change, I'll never be able to lead change. Since the only person we can change is ourselves, as change leaders we have to model the way. Recognizing that we're ready for something new to happen may be the first step, but recognizing our own contribution to the problem is crucial. We may not be *causing* the need for change, but we may be *cooperating* or *complacent* about the need for change. To address personal change, we have to keep asking the big questions.

To affect change, we strengthen our own voices before moving out into other's space. That means working through differences, debating the issues, and addressing fragmentation. Disagreement helps us find our voices. Openness to new ideas and new ways of thinking helps us create a new collective identity, a new way of seeing what's unfolding. This generative process allows unexpected elements to emerge that foster change.

Most people don't have the liberty to assess readiness for change because they get pushed into implementing a change initiative that someone else developed. Even if you find yourself in that position, it helps to determine the organization's readiness for change so that you identify the strengths and address potential obstacles. To assess your organization's readiness for change, ask:

- *What forces are driving the change? Market? Business? Environment? Culture? Organization? Behavior? Politics?*

- *What shared values will help people embrace the change?*

- *What track record do you have for handling change?*

- *What level of cooperation and trust exist that will support a culture of risk taking and change?*

- *What evidence shows that people have the capacity to handle more change?*

- *How will people continue the day-to-day operations during the transformation?*

- *Do the leaders have the capacity to lead the change?*

- *Do the employees have the capacity to make the change successful?*

If you've had three new CEOs in the past five years, and as many failed change initiatives, then your organization needs some recovery time before embarking on yet another change process.

Top-driven change initiatives rarely succeed. White knight leaders may have a short-term impact, but they ravage the organization unless they build capacity in the ranks. Hero CEOs get paid exorbitant amounts of money and have tremendous power over others, but that only serves to separate and disconnect them from the people they so need to succeed.

Richard Beckhard, a pioneer in organizational development wrote the book *Organizational Transitions*. Peter Senge recalls that Beckhard once said, "When one person wants change in an organization, he gets clobbered. When two people want change, they can commiserate. But when three people want change, they have a full-fledged conspiracy." Ultimately, any organization needs a cadre of leaders to implement long-lasting cultural change.

Determining readiness for change helps you identify the organization's ability to embrace new opportunities. So choose a pace that allows people to flourish. Most change initiatives take years or even decades to realize. Some people find the bumps along the way daunting, but others find the challenges exhilarating.

When assessing readiness for change, don't just look for problems. Use an Appreciative Inquiry approach to explore your organization's history of change and determine what forces have made past changes successful.

Once you've assessed the organization's readiness for change, you may need to build capacity before implementing the change. Developing transformational change leaders and creating a strategy to build a culture that is ready for change have to come first.

Many people think the Civil Rights movement started when Rosa Parks' feet got tired and she refused to give up her seat on the bus. In actuality, it started decades before. Black Americans used gospel singing, education, registering to vote, discussions in homes, bible study, and the teachings of Gandhi to plant the seeds of change. The movement really gained momentum when leaflets were distributed in beauty parlors. Women and youth engaged in the struggle. By the time charismatic Martin Luther King, Jr. spoke at the 1963 March on Washington, Catholics, Jews, Orthodox Greeks, and the United Auto Workers all identified with the Civil Rights movement. Inclusion is the key to galvanizing any change initiative.

Building a Case for Change

The heart of profound change doesn't always stem from conflict. When the ignition for change doesn't come from crisis, we have to build awareness of the sense of potential.

To build a case for change we establish a sense of urgency and take a fierce stance for bettering the future. That means identifying prominent threats and opportunities and determining potential outcomes. We establish the business case for change by converting threats and opportunities into dollars and cents.

To build a broad base of support, we discuss the options with key interest groups. A coalition of key stakeholders will reveal the rewards and benefits that people anticipate as a result of the change. In addition to building alliances, we determine whether the benefits of the change outweigh the detriments.

We need more than statistics and profit and loss statements to convince others that change is needed. People endorse change at an emotional level, so we find out what matters most to them. We listen for the stressors connected to crises and opportunities. We determine the market trends and discover what competitors are doing that will drive the change process. But we also build a case for change by connecting with people's hearts and engaging them in what's possible. If current practices and systems won't produce the desired results, then we determine the solutions that will. If we don't change, that doesn't mean things will stay the same, so we explore the ramifications of what happens when we keep doing what we've always done.

Most change efforts begin when outside forces change, such as the market shifts, a competitor gets a jump, technology takes a leap, or the economy sputters. Outside forces influence people's thinking, but rarely is that sufficient to get people on board with the change. When you establish an emotional feeling of urgency, that's when people begin to understand the need to change their behavior and collectively awaken to full potential.

What happens if the change doesn't go through? Nobody appreciates scare tactics, so tell the truth about what might happen. Without exaggerating, without trying to manipulate people, paint the picture of the future with the change or without it. Are you selling the nightmare or are you selling the dream?

When I asked Gita, a consultant, about the most visionary people she knows, she told me the story of a company headed toward failure. She talked about her relationship with Ram, the CEO of a clothing manufacturer in India. He felt shocked by the data that Gita presented after she'd interviewed the executive team, many employees, and several customers. Known for her loving approach and fierce, direct conversations, she delivered unequivocal evidence that the company was headed toward failure. An extraordinary listener, not once did Ram show any signs of defensiveness as Gita presented her findings.

In her discussions with executives, they shared their fear that Ram lacked the confidence to lead the company. Their biggest concern was that one major customer responsible for more than half of their revenue had dictated terms that threatened the survival of the company. In essence, the company manufactured shirts that cost a dollar to produce and sold them at a loss for ninety cents. This strategy helped them to increase sales, but no one wanted to tell the boss that higher sales would only speed up their eventual demise.

Hundreds of employees had been fired and rehired as contract employees at half their wages and no benefits. For those who remained employed, trust levels hit rock bottom as people clung to the hope that the company could survive, but not one person had any answers to stop the bleeding.

Massaging his temples as he spoke, Ram asked Gita, "What should I do?" An empowering consultant, she refused to answer and they sat with the silence as he listened for the answers to emerge from within. As his ideas started to take shape, Gita asked powerful questions until he said, "I'd rather close the company than turn our workers into slaves. We value our workers, and we don't need customers who don't share our values."

"So you're willing to give up your best customer?" asked Gita. He winced and then sat up tall. "Yes," was all he said.

The next day Ram asked Gita to present her findings to the customer. With great passion, Gita painted the picture for the customer. She didn't just talk about slave-like conditions; she quoted employees verbatim, "My whole family, including my 3-year-old, works all day to make these shirts, and still we only have a handful of rice and a bit of dhal to eat each night."

When Gita saw the customer choke back tears, she handed him a box of tissues and continued. Unflinchingly, she laid out the only path the company could take. Deeply moved, the customer hammered out a new contract that would allow a decent living wage for all workers.

Inspired by Gita's delivery, Ram intensified the process of connecting with his inner passion. Over time, he learned to communicate his anguish and his hopes. He worked with everyone in the company to create a radically honest culture, where people learned to speak up when things were not going well. Their forthrightness extended to external relationships with customers. Ram became an inspirational visionary who lives his values and expects employees to live theirs. He says his next step is to help the members of his team "get in touch with their personal visions and what is most alive in them so that they can bring passion to their work."

Enlisting Change Agents

I've learned the hard way that building participation is not optional. As leaders, we have no choice but to figure out how to invite in everybody who is going to be affected by change.

— Margaret Wheatley

People respond to change very differently. Some feel overwhelmed by the simplest change, even when it's a promotion accompanied by a raise. Others relish change and live for the adventure of new opportunities.

For a change initiative to succeed, enlisting key players is vital. Champions, sponsors, change agents, and those affected by the change all contribute to the transition. CEOs should back every change initiative, but that doesn't mean they lead every change effort.

The champions are those who see the value and instigate the change, but they usually lack the resources to execute the changes. That's why they need a change sponsor, someone from a high level who commands the resources necessary to succeed. The sponsor authorizes the change, commits resources, demonstrates ownership of the change, and reinforces the change process. Holding the container for change, the sponsor empowers people to take initiative and take risks. Another responsibility of the sponsor is to address resource constraints. The change sponsor takes the leadership role in the change initiative including recruiting key players.

The sponsor pulls in the right people based on their ability to influence, build team spirit, and lead the change effort. Sponsors choose change agents who have the natural inclination and skills to get people on board.

The role of change agents is to align people, resources, and culture. They bolster the confidence of the team, build momentum, and remove barriers along the way. Although critical events usually *start* the change, a team of change agents ensures the planning and execution of the change. To identify the change agents, choose credible people who understand the culture of the organization. Change agents have strong networks and know how to build trust.

The people most affected by the change are clearly the most important players of all. These are the people who have to change their behavior and deal with the emotional aspects of change.

Only 2 percent of the people in the workplace are *innovators*, those venturesome souls who eagerly develop new ideas and try new approaches. You can rely on them to identify improvements and come up with unique ideas, but don't expect them to communicate the change initiative to the rest of the organization. Daring and bold, they willingly invest time and energy in untested, uncertain ideas.

Early adopters, who typically represent 14 percent of the workforce, make the best change agents, because they have excellent communication and facilitation skills. Socially oriented, they usually are the opinion leaders of the workplace. Eager to share their knowledge with their network, they take an active role in the change because they perceive low risk and high opportunity.

The *early majority*, who represent 34 percent of the workforce, don't get too excited about new ideas and approach change with caution. They need evidence that the proposed change will work, and they want plenty of time to test the soundness of the change and absorb the implications. They almost never take a leadership role in a change initiative, but they will follow others once ideas have been proven.

The *late majority* reluctantly endorse the change. They represent 34 percent of the workforce. They're skeptical about change, but they'll endorse the change once the change has demonstrated success, and most of their peers have gotten on board. They retain a lot of influence, and will distort information if they feel coerced or pressured to adapt. This group needs repeated information about the change and regular progress updates. They need business reasons to accept the change, but more importantly, they look for personal reasons. Pushing them to become involved or punishing them only invites more resistance.

Traditionalists, who represent 16 percent of the workforce, tend to take a hostile stance toward change, but their love of tradition provides a stabilizing influence. They won't allow people to change for the sake of change, and they take a stand for keeping best practices from the past. This group is most likely to derail the change effort because they like steadiness and prefer traditional, proven ways of doing things. They will eventually adopt, but only when they understand the ramifications of non-compliance. They play an important role in helping change agents examine the underbelly of change. Although you're wasting your breath trying to get them excited about the benefits the change will bring, don't ignore their concerns.

Eventually all five groups need to pull together to make the change work, so bring all their hopes and concerns into the fold. When a loose core of allies, people who resonate with the change, evolves into a committed core, their energy and sense of potential galvanizes others to see the change through to fruition.

Developing a Change Communication Plan

You're never going to eliminate the grapevine during a transition. However, you can ensure that rumor and speculation aren't the *only* sources of information. A strong communication plan helps you stay focused and prevent unwanted surprises. The primary purpose of the change communication plan is to share the vision and address the people side of change.

Providing information is not the same as communicating. By thinking about the people the change will affect, and how they feel threatened, you can proactively address questions and concerns. That means sharing honestly the potential benefits *and* the drawbacks of the change. By sharing information early that directly affects all the players, you turn the rumor mill into a source of support.

The biggest mistake leaders make is in thinking that communicating the change only once should suffice. One team member sounded irate and said, "We didn't know this was going to happen!" The plant manager countered, "That's not true. I told everyone back in January!" Telling people once is not enough. People need frequent updates about progress and they want to know about any changes in the plan. That means allowing time for two-way communication, where people listen and understand each other's deepest concerns and greatest wishes. People will chew you up and spit you out if they believe that they have not been heard, so a two-way communication process is vital. To develop a change communication strategy, organize facilitated sessions that get people talking about both the apprehension and the benefits of change. When you encourage venting, you get to hear their reactions and together you can come up with ways to address concerns in the moment.

People want reassurance that senior leaders know what they're doing, so it's important to express confidence in the change initiative and in the people leading the change. At the same time, you need to solicit ideas actively to implement the change smoothly. One change leader said, "It's a delicate balancing act to offer assurance and ask for help at the same time." You promote buy-in when you describe the change you envision, allow people to vent and encourage them to expand on the vision. That way you gain insights into what holds people back and generate ideas to overcome potential roadblocks.

If you only talk about the *positive* aspects of change, you will lose people from the start, so talk openly and honestly about the potential downside of the change. At the same time describe the upside by talking about who will benefit and how.

Your communications should result in an emotional connection, allowing you to explore the collective frustration, disappointment, anxiety, and despair. Don't stop there; explore the feelings of relief, hope, trust, faith, passion, and excitement. To get buy-in, connect each emotion to the vision and create the space for dramatic shift of emotions.

The communication plan isn't complete unless you share your strategies and action plan for working through the transition phases. Another component of the communications plan is to share how you plan to support people as they move through the change, whether it's with coaching, training, or new tools.

Managing Resistance to Change

Highly successful organizations know how to overcome antibodies that reject anything new.

—*John Kotter*

Living through difficult times gives us a big advantage. Highly successful companies often have an early history of difficulty. If the vision doesn't cause a stir, if it meets no resistance, then it probably won't have much impact. To stimulate change, we need to identify the barriers and outline the actions required to break down those barriers. In the early stages of creating a new vision, when we anticipate, accept, and honor resistance to change, we help people embrace the past and the future. In contrast if we judge the laggards or treat them as obstacles, we get what we deserve, more resistance to change.

The change process invariably generates conflict, and a tremendous amount of energy can go into taking sides and evaluating positions. Instead of trying in vain to determine who is right or wrong, to resolve conflict, we help people understand and appreciate differences.

Theodore Steinway said, "In one of our concert grand pianos, 243 taut strings exert a pull of 40,000 pounds on an iron frame. It is proof that out of great tension may come great harmony." Creative tension serves as the driving force for realizing the vision.

Dealing with resistance often seems like the most difficult part of the project. Surprisingly, the people who initiate the change often put up the biggest obstacles to success. Loss of what feels comfortable or familiar leads to loss of confidence and the change initiative sometimes becomes the target of frustration and doubt.

When you discuss the upcoming changes, encourage people to take ownership and alter the change initiative, which helps get others on board. Whether people perceive the change positively or negatively, expect resistance. Overt resistance is much easier to manage than covert resistance, so encourage open and honest dialogue about resistance to change. Organizations commonly use consultants or facilitators to provide an objective presence and avoid political agendas and biases from within.

There are hundreds of great reasons for resisting change, but the most common reasons include:

1. The change will negatively affect me personally.

2. Things are fine, and we don't really need change.
3. No one really values our contributions and ideas.
4. The detriments of the change far outweigh the benefits.
5. People don't have the skills, knowledge, or confidence to implement the change.
6. The change probably won't succeed.
7. The change will be poorly managed.
8. I don't trust the people implementing the change.
9. The familiar is more comfortable than the unknown.

Many people enjoy the role of devil's advocate, but they do not want the label of naysayer or stick-in-the-mud. So most resisters keep their reasons to themselves, and quietly, sometimes unconsciously, sabotage the plan for change. When we ask people to take part in the change, to be part of a bigger vision, we have to remember that some people just want to earn a living. Pretending that resistance to change doesn't exist is the most common way for dealing with it, but getting people to talk about their resistance is crucial to the change process. When people in power use force to try to suppress guerrilla fighters, indignation and determination usually rises, which helps them build support for their cause and generates even more resistance.

Even if we consider ourselves progressive change agents, some part of ourselves always objects to change. Richard Beckhard, a pioneer in organizational change once said, "People do not resist change; people resist being changed."

When we acknowledge resistance to change, we build awareness of the underlying positive intent. The chain stitch on a sewing machine is one of the strongest because for every two stitches forward, there is one stitch backward. As you walk the path of change, and you find yourself taking a step backward for every two steps forward, notice the same strength and flexibility of the chain stitch. Full steam ahead is a poor way to manage change. Resistance to change strengthens us.

A great way to deal with resistance to change in others is to build awareness of resistance to change in yourself. Sometimes the part of you that objects to change has 95 percent of the influence and sometimes it's only 5 percent. That 5 percent can wield enormous power, and simply overruling it does a lot of damage. When you "go inside" to find the voice of objection, ask, "What would satisfy the objection?"

Often the objection appears first as fear or anxiety, so the next step is to ask what could change. What would make you feel comfortable as you make the change? Instead of dismissing the objections, listen to the arguments and explore available resources to help you meet all your needs. Satisfying the objections helps you as an individual move forward, and you can then use the same process with other individuals and groups. When you fully experience resistance to your own progress, you learn to appreciate and honor resistance in others.

In T'ai Chi, opponents spar by pushing hands. As one pushes, the other yields, giving no resistance. Each push demands that the opponent relax completely. The more relaxed you become, the more you can control. The winner isn't the strongest, but rather the one who stays relaxed longer. That means staying alert and ready, not limp and flaccid.

At first, the concept of "flowing with resistance" feels like moving in the wrong direction. However, at least you're moving. You're moving together. You have a start. An Aikido exercise to do with a partner starts with one person holding her arm very rigid, and the other tries to move the arm with brute force. Notice the resistance gets stronger. However, when the finger tips land gently on the wrist like a butterfly, you'll notice that the resister's arm always moves ever so slightly, simply because it is alive. As the butterfly moves with the resister's movement, it gently influences the direction. Moving in the wrong direction first invites movement, reduces the brace against the change, and opens the energy to moving in the right direction.

Many managers see resistance to change as a cancer to irradiate. So they fire the loudest resisters and are taken by surprise when even more powerful resisters emerge. The people leave but the roles remain. Firing a resister is like chopping the head off a fluffy dandelion seed head—many more appear in its place. People usually have good reasons for resisting change. They don't hold on to traditional ways because they're stubborn, old-fashioned, or stupid. Resistance is a habitual, inevitable reaction to change. When you expect resistance, you can plan for it. Remind yourself not to take resistance personally.

Resistance to change manifests as:

- Holding onto tradition
- Ridiculing or shaming
- Stereotyping people
- Settling for complacency
- Demonstrating fatigue or boredom
- Thinking about the short-term
- Nay saying or squashing hope

Do you recognize these voices of resistance?

- "We can't afford it."
- "It'll never happen."
- "Sounds like flavor of the month to me."
- "I'd like to see it happen, but you'll never get others on board."
- "Jobs will be lost."
- "Quality will go down hill."
- "We don't have time for this crap."

When you hear the voices of resistance, listen for the values and the underlying positive intent. Resisters typically value safety, calm, steadiness, comfort, and security. So challenge yourself to figure out how to uphold the traditions worth keeping. At the same time, embrace the advantages of change. The biggest resisters sometimes become the greatest champions, but only if you encourage them to voice their fears, doubts, and frustrations. Eventually, their staunchly held beliefs and persuasive powers help to get other resisters on board.

Building Momentum

To build momentum we pay attention to the tone and rhythm of change. We line the womb, nurture the seeds, and allow for the natural gestation before giving birth to the change. Instead of hurrying the change, we listen for the clues that allow the change to evolve naturally in its own time.

As change agents, we collectively establish milestones worth celebrating. In that way we generate creative, inclusive ways to recognize success. If we wait until the change initiative is complete before we celebrate, we probably won't reach the destination at all. We manage the momentum by paying attention to the rate that people accept change and by reinforcing accomplishments every step of the way.

Early successes create opportunities for reassurance and recognition, which builds faith in the process. You can bolster every change initiative with milestones and celebrations to validate the extraordinary effort that goes into the process. The surest way to deepen commitment to the change initiative is to remind people of their success on a regular basis. Reinforcing small steps that support the change initiative has a positive impact on morale and helps people stay focused on the big picture.

Recognition of success should come early and often. To reward breakthroughs, change leaders use all kinds of incentives including lunch, movie tickets, bonuses, promotions, days off, and celebration parties. Not every group wants prizes or gimmicks. Some teams are so engrossed in their work that their idea of celebrating success is to brainstorm new ideas for growth. Most people enjoy the break from the routine, and find the opportunity to celebrate together invigorating and worthwhile. Visual reminders of recognition such as awards, bulletin board postings, or gifts reinforce the sense of success. Gag gifts, roasting the key players, or telling humorous stories about low points, aligns people with their hopes for the future. More important than any extrinsic motivators are the intrinsic motivators, the key to any successful change initiative.

Sustaining a Culture that is Receptive to Change

> *Never doubt that a small group of thoughtful, committed citizens can change the world; indeed, it's the only thing that ever has.*
> — *Margaret Mead*

More than 27,000 children die daily from hunger-related complications. Some people say the situation is hopeless. But global anti-poverty activist Lynn McMullen says, "The women of Africa have not given up, and they're not going to. That's emboldened me and makes me proud to be a human being."

Lynn insists the solutions to poverty are available, if only people would invest. Her vision is to see people all over the world give away three times more money than they do currently. She wants people to triple their impact and take a stand for a new vision, using their money as a vehicle for creating the world they want.

According to Lynn, people spend money on things that don't really matter, including $21 billion on plastic toys, $43 billion on computer games, and even more on cosmetics. Working with organizations all over the world, she brings sustainable tools like microfinance and training programs to lift destitute people out of poverty. Lynn inspires people to live more consciously and to shape the world they are longing for.

As the waves of change keep rolling in, visionaries like Lynn lead people who change the world. To make change stick we have to build a culture that supports change. Tradition is like a comfortable, inviting hammock, so we can't just announce that tradition is off limits; we have to weave the old into the new. Flexibility and celebrating repeated success are the active ingredients in sustaining change.

We need to create a culture where continuous improvement and course corrections are the norm. Due to wind, turbulence, and other aircraft, airplanes fly off course by a few degrees most of the time. So the pilot constantly makes course corrections to keep the plane headed toward its destination. Likewise, our lives and our organizations do not always go according to plan, and we change direction routinely.

Critics of an ordinary vision process consider it impractical because the resulting vision statement sounds canned and doesn't inspire people to change. However, a robust vision process engages and energizes people throughout the organization and helps them break out of a limited view of the future.

Tuning up the vision should be a continuous process. In some organizations, revisiting the vision on a yearly basis becomes rote or perfunctory. In other organizations, a retreat or a future search conference re-energizes people as they set high-level directions. Instead of embarking on 15 change initiatives at once, visionaries consolidate projects so that the changes are more manageable and easier to embrace.

Finding alignment between our purpose, values, and vision provides both the foundation and the direction. Even if we don't completely realize our destination, our vision pulls us forward in specific, tangible ways.

Incentives and compensation rarely sustain a large-scale change. A common misconception is that if we change the culture we'll be successful. In actuality, culture doesn't change easily. When changes bear fruit, that's when the new culture takes root. A new culture comes as the result of success, not before. So take great pleasure in telling your success stories along the way.

We need to manage the changes in culture, behavior, and attitude, especially our own. Any leader can tell you that the only way to lead change effectively is to do the inner work of change. Continuously.

With the world changing at the speed of light, we need to keep ourselves wide open to dramatic modifications. Goethe said, "One never goes as far as when one doesn't know where one is going." As open-minded leaders, we entertain a delicate balance between knowing where we are going, and remaining open to new possibilities. If we limit ourselves to what our minds can imagine, we miss huge opportunities.

To sustain change, we build awareness of transformational opportunities. That means we commit to a path of life-long personal development. By expressing our passion, we unleash potential and invite others to help us create a better future.

Epilogue

Sharing an Evolving Vision

Choice, not chance, determines your destiny.

— *Jean Nidetch*

Envision a world full of passionate people who boldly choose to paint a brighter future. Imagine teams of change catalysts, venturing out into far corners, helping people awaken to their potential, and helping them execute their plans for making the world a better place.

When we explore our personal visions, we awaken opportunities for engaging in organizational visions. Throughout this book, I have challenged you to dream, to forge visions that will bring about amazing change. My greatest wish is to see people all over the world delve into their personal visions as the driving force that energizes larger, far-reaching organizational visions.

My vision is not for the few or the elite, but for anyone with a desire to improve the future. Whether we are members of organizations, families, spiritual communities, or neighborhoods, we can all elevate each other's hopes and support each other's visions. We can release the passionate energy that arises from personal vision and apply the same principles to awaken passion in the workplace.

Most vision work is not a solitary process. Together we explore our hopes and fears, and form alliances to realize our visions. We do the deep inner work that whispers our highest aspirations, and we work in groups, organizations, and corporations to discover new options and voice new choices. The role of a leader is not to dictate the direction, but to unleash the collective aspirations. I'm especially eager to see people tell stories about the future that awaken new possibilities, build heart-centered relationships, acknowledge each other's gifts, and celebrate success in creative ways.

In my ideal world, we eagerly invest in each other's personal and professional growth and collectively shape the future. We live purposely, yet we're not glued to the plan. We continue to open ourselves to new creative opportunities. We communicate compellingly, unleash passionate energy, and call people to action. We spawn support systems that nurture the soul, build wealth, and help people get what they need.

Because we honor the individual, team spirit has a life of its own, and people truly enjoy their work. Most importantly, we know how to make it all happen. We say no to life-draining forces and choose to serve as leaders and followers who stimulate positive change. We get the help we need to overcome barriers, dance with change, and stay open to continually reshaping the vision. The greatest gift we can give is to invite others to join our quest for creating a better future.

More about Courageous Visions

Many, many people contribute to an evolving vision, helping each other create new opportunities. To join us and expand your vision, visit the Web forum at: www.CourageousVisions.com

Bibliography

Albert, Susan Wittig. 1997. *Writing from Life: Telling Your Soul's Story*. J. P. Tarcher.

Alessandra, Tony. 2000. *Charisma Seven Keys to Developing the Magnetism That Leads to Success*. Warner Books.

Anderson, Nancy. 1995. *Work With Passion: How to Do What You Love for a Living* . New World Library.

Andreas, Connirae and Andreas, Tamara. 1996. *Core Transformation: Reaching the Wellspring Within*. Real People Press.

Angeles Arrien. 1993. *The Four-Fold Way: Walking the Paths of the Warrior, Teacher, Healer, and Visionary*. Harper San Francisco.

Anundsen, Kristen; Shaffer, Carolyn; Peck, Scott M. and Backlar, Patricia. 1993. *Creating Community Anywhere: Finding Support and Connection in a Fragmented World*. Perigee.

Axelrod, Alan. 2002. *Profiles in Leadership*. Alpha Communications.

Barrett, Richard. 1998. *Liberating the Corporate Soul: Building a Visionary Organization*. Butterworth-Heinemann.

Beckhard, Richard and Harris, Reuben. 1987. *Organizational Transitions: Managing Complex Change*. Addison-Wesley Publishing Co., Inc.

Bennis, Warren G. 2003. *On Becoming a Leader*. Perseus Publishing.

Block, Peter. 2003. *The Answer to How is Yes: Acting on What Matters*. Berrett-Koehler Pub.

Borysenko, Joan. 1994. *Fire in the Soul: A New Psychology of Spiritual Optimism*. Warner Books.

Canfield, Jack and Victor Hansen, Mark. 2003. *Chicken Soup for the Soul: Living Your Dream*. Health Communications.

Capacchione, Lucia. 2000. *Visioning: 10 Steps to Designing the Life of Your Dreams*. J. P. Tarcher.

Clemmer, Jim. 1995. *Pathways to Performance: A Guide to Transforming Yourself, Your Team, and Your Organization*. Prima Lifestyles.

Collins, James C. and Porras, Jerry I. 1997. *Built to Last: Successful habits of Visionary Companies*. Harper Business.

Covey, Stephen. 1996. *First Things First: To Live, to Love, to Learn, to Leave a Legacy*. Free Press.

Csikszentmihalyi, Mihaly. 2003. *Good Business: Leadership, Flow, and the Making of Meaning*. Viking Press.

Fritz, Robert. 1989. *The Path of Least Resistance: Learning to Become the Creative Force in Your Own Life*. Fawcett Books.

Gallwey, Timothy. 2000. *The Inner Game of Work.* Random House.

Gershon, David and Straub, Gail. 1989. *Empowerment: The Art of Creating Your Life as You Want It.* High Point Press.

Goldberg, Natalie. 1986. *Writing Down the Bones.* Shambhala.

Goleman, Daniel. 1993. *Emotional Intelligence.* Bantam Books.

Hendricks, Gay and Ludeman, Kate. 1997. *The Corporate Mystic: A Guidebook for Visionaries With Their Feet on the Ground.* Bantam.

Heuerman, Tom. "True Spirit at Work" *The Systems Thinker.* August 2002. Pegasus Communications.

Hultman, Ken. 1998. *Making Change Irresistible: Overcoming Resistance to Change in Your Organization.* Davies Black Publishers.

Hultman, Ken. 2001. *Balancing Individual and Organizational Values: Walking the Tightrope to Success.* Jossey-Bass/Pfeiffer.

Izzo, John and Klein, Eric. 1999. *Awakening Corporate Soul: Four Paths to Unleash the Power of People at Work.* Fair Winds Press.

Kornfield, Jack. 1993 *A Path with Heart: A Guide Through the Perils and Promises of Spiritual Life.* Doubleday.

Kotter, John. 2002. *The Heart of Change.* Harvard Business School Press.

Kouzes, James and Posner, Barry. 2003. *Encouraging the Heart: A Leader's Guide to Rewarding and Recognizing Others.* Jossey-Bass.

Kouzes, James and Posner, Barry. 2003. *Leadership Challenge.* Jossey -Bass.

Kubler-Ross, Elisabeth. 1997. *On Death and Dying.* Scribner. www.elisabethkublerross.com

Leider, Richard. 1997. *The Power of Purpose: Creating Meaning in Your Life and Work.* Berrett-Koehler Publisher.

Levoy, Gregg Michael. 1998. *Callings: Finding and Following an Authentic Life.* Three Rivers Press.

Linn, Denise. 1997. *The Hidden Power of Dreams.* Ballantine Books.

Linn, Denise; Linn, Meadow. 1999. *Quest: A Guide to Creating Your Own Vision Quest.* Ballantine Books.

Maurer, Rick. 1996. *Beyond the Wall of Resistance: Unconventional Strategies That Build Support for Change.* Bard Press.

Maxwell, John C. 2000. *Developing the Leader Within You.* Thomas Nelson.

Medicine Eagle, Brooke. 1991. *Buffalo Woman Comes Singing.* Ballantine Books.

Muller, Wayne. 1997. *How, Then, Shall We Live? Four Simple Questions That Reveal the Beauty and Meaning of Our Lives.* Bantam.

Nachmanovitch, Stephen. 1991. *Free Play: Improvisation in Life and Art.* J. P. Tarcher.

Nanus, Burt; Bennis, Warren. 1995. *Visionary Leadership: Creating a Compelling Sense of Direction for Your Organization.* Jossey-Bass.

O'Reilley, Mary Rose. 1998. *Radical Presence: Teaching as Contemplative Practice.* Boynton/Cook.

Pearce, Terry. 2003. *Leading Out Loud: The Authentic Speaker, the Credible Leader.* Jossey-Bass.

Peck, Scott. 2003. *The Road Less Traveled: A New Psychology of Love, Traditional Values and Spiritual Growth.* Touchstone Books.

Pierce, Gregory. 2001. *Spirituality@Work: 10 Ways to Balance Your Life On-The-Job.* Loyola Press.

Quinn, Robert, 1996. *Deep Change: Discovering the Leader Within.* Jossey-Bass.

Roberts, Monty, 1998. *The Man Who Listens to Horses.* Ballantine Books.

Rosenberg, Marshall. 2003. *Non-Violent Communication: A Language of Compassion.* PuddleDancer Press. www.cnvc.org

Samuels, Neil. 2002. "A Guide to Appreciative Upward/360° Feedback Conversations." Appreciative Inquiry Commons.

Sanders, Tim and Stone, Gene. 2003. *Love is the Killer App: How to Win Business and Influence Friends.* Three Rivers Press.

Senge, Peter. 1994. *The Fifth Discipline.* Currency.

Senge, Peter; Kleiner, Art; Roberts, Charlotte; Roth, George; Ross, Rick; Smith, Bryan. 1999. *The Dance of Change: The Challenges to Sustaining Momentum in Learning Organizations.* Doubleday.

Sher, Barbara. 1997. *Live the Life you Love.* DTP.

Thomas, Bob. 1994. Walt Disney: *An American Original.* Disney Editions.

Watkins, Jane Magruder and Mohr, Bernard J. 2001. *Appreciative Inquiry: Change at the Speed of Imagination.* Jossey-Bass/Pfeiffer.

Wheatley, Margaret. 2002. *Turning to One Another: Simple Conversations to Restore Hope to the Future.* Berrett-Koehler Publishers.

Whitmore, John, 2002. *Coaching for Performance: Growing People, Performance and Purpose.* Nicolas Brealey.

Whyte, David. 1996. *The Heart Aroused: Poetry and the Preservation of the Soul in Corporate America.* Currency.

Williams, Oliver. 1986. *The Apartheid Crisis: How We Can Do Justice in a Land of Violence.* HarperCollins

Williamson, Marianne. 2002. *Everyday Grace: Having Hope, Finding Forgiveness, and Making Miracles.* Riverhead Books.

Yudkin, Marcia and Laurie Schloff. 1992. *Smart Speaking: 60 Second Strategies for More Than 100 Speaking Problems and Fears.* Plume.

Index

About the Author

Executive coach **Martha Lasley** is a founding partner of Leadership that Works, a firm that develops dynamic leaders at all levels. As Chief Choreographer, she custom-designs programs to facilitate profound personal and organizational growth.

Martha's work focuses on:

- Coaching leaders to develop visionary strategies, manage change, improve interpersonal communications, and foster team spirit.

- Designing and delivering leadership development programs and retreats that improve productivity and open the way to exciting opportunities and new perspectives.

- Facilitating organizational assessments, interventions, conflict mediation and group process facilitation.

She empowers leaders to develop compelling visions and communicate excitement about the future. A member of the International Association of Facilitators, the American Society for Training and Development, and the International Coaching Federation, she travels internationally as a coach, speaker, trainer, and facilitator. On the faculty for the Capella University MBA program, she teaches courses in Coaching, Negotiating, Leading Teams and Leveraging Diversity.

Always up for an adventure, Martha likes to windsurf, telemark ski, kayak, and play. She's passionate about food, gardening, reading, and cooking up new ideas in the hot tub.

To reach her, write: Martha Lasley, Leadership that Works, PO Box 224, Troy, PA 16947 or email info@LeadershipthatWorks.com

Quick Order Form
Give the gift of *Courageous Visions* to Friends, Family and Colleagues

Check your favorite bookstore or order here.
Fax orders: Fax this form to 570-297-2727.
Telephone orders: Call toll free: 86-MY-FUTURE. Please have your credit card ready.
Web orders: http://www.CourageousVisions.com
Email orders: orders@CourageousVisions.com
Postal orders: Discover Press, PO Box 5, Burlington, PA 18814, USA.

Please send more FREE information on:
❑ Speaking   ❑ Seminars   ❑ Consulting   ❑ Team Vision

Name: _____

Address: _____

City: _____

State: _____ **Zip:** _____

Phone: _____

Email: _____

Please send _____ copies of *Courageous Visions* @ $19.95 each. I understand that I may return any of them for a full refund—for any reason, no questions asked.
Sales tax: Please add 6% for products shipped to PA addresses. _____
Shipping: U.S.: $4.00 for first book and $2.00 for each additional product.
International: $9.00 for first book; $5.00 for each additional.
Total Due: _____

Payment:
❑   Check
❑   Credit Card: _____ MasterCard   _____ VISA

Credit card #: _____ Exp Date: _____

Name on card: _____